A Political History of Literature

A Political History of Literature

Vidyapati and the Fifteenth Century

Pankaj Jha

OXFORD
UNIVERSITY PRESS

OXFORD
UNIVERSITY PRESS

Oxford University Press is a department of the University of Oxford. It furthers the University's objective of excellence in research, scholarship, and education by publishing worldwide. Oxford is a registered trademark of Oxford University Press in the UK and in certain other countries.

Published in India by
Oxford University Press
2/11 Ground Floor, Ansari Road, Daryaganj, New Delhi 110 002, India

First Edition published in 2019

ISBN-13 (printed edition): 978-0-19-948955-8
ISBN-10 (printed edition): 0-19-948955-6

ISBN-13 (eBook): 978-0-19-909535-3
ISBN-10 (eBook): 0-19-909535-3

Typeset in Scala Pro 10/13
by Tranistics Data Technologies, Kolkata 700 091
Printed in India by Rakmo Press, New Delhi 110 020

Acknowledgements

The doctoral dissertation on which this book is based had been long in the making. Part of the reason for this long gestation was the need for a tolerable level of competence in several languages other than Hindi and English. I was very slow to acquire that. It appears to be ages ago when I suggested somewhat hesitantly to Sunil Kumar that I was thinking of working on Vidyapati. The excitement with which he responded made it impossible for me to consider any other topic of research. I was already teaching undergraduate students in the University of Delhi at the time. Little did I know that it would take me a few years and several trips to libraries in Darbhanga, Patna, and even Delhi to collect all the published works of Vidyapati. It took a further few years before I could get leaves sanctioned from my college and focus solely on the project. Staying with a subject for so long had its advantages inasmuch as it allowed me to think and rethink through issues at length. It also allowed my ideas to brew over time. I hope this shows in the book.

I have had the fortune of being in the company of and learning from Sunil Kumar for more than two decades now. He has been my guide, mentor, philosopher, friend, and much more. Had it not been for the faith that he put in me, I would probably have chosen a different career. I have had the fortune of being taught by some of the most competent and inspiring undergraduate teachers before I met him. Yet, it was with his guidance that I started picking up the elementary techniques of research. I do not have the words to express my gratitude for a relationship so enriching as this one.

All through these years, I also received help from numerous colleagues, friends, relatives, and institutions. I do not think I can remember them all. But those that I do, I would like to thank. First of all, I record my gratitude to my debate adviser in high school, R.K. Singh who introduced me to the joys of reading literature. History was too boring for me at the time. When I landed up, by accident, in the history honours programme for my bachelor's at Ramjas College, the discipline dramatically rose overnight in my esteem. Such was the passion with which Sudhakar Singh taught it in the class. Among my undergraduate teachers, I must also mention Dilip Simeon, whose insistence that history was always political and mostly about the present has stayed with me for good. The brilliant lucidity of Hari Sen's lectures in the classroom was a source of inspiration.

Fortunately, I got an opportunity to interact with some of the leading scholars in the broad area of my research. Conversations, formal and informal, with them have been a source of questions, ideas, and inspiration. I would particularly like to thank Sanjay Subrahmanyam, Muzaffar Alam, Whitney Cox, Sumit Guha, Daud Ali, Katheryn Hansen, Francesca Orsini, Allison Busch, and Indrani Chatterjee. Among younger scholars and friends, my research has benefitted from conversations with Samira Sheikh, Ravikant, Nilanjan Sarkar, Mayank Kumar, Anubhuti Maurya, and Anand Vivek Taneja.

At Lady Shri Ram College, most of my colleagues were there to help me in times of need. Each member in the Department of History extended their unconditional support to me at all times. I must especially mention Meera Baijal, Vasudha Pande, and Nayana Dasgupta, who have been a source of emotional as well as intellectual support. I also formally note my appreciation for Lady Shri Ram College for granting me study leave for three years so that I could pursue the PhD programme.

I spent nine months of the study leave at the University of Texas, Austin. I must gratefully acknowledge that my stint at the University of Texas was arranged for and financially supported by the Fulbright–Nehru Doctoral Research Fellowship. I take this opportunity especially to thank Sudarshan Dash and Pratibha Nair of the United States–India Educational Foundation, New Delhi, for their help. Thanks are due also to Zachary Alger of the Institute of International Education, New York, for prompt help on all official issues related to the Fulbright Fellowship during my stay in the USA.

Cynthia Talbot, my research adviser while I was at the University of Texas, was extremely generous with her time, suggestions, and encouragement. She brought very useful readings to my notice and gave invaluable suggestions, especially regarding the way I needed to organize the chapters in my thesis. I express my sincerest gratitude to her.

While I was at the University of Texas, Edeltraud Harzer Clear very kindly allowed me to sit in her Sanskrit classes for the entire semester. I owe my sincerest thanks to her. The staff at the Perry-Castañeda Library, Austin, were invariably prompt in their help. I would particularly like to thank Merry Burlingham, among others.

Gratitude is due also to the library staff of Sahitya Akademi and Indian Council of Historical Research, New Delhi; K.P. Jayaswal Research Institute and Khuda Baksh Library, Patna; and Lalit Narayan Mithila University, Darbhanga.

Among friends, who always stood strongly by me, often in spite of complete disinterest in the precise nature of my work, I must gratefully mention Anil, Baba, Sanjay, Anil Chapoliya aka Sethji, Suman, Sunilji, Topi, and Vijay Singh. Recently, I have also discovered some old friends in new avatars: Rakesh Niraj and Samita among them. My housemate-turned-friend at Austin, Aniruddhan Vasudevan, was one of my most precious finds during my stay in the USA.

Scholars of humanities do not work in laboratories. But for those of us who teach in a university/college, our classrooms are no less than the place where we test our ideas and pick up new ones, frame arguments and hone them. I have had the good fortune of learning from a whole generation of students at Lady Shri Ram College.

My interactions with them have been a singularly enriching experience. I register my gratitude to every student who ever shared an idea with me in the class or asked a question.

My parental family has always been a great source of strength for me. Baby, Ruby, Anmol, and Manoj have been resolute in their affections. My parents-in-law have never been less than indulgent towards me. My stay away from my family for nine months would not have been possible without their support. I express my gratitude to them too. My parents are proud that their son earned a doctoral degree. They are happy that I am publishing a book based on it. I know no one's satisfaction would be deeper on the mere publication of a book.

It is not possible to adequately acknowledge Sneh, my closest friend, companion, spouse, critic, and fellow academic. It was on her insistence that I applied for the Fulbright Fellowship. She took the responsibility of looking after our two rambunctious kids for nine months while I was at Austin. This book is also hers in part. It is indebted to her in a thousand ways and more. I wouldn't risk belittling all that she has been to me by trying to thank her. My son, Malhar, and my daughter, Tamanna, have been a delightful source of distraction. They duly resented my unending homework. I earnestly hope that my work was worthy also of the time that they rightfully thought was theirs.

Notes on Transliteration

All translations from Sanskrit, Apabhraṃśa, and Hindi are mine, unless otherwise specified. In the case of Persian, I have indicated in the footnotes where I have consulted the original and where I am using translation(s) by others.

All non-English words have been italicized except those that occur too frequently. I have not used diacritics for place-names that are still in official or/and popular use. However, the older variants of the same have been marked with diacritics. Thus, I refer to the village of Vidyapati's birth, which is still there in north Bihar, as Bisfi. However, its old name is referred not as Bispi but as Bisapī.

All dates in the book are in the Common Era (CE) unless otherwise specified.

For Persian words, no diacritics have been used, partly in order to avoid possible confusion between the standard methods of transcribing Persian words into English and those for transcribing Sanskrit words into English. Hence, while rendering the Persian words into

English, only readability has been kept in mind, which often led me to adopt the most commonly used spellings.

The transliteration scheme followed for Sanskrit, Apabhraṃśa, Hindi, and Maithili words are given below:

अ	*a*	आ	*ā*	इ	*i*	ई	*ī*
उ	*u*	ऊ	*ū*	ए	*e*	ऐ	*ai*
ओ	*o*	औ	*au*	ऋ	*ṛi*		
क	*ka*	ख	*kha*	ग	*ga*	घ	*gha*
ङ	*ṅ*	च	*ca*	छ	*cha*	ज	*ja*
झ	*jha*	ञ	*ñ*	ट	*ṭa*	ठ	*ṭha*
ड	*ḍa*	ढ	*ḍha*	ण	*ṇa*	त	*ta*
थ	*tha*	द	*da*	ध	*dha*	न	*na*
प	*pa*	फ	*pha*	ब	*ba*	भ	*bha*
म	*ma*	य	*ya*	र	*ra*	व	*va*
श	*śa*	ष	*ṣa*	स	*sa*		

anusvāra	*ṃ*
visarga	*ḥ*

Introduction

This book has been conceived as a political history of literature in the fifteenth century. It is neither an exhaustive consideration of all literature produced in that age in North India, nor does it claim to be a treatment of a 'representative' sample of all such compositions. Rather, I have focussed on three sharply different texts of a prolific poet, Vidyapati, from an atypical region, Mithila. I have tried to use the three texts under consideration to open up the wider world of literature in the fifteenth century. Thus, I relate Vidyapati's compositions to the existing traditions of literary production of the time, with a view to unearth the deeper histories that lay behind them. Given the state of the relevant historiography, this was a huge methodological challenge.

The book is organized in five chapters, which are unevenly divided in two parts, preceded by a short introduction, and followed by a conclusion. The conclusion ties up the points made by the different chapters both at a general, methodological level, as well as in the specific context of the long fifteenth century, in a way that might connect its details with certain larger questions of contemporary as well as historical significance.

The first part of the book has two chapters: the first provides basic information about Vidyapati, his compositions, and his immediate geopolitical and intellectual milieu. The second chapter takes critical stock of the more dominant and recent strands of historiography of the 'long' fifteenth century. But it also uses this critical stock-taking as a step towards (*a*) broadly mapping the literary cultures of the fifteenth century, and (*b*) thinking about issues of historical method, historians' possible engagements with literature, knowledge formations, and power, as a set of related themes. The second part of the book has three chapters, each centred around, but not limited to, one of the texts of Vidyapati, namely, *Likhanāvalī*, *Puruṣaparīkṣā*, and *Kīrttilatā*, out of more than a dozen of his compositions available in print whose authorship is not disputed. While I do refer to the poet's other compositions whenever the context requires me to, these are not taken up for detailed exploration.

Before I move to the next section, let me put in an explanation for why I treat Mithila as an 'atypical' region. The 'region' of Mithila was atypical in two distinct ways. First, at a moment when a robust system of long-distance trade had developed in most parts of the subcontinent, Mithila lay on none of the major trade routes of the time. Second, for related reasons, Mithila continued to survive as either an independent chieftaincy or as a semi-autonomous principality of the three major sultanates of the long fifteenth century in its neighbourhood: Delhi, Jaunpur, and Bengal. It was only in the mid-sixteenth century that it emerged as an integral and separate territorial unit of a major imperial power, namely, the Mughal state. As such, it figures only marginally in the standard narratives of the Delhi Sultanate or the other sultanates up to the first half of the sixteenth century.

Why Vidyapati?

When I started researching the enormous corpus of literature left behind by Vidyapati, all I knew was that I wanted to focus on non-Persian textual productions of the fifteenth century. Medieval historiography has hitherto shown little patience with the fifteenth century, and precious little interest in non-Persian 'sources'. Vidyapati, however, was doubly attractive because he was multilingual and lived in Mithila, an area that modern historians, like most Persian chroniclers of the middle ages, often passed by quietly. And yet, Vidyapati's literary corpus was vast, disparate, and straddled a range of what appeared to be unconnected worlds. There was law, love, writing, political ethics, biography, rituals, tantricism, 'geography', romantic play, ritual donations (*dāna*), and a vast corpus of songs for a variety of occasions. My problem was to focus on specific issues, and accordingly on certain texts, so I could study the author and his oeuvre more intimately.

After weighing in all my options, I decided to focus on the following three of Vidyapati's compositions. *Kīrttilatā* was a text I could not have avoided for the simple reason that it was the only major extant work of Vidyapati that was composed in Apabhraṃśa. Since one of my concerns was to examine the relationship between language, literature, and politics, this explicitly political text—a biopolitical narrative in 'vernacular' with a local prince as its protagonist—suggested itself 'naturally'. *Puruṣaparīkṣā* was another work that appeared unique in the history of Indic literatures, being possibly the only known early modern text that so directly propounded what might be termed a theory of masculinity. That it was simultaneously a work on *naya/daṇḍanīti*, or political ethics/ state policy, also suited my proposed engagement with issues of literature and state formation, or more generally, knowledge and power. No less compelling for me was the choice of *Likhanāvalī*, again for the simple reason that it was possibly the first text of its kind in Sanskrit. Being so centrally concerned with the state, this work too could add variety to my investigation of matters related to another 'literary' dimension of state power, namely, documentation. As I hope to demonstrate in the third chapter, however, *Likhanāvalī* turned out to be much more than what it claimed, a manual for those interested in cultivating the craft of documentation. A first-of-its-kind Sanskrit text that borrowed imaginatively from a range of literary traditions including Persian, it provides a glimpse into the eclectically constituted ways of making literature and imagining imperium in the fifteenth century.

If I mention the process by which I arrived at my choice of these compositions, it is because they are not in any way meant to be 'representative' works of Vidyapati. It would be virtually impossible to make such a list for an author as varied in his choice of subjects as the scholar from Mithila. What was important about my choice of the three texts was the way in which they treated the issues I wanted to explore, each in its own distinctive way. From the point of view of genre, or language and literary strategies, they represent very divergent authorial exercises. This allowed me the opportunity to explore afresh how a historian's literary engagement with her/his 'source texts' was crucial for a nuanced reading.

The argument that the centuries after the thirteenth in North India were fast turning out to be riotously multilingual in literary practice and everyday speech is much more convincing today than it was ten years ago. Equally strong is the case now for this period being diverse and dynamic in its literary themes, genres, and sheer volume.[1] In several ways, Vidyapati seems to embody the spirit of the long fifteenth century more substantively than any other literary figure of the time. He wrote in at least four languages, and probably knew a few more. If many before him wrote vernacular verses in a style that celebrated 'male' heroism, he too did that; if the fifteenth century was the period of the so-called bhakti movement, he represented one of the most irresistible voices of that trend; if the *dharmaśāstra*s continued to be important, he too wrote one; if tantric cults were gaining popularity, he wrote a play with one of the most prominent protagonists of tantricism as its hero; and he was surely not the only Brāhmaṇa scholar of the period who drew patronage from a host of minor princes of more than one royal household. He composed in a dozen genres including some that he almost invented himself; he lived in a local chieftaincy that seemed to be farthest from big imperial formations. I do not, however, claim to study Vidyapati as any sort of a 'representative' of the fifteenth century. Rather, I use his compositions to reach out to other related ones, and eventually to open up the times he lived in.

[1] For a detailed argument of the case, see Jha, 'Literary Conduits for "Consent"'. Also see Orsini and Sheikh, 'Introduction'.

Political History of Literature or a Question of Method

For long, historians have believed that it is important to study an author before one studies his/her work. It is equally important, however, to explore the implications of an author's choice of language and of genre. In choosing to compose in a language, authors chose a certain readership/audience, along with a whole system of idioms constituted culturally. In doing so, they might, as indeed Vidyapati did, simultaneously expand (or narrow down) the horizons of that language in multiple ways. The manner in which it would be read/recited and the usage to which their authors hoped their texts would be put also depended largely on the choice of language and register. A composition could be used for performative purposes, for public recitations, for popular retelling, or for quiet and private study by peers. Equally, in choosing a genre, authors chose to be bound by the conventions of that genre, whether flexibly or strictly. The content of the compositions would tend to reflect the authors' concerns and issues. But the authors would often also feel obliged to speak to, and speak in, the voice of past authors in the chosen genre.

My attempt, however, is to relate this literary corpus to 'mainstream' history, and attempt a political history of literature. How does one contextualize internally coherent and apparently monolingual texts like *Likhanāvalī*, *Puruṣaparīkṣā*, and *Kīrttilatā* in a milieu that was so pervasively multilingual? I trace the parallel and comparable developments elsewhere in North India during the time, while diachronically excavating the deep histories and multilingual debts of apparently monolingual texts.

Locating the texts within the long-term patterns of development of languages and literature in North India could only be one aspect, a first step towards writing a political history of literature. This first step involves, among other things, looking carefully for tangible traces of intertextuality in them, but also for the not-so-tangible (often unacknowledged) signs of 'influences' from other languages and genres. It is well established, if seldom realized by historians, that texts on a theme become intelligible only to the extent that they are part of ongoing streams of conversation with other texts on that theme. Even the novelty of a literary composition lies in its ability to adapt, respond to, or rebut already existing propositions in other texts. The 'originality' quotient of a new work may also lie in its response to changes 'outside' the text, say, in material conditions of life or changes in political culture. Even when the poetic imagination breaks 'fresh' ground by articulating an aspiration or conjuring up fantastic images, the use of familiar terminologies can hardly be avoided. That is why I find it useful to historicize the texts, and determine the nature and variety of streams that feed into them.

For long, historians treated literature like enemy territory. Their standard modus operandi was to conduct surgical strikes on texts to extract 'history' (read 'facts' and suggestive pieces of information) from them. This fundamentally violent approach bypasses the literariness of a composition that one cannot access without placing it within its own textual tradition. My explorations suggest that emplacement of an imaginative work within the deep histories of its own language–genre–theme tradition makes the work reveal much more than pieces of information. Such an approach helps us locate those aspects, which are unique to the text, as well as identify alternative ideas, which the text might have been responding to. After all, a literary expression is also, among other things, an intervention in the dynamic flow of history: a wager in an ongoing conversation—real or imagined.

This requires historians engaging with their 'sources', irrespective of what aspects she/he is looking into, to look deep and wide into other texts so as to see the work at hand itself as a historical product. Within a multilingual literary culture, this is a very difficult task. It requires us to look for relevant practices in several languages simultaneously.

And this leads to the second step in my reading of Vidyapati. If the first step helps me find out 'where the texts are coming from', the second step involves the issue of 'where they are going'. The question that I put across is this: what kind of socio-political order did these texts uphold? What visions of power did they describe, proscribe, or prescribe? To put the question prospectively, what political possibilities could the literary cultures of Mithila prepare the ground for?

As far as medieval studies are concerned, this was a bit of a leap in the dark. Typically, premodern historians relate literature (as also other cultural products) to politics by looking at patterns of patronage, and immediately hitting the dead end of (often instant) legitimation. This approach sees culture as a by-product of politics and (more often than not, state) power.[2] I discuss the limitations of this approach in the second chapter. I do not, however, imply 'literary determinism of political action'.[3] Nor do I assign, as Sheldon Pollock does, an 'autonomous aesthetic imperative' to literary initiative.[4]

Methodologically, there are four interrelated components to my approach to literature: first, I treat literary compositions as historical products, and seek to trace their antecedents not in an isolated history of ideas but in the cultural politics of the past and (the then) present; second, I keep the possibility alive that an author's location in a small or 'local' principality might not be the sole or even the major determinant of her/his political vision; third, that in a place where there was no established institutionalized space (unlike, say, the church in Europe) for regular communication with people, literature, especially its durable forms (for example, stories and poetry that could be remembered and related more easily) in a largely oral culture, would play an extremely important role in enunciating the terms of cultural discourse. Finally, I ask the simple but perhaps the most important question of all: what is the political value of literature? Alas, historians (unlike philosophers!) can never hope to answer that question once and for all. I pursue the question, fully cognizant of the fact that the meaning of 'political', very much like the character of literature, is historically variable. One can map the complex relationship between the two only in the long duration. I briefly discuss the dynamics of this relationship in the later part of Chapter 2 in this volume.

[2] There are occasional exceptions though. In a study of the oeuvre of the famous Telugu poet Ṣrīnātha and the Telugu literary traditions in the fourteenth and the fifteenth centuries, for example, Velcheru Narayana Rao and David Shulman offer the opposite view. They note that in an 'unstable and fragmented political climate', 'the patron and the poet were locked in a relation of asymmetrical dependence—the former being essentially dependent upon the good grace and poetic talent of the latter, who nevertheless needs the patron for his economic survival'. See Rao and Shulman, *Śrīnātha*, p. 6.

[3] I have borrowed the phrase from Jene Andrew Jarrett. See Jarrett, *Representing the Race*, p. 7.

[4] Pollock, 'India in the Vernacular Millenium: Literary Culture and Polity', p. 44.

In this endeavour, my debt to Sheldon Pollock should be obvious. The excitement generated by his study of the literary cultures of Sanskrit and other Indic languages has refused to subside, even two decades after he first proposed a millennium-by-millennium binary paradigm of Sanskrit cosmopolitanism and vernacularization. If excessive focus on Persian 'authorities' was my problem with medieval studies, here was a scholar whose engagements with non-Persian literature and literary cultures of the middle ages marked out a 'parallel' archive. It was a massive archive, replete with all possible genres, and tantalizingly diverse in its themes, locations, and patronage patterns.

Paradoxically, however, if the 'mainstream' historians of medieval India had, to a large extent, failed to account for the massive presence of Sanskrit and vernacular sources, Pollock's engagements with this archive reduced the Persian ecumene along with the Delhi Sultanate, Mughal state, and other 'regional' states (seen to be exclusively) invested in Persian culture to minor footnotes. If the claims of Persian chroniclers enjoyed a positivistic salience in the historiography of the Sultanate and Mughal state, Pollock and his adherents too, followed the same methodological track: Sanskrit was reported dead on arrival (or localized) by the second millennium; vernacularization of politics reigned sway in complete innocence of the presence of Persianized conceptions of imperium; and monopolistic truth-claims of the language of the gods passed uncritically into histories of literary cultures.

Ironically, these two neat archives (Sanskritistic and Persianate), corresponding broadly to two parallel historiographies, fell into the same isolated territories of investigation that Pollock, trained in Sanskrit philology, himself had warned against: 'What the theorists [and presumably historians] say about us, "all dressed up and nowhere to go," hits a lot harder than what we say about them: "lots of dates and nothing to wear"'.[5]

My work, however, is humbler in scope, and I would like to believe, more historicized in method. That is why, instead of bunching texts together in hundreds and ticking them off as monolingual/bilingual

[5] Pollock, 'Future Philology?', p. 947.

and local/universal, I focus 'only' on three texts. This allows me to carefully examine the framing, language, literary techniques, content, genre, and genealogy of each. In the process, many inherited categories that one was used to taking for granted proved to be miserably inadequate (or in need of modification) to describe the worlds of complexity that these texts revealed. Thus, for example, my examination of *Puruṣaparīkṣā* shows that the text deployed narratives of recent history in novel ways to justify ethics that are simultaneously validated with reference to Vedic lore. The entirely modern distinctions between secular and religious appeared inadequate.

The evidently multiple forms of multilingual literary cultures in the fifteenth century—lexical, generic, idiomatic, thematic, authorial, among others—at one level are interesting in themselves. Yet, the follow-up questions are equally important: what kinds of power relations did the textual productions of the time try to uphold? What sorts of future political enterprises could this kind of literary culture prepare the ground for? To put the question in a simplistic and linear sequence, if literatures created/disseminated 'knowledge', and if knowledge formations are bedrocks on which fields of power are laid and exploited, then what could all this mean politically beyond the actual existing polities, in the long term?

As a prelude to answering that question, I also pose, in Chapter 2 in this volume, the intermediate theoretical problematic of what the categories of literature, history, and power mean to a historian now (in the 'emic' sense), and what they could have meant to someone in the fifteenth century following various literary traditions (in the 'etic' sense). My exploration of each of the three texts in the second part is also an empirical way of opening up these larger theoretical questions. These apparently theoretical engagements are crucial for reconstituting the space for a political history of literatures and languages.

In the end, it is of critical significance for me to clarify that while trying to work out the contours of a knowledge formation by mapping the literary culture of the long fifteenth century, I am making assumptions about a slow-moving but tangible relationship between literature and knowledge formation on the one hand, and power and political possibilities on the other. In this analysis, however, I make a clear distinction between relations of power and institutions of governance. Governance is a tangible, everyday practice, undertaken by particular institutions like family, caste-bodies, guilds, and above all, the state. These and other institutions governed subjects as per written and unwritten codes of law, ethics, morality, and tradition. However, I use the word 'power' primarily as a disciplining mechanism through discourses about 'correct' and 'incorrect', moral and immoral, or acceptable and non-acceptable. It is this disciplining wiring of society that a new dynamism of literary culture could enter and alter. And it is this slow process of changes in disciplinary formations that I seek to unravel.

While institutions of governance surely need to be studied, my interest in this volume is limited to a study of the ways in which the basis for changes in power relations was being laid in the fifteenth century, without any individual or institution having willed consciously to do so: Particular kinds of stories being told in specific ways, for example, could play an important role in spreading and reconstituting knowledge formations. To the extent that I succeed in doing this by exploring literary productions of the time, I will have succeeded in highlighting the political value of literature.

Part I

Contexts

1 *Vidyapati and Mithila*

In February 2013, I visited Bisfi, the village of Vidyapati's birth in Madhubani district of north Bihar.[1] As I asked around, an old man remarked in Maithili that there were many Vidyapatis.

> One was Raja Śivasiṃha's Rājapaṇḍita who was a great scholar of Sanskrit and wrote many books. The Mughals took away all of them for their own use. Another was the devotee [*upāsaka*] of Bhagavatī, her *asthāna* [*sthāna*, place] is still there. Then, there was the Vidyapati who Mahādeva himself came to serve as his personal attendant [*khawāsa*].

[1] Recently it has also been made a block, that is, an administrative unit below the district, and it gives its name to the local Vidhan Sabha constituency as well. It is a large village, compared to the average size of villages in Bihar and North India. As per the Indian government's Census of India website, Bisfi had a total of 2,832 households with 13,981 persons living in them in 2011. See http://censusindia.gov.in/pca/cdb_pca_census/Houselisting-housing-BR.html, accessed 11 June 2015.

> Yet another Vidyapati composed beautiful Kṛiśṇa līlā songs, and those are still sung by Vaiṣṇava bhaktas all over the world. There is another one who politicians resurrect every now and then. Have you seen his memorial?

'Yes, I have', I assured him. But, did he really think these were all different people? He shook his head in exasperation. 'You do not understand', he said, 'Vidyapati was not a man like you and me. He was a *jugapurusa*.'[2] I thought of my uncle in my native village in the district of Samastipur, about fifty miles to the south of Bisfi. 'You are going northwards', he had warned me, 'be very careful. Everyone there fancies being a scholar. *Māthā ghumā detau tauhar*, they will send your head spinning.'

In saying that there were many Vidyapatis, however, the old man could not have put it better for me. The range of Vidyapati's compositions, as well as the diversity of ways in which he has been remembered and appropriated since, is indeed stunning.

Life, Literary Compositions

Vidyapati is a household name in Mithila, the region in north Bihar where he flourished in the late fourteenth and early fifteenth centuries. As noted, he was born in the village of Bisapī (now Bisfi). His father Gaṇapati Ṭhakkura was a court priest of Rāya Gaṇeśvara, the reigning chief of Tirhut and father of the famous Kīrttisiṃha. Vidyapati is believed to have had two wives, three sons, and four daughters.[3] But there are other details of his life that are more elusive.

We do not know when exactly he was born. The multiple references in his numerous works (as well as in those of his contemporaries) to his patrons, some of whom it is possible to date with precision, introduce more confusion than clarity, and we are still unable to date the poet's birth with certainty. The irony should not be missed; Mithila is probably the only area in the subcontinent that boasts of a tradition

[2] From Sanskrit: *yugapuruṣa*, literally, Man of the Age. The word has an implied connotation of one whose being changes the course of time and history.

[3] Chaudhary, *A Survey of Maithili Literature*, p. 57.

of maintaining genealogies of each and every Brāhmaṇa family in the form of *pañjī* records maintained by professional record-keepers, the *pañjīkāras*.[4] And yet, while information on Vidyapati's birth is available in these records, it does not always match with the 'evidence' from his own compositions.

A related problem in arriving at a definite time of his birth is the fact that most references to time in Vidyapati's texts were given in the Lakṣamaṇa Era.[5] Unfortunately, the precise date when this era started is not known beyond dispute. While a large number of scholars writing in Hindi and English agree with Kielhorn's meticulous calculation that places its beginning in the year 1119 of the Common Era, many scholars in Mithila believe that the era started ten years earlier, in 1109.[6] In this volume, I have used 1119 CE as the year in which the Lakṣamaṇa Saṃvat started.

Scholars have debated these issues endlessly. They now accept one of two positions: those who go by the pañjī records believe that Vidyapati was born in 1350.[7] Others see 1374 as a more likely year

[4] The records have been maintained from early-fourteenth century onwards. Legend has it that Harisiṃhadeva, the reigning Karṇāṭa chief in Mithila at the time, instituted it.

[5] See note 53 of this chapter for a detailed explanation of Lakṣamaṇa Era.

[6] Kielhorn, 'The Epoch of the Lakshmansena Era'. Maithili-speaking scholars have relied on a verse attributed to Vidyapati in which dates are cited simultaneously in the Lakṣamaṇa Era and the Śaka Era. For a good discussion of arguments for and against the proposition, see Singh, *Vidyapati*, pp. 38–47. While it is difficult to be definitive, Kielhorn's calculation, based as it is on a cross-examination of a larger chunk of data, appears more plausible.

[7] Most of the scholars from the Mithila region fall in this category. This includes scholars like Ramanath Jha, Govind Jha, Dineshwarlal Anand, Shashinath Jha, Indrakant Jha, and a host of others who have edited Vidyapati's works. See, for example, R. Jha, 'Introduction', in Vidyapati, *Puruṣaparīkṣā*, p. 16; Jha, 'Bhumika', in Vidyapati, *Vibhāgasāra*, p. 4; Anand and S. Jha, 'Bhumikā' (Preface), in Vidyapati, *Padāvalī*, vol. 2, pp. 15–16; I. Jha, *Vidyapatikālīn Mithila*, pp. 3–31. However, there are a few scholars, among them Radhakrishna Chaudhary, who believe that Vidyapati must have lived a long life, roughly between 1360 and 1480. See Chaudhary, *Mithila in the Age of Vidyapati*, pp. 13–20.

for his birth.[8] There is no agreement on the date of his death either. Estimates vary between 1430 and 1480. Fortunately, however, the broad timing and sequence of his compositions are not disputed. It is understood that most of his major compositions span, roughly, the period between 1400 and the 1430s.

Vidyapati was a prolific scholar and a popular poet, a *dharmaśāstra* expert and a story-teller, a courtier and royal priest, a Śiva *bhakta* (devotee of Śiva), and a gifted composer of Vaiṣṇava and ṣringār songs, all rolled in one. Apart from Sanskrit, he knew Prakrit, Apabhraṃśa, and Maithili, and composed with equal facility in all of them. His oeuvre includes erotic allegories, a law book, praise-biographies, a tantric play, a writing manual, a treatise on political ethics and masculinity, compendia of rituals, and more (see Table 1.1). Above and beyond this were his Maithili and 'Brajabuli' songs, on a vast diversity of themes: sowing and harvesting seasons, love and erotica, separation, Kṛiṣṇa's love-play with the *gopīs*, Vaiṣṇava and Śaiva bhakti, and various *saṃsakāras* like birth, *upanayana* (sacred thread ceremony), and marriage. Indeed, these songs appear to be the mainstay of Vidyapati's glory, both in the middle ages and now.

Fame and Legends

Over the last six centuries or so, Vidyapati has been mythologized as well as memorialized in interesting ways. His admirers credit him with having performed miracles and received divine favours in ways that a 'rational' approach fixated on facts may be inadequate to understand. The most popular of these legends holds that Lord Śiva was so moved by his piety that he took the guise of a poor man, calling himself Ugna, to become a personal attendant to the poet. Almost all of Vidyapati's myriad biographies relate this 'episode' in his life. Any conversation about him with a Maithil is bound to refer to the story. Although there are many versions of this story, the core narrative remains fairly stable: Lord Śiva lived with Vidyapati disguised as his attendant,

[8] A majority of the scholars who believe that Vidyapati could not have been born long before 1374 are scholars of Hindi literature from outside Mithila. See for example, Singh, *Vidyapati*, p. 43.

Table 1.1 Vidyapati's Compositions with Their Language, Script, Patrons, and Themes

Title	Language and Script	Earthly and Divine Patrons	Genre and Theme
Maṇimañjarīnāṭikā	Sanskrit (with blank spaces for songs, presumably in another language) Script: Tirahutā	No earthly patron Salutations to Umā–Śiva	A minor play, *nāṭikā*, that followed the rules laid by Bharata's *Nāṭyaśāstra*. It tells a fictive story of a married king, Candrasena's love for a young Vaṇija girl
Bhūparikramaṇa	Sanskrit Script: Devanāgarī	Written for Devasiṃha (who is not referred to as Raja) Salutations to Gaṇeśa, Sāmba, Viṣṇu, Ravi (sun), and Ambikā	Collection of stories, *kathā*s, set in different locales, *deśa*s, as a means of information about each of the locales. It was originally meant to have sixty-five such stories set in as many deśas, but it seems the author managed to finish only eight stories. All are in prose though individual characters frequently cite verses. The same composition was later 'reframed' differently with an addition of thirty-six stories to compose the famous *Puruṣaparīkṣā*

(*Cont'd*)

Table 1.1 (*Cont'd*)

Title	Language and Script	Earthly and Divine Patrons	Genre and Theme
Kīrttilatā	Avahaṭṭha/ Apabhraṃśa Script: Devanāgarī	Written for Kīrttisiṃha Invocations of Gaṇeśa, Pārvatī, Śiva, and Sarasvatī	A praise-biography in verse, with occasional prose in between, composed broadly in the style of the Sanskrit genre *ākhyāyikā*. It tells of the travels, travails, and the eventual victory of its protagonist (also the patron of the text), Kīrttisiṃha, over Malik Arsalan. Contains detailed account of the city of Jaunpur (Joṇāpura), the capital city of the Sharqi Sultanate, where Kīrttisiṃha travelled with some of his companions (including Vidyapati) to ask for the Sultan's help in overcoming Arsalan
Puruṣaparīkṣā	Sanskrit Script: Devanāgarī	Written for Śivasiṃha Salutations to Ādiśakti (but Brahmā, Mahādeva, and Viṣṇu too are mentioned)	Compendium of stories told in simple prose with *śloka*s frequently cited by various characters. Composed broadly in the kathā genre of Sanskrit. According to author himself, it is a treatise on *naya/nīti*, that is, political ethics. However, it is framed as a text on the ideals of 'masculinity', where the seed story is about a king being instructed by a sagely minister on how to identify/become an ideal man

Gorakṣavijaya	Multilingual with Sanskrit, Prakrit, and Maithili Script: Mithilākṣara	Written for Śivasiṃha Salutation to Lord Śiva	A play that narrates the story wherein the famous tantric saint Gorakhanātha (Sanskrit: Gorakṣanātha) rescued his preceptor Machendranātha (Sanskrit: Matsyendranātha) from a life of bhoga back to a life of yoga. The play starts with a conversation between a naṭa and a naṭī in Sanskrit and Prakrit. The story actually unfolds through a series of songs in the Maithili language. The rāgas in which the songs are to be sung are also mentioned
Kīrttipatākā	Avahaṭṭha/ Apabhraṃśa Script: Tirahutā	Written for Śivasiṃha Salutation (*maṅgalācaraṇa*) page is missing in the damaged manuscripts	Another praise-biography in verse. This has Śivasiṃha as its chief protagonist. The extant manuscript is damaged badly, and only a small portion of the text has survived, which depicts a battle in which Śivasiṃha emerges victorious against an unidentified Turkish sultan
Harikeli	Avahaṭṭha/ Apabhraṃśa Script: Tirahutā	Written for Rāya Arjuna Salutation (maṅgalācaraṇa) page is missing in the damaged manuscripts	Another text that has come down to us in a damaged manuscript. Its protagonist is Rāya Arjuna or Jagat Siṃha, most probably a cousin of the more famous Śivasiṃha. Much of the available text is an erotic, probably allegorical, description of Kṛiśṇa's love-play with the gopīs

(*Cont'd*)

Table 1.1 (*Cont'd*)

Title	Language and Script	Earthly and Divine Patrons	Genre and Theme
Likhanāvalī	Sanskrit Script: Devanāgarī	Written for Purāditya Girinārāyaṇa of Droṇāvāra Salutation to Lord Gaṇeśa	Written in the form of a manual for scribes. It carries model letters (official and personal), as well as model documents recording business transactions and affidavits on oath
Śaivasarvasvasāra	Sanskrit Script: One manuscript in Mithilākṣara and two in Devanāgarī	Written for Viśvāsadevī Salutations to Lord Śiva	Describes the cosmic significance, religious merits, and prescribed rituals of worshipping Śiva. Cites extensively from the Purāṇas
Gaṅgāvākyāvalī	Sanskrit Script: Not available	Written for Viśvāsadevī Invocation of Ganga and Lord Śiva	Another text that cites from the Purāṇas; it glorifies the religious significance of River-Goddess Ganga
Vibhāgasāra	Sanskrit Script: Tirahutā	Written for Darpanārāyaṇa (aka Narsiṃhadeva) Invokes Hari, Śiva, and Ganga	A dharmaśāstra that focusses chiefly on the laws of property. It cites copiously from a number of smṛitis including those of Manu, Bṛhaspati, Nārada, Yājñavalkya, Kātyāyana, and Gautama

Dānavākyāvalī	Sanskrit Script: Devanāgarī	Written for Rani Dhīramatī (Queen of Narsiṃhadeva) Invokes Lord Śiva	Tells of different kinds of ritual donations and the spiritual merits each would earn for the donor
Durgābhaktitaraṅginī	Sanskrit Script: Devanāgarī	Written for Bhairavasiṃha Invokes Goddess Durga	Describes the 'due' procedure for worshipping the goddess Durga, especially during the nine days of the *navarātra* in the month of *āśvina*
Gayāpattalaka	Sanskrit Script: Devanāgarī	No patrons mentioned	A booklet that provides the rituals relating to funerals
Varṣakṛitya	Sanskrit Script: Not available	Not dedicated to anyone but mentions Raja Rupanārāyaṇa	Another minor work that details the festivals to be observed (probably those that *were* observed by people in Mithila in those days) through the year
Padāvalī	Maithili Script: Tirahutā/ Bangla/Devanāgarī	Not originally compiled by the author in the form of a book, hence has no specific patron. The most frequently occurring name in the songs is probably Raja Śivasiṃha	Compilation of Vidyapati's songs on a variety of themes. Doubtful if the author himself put these songs together in book form. We have at least one medieval manuscript, a collection put together from oral sources by Grierson, and a few songs taken from citations in Locan's *Rāgataraṅgiṇī* (seventeenth century). Published in several overlapping volumes

Source: Author's compliation.

Ugna, for a finite but unspecified period of time. Once when the two of them were stranded in a forest, Vidyapati asked Ugna to fetch water. Finding no source of water anywhere in the vicinity, Ugna assumed his original form and drew a pot of fresh Ganga water out of his own tresses. However, the Brāhmaṇa bhakta of Śiva recognized the taste of Ganga water. Knowing that River Ganga flowed nowhere near the place, he got very suspicious. He insisted that Ugna must reveal his real identity or else he will be abandoned. Thus forced, Lord Śiva revealed himself but agreed to live with Vidyapati on the condition that Vidyapati would continue to treat him as his servant, and that he would never reveal the secret to anyone. One day after some time, however, Vidyapati's wife happened to be very annoyed with the servant. In anger, she took a piece of wood and charged towards Ugna in the presence of her husband. Thus, the recipient of Lord Śiva's grace had to reveal the real identity of his attendant with the result that Ugna disappeared before his eyes, forever.

A second legend holds that at the time of his death, Vidyapati decided to move southwards to meet the goddess Ganga. However, a few miles away from the sacred river, he felt too tired to continue his journey. He decided to remain there, and resolved that if his piety was pure, the sacred Ganga would herself come to him. Very soon, the River-Goddess obliged the great poet, and the water level of the river started rising miraculously until he could take a final holy dip. The place where this 'happened' was renamed Vidyapati Nagar at an unidentified time in the past. A temple dedicated to Śiva came up here.

Presently, it stands a few kilometres from the subdivision of Dalsinghsarai in the district of Samastipur, about sixty miles southwest of Bisfi. Interestingly, Vidyapati himself related a version of this story in his *Puruṣaparīkṣā*, wherein the protagonist was a Kāyastha by the name of Bodhi from Mithila.[9]

That Vidyapati himself came to have so many legends posthumously woven around his character is probably befitting. In the aforementioned story about the *tātvika*, Bodhi, he made the protagonist Bodhi recite a śloka to the effect that 'one's body is destroyed,

[9] See '*Tātvika Kathā*', *Puruṣaparīkṣā*, pp. 166–8.

riches disappear and friends go away, in the end it is only stories that are left behind, *kathāsāre hi saṃsāre*, and only fame that is permanent, *kīrttireva sthirā bhavet*!'[10] Vidyapati's own glory appears only to have grown with the passage of time. Popular memory has kept him alive by singing his songs, circulating 'appropriate' legends, and even crediting him with a form of folk theatre.[11]

Meanwhile, in Bisfi, a temple of Bhagavatī claims to ensconce the idol the poet 'had himself worshipped'. Another temple stands at the far end of the village, duly named Ugna Mahadev, after Vidyapati's famous personal attendant (Image 1.1). A feeble attempt by the state at 'nationalizing' Vidyapati can be seen in the memorial constructed for the poet in 1983 (Images 1.2a and 1.2b).[12] Yet, the village of Vidyapati's birth is not really overwhelmed by the presence of the legendary scholar. The attempt at monumentalizing remains humble, even indifferent.

However, the temple complex at the eponymously named *qasba* of Vidyapati Nagar, recently renamed Vidyapati Dhāma, presents a picture in contrast. In the 1980s, local residents told me, it was just a single building and though it was popular even then, it did not attract so many visitors. In the last thirty years or so, the temple has grown into a much larger structure, with a museum, halls for

[10] Vidyapati, *Puruṣaparīkṣā*, p. 168.

[11] *Bidāpat Nāch*, a form of street theatre, was performed in certain villages of Purnea district of north Bihar in the last century. *Mailā Āñcal*, the famous novel by Phaṇīśvar Nath Renu describes one such performance, set in a village in Purnea. For a discussion of the tradition of *Bidāpat Nāch*, its history, and its state at present, see unpublished PhD dissertation, Woolford, 'Renu Village', especially 'Chapter 4', pp. 195–268.

[12] It is a walled compound of modest size with a single-storey building in the middle, a raised platform in a corner, and a bust of the village's most famous ancestor in front. The building had a single chamber with two framed and fading photographs, indifferently reclining against the wall: a portrait of Vidyapati and a smaller frame of Mahatma Gandhi flanked by tiny heads of Jawaharlal Nehru, Rajendra Prasad, Subhas Chandra Bose, Chandrashekhar Azad, Bhagat Singh, and Sardar Patel. A few paces from the memorial was a notionally marked birthplace where, I was told, his havelī must have stood once upon a time.

Image 1.1 Ugnā Mahādeva Temple at Bisfi
Source: Author.

Image 1.2a Vidyapati Memorial at Bisfi
Source: Author.

Image 1.2b A Bust of Vidyapati at Bisfi
Source: Author.

pilgrims to rest, and a fairly wide courtyard.[13] The footfalls have registered a sharp increase. Occasionally, there is a stampede-like situation, especially in the rainy month of *Sāvan*, a month considered particularly auspicious for worshipping Lord Śiva. A veritable market has come up around the temple wherein Vidyapati gives his name to almost every shop including eating joints and medicine counters (Images 1.3a, 1.3b, and 1.3c). A marble plaque outside traces Vidyapati's lineage from his own time to the present. Another one records the inauguration of a temple renovation project by the chief minister of Bihar in 2010.

Parallel initiatives by the government of Bihar also helped recover the historical Vidyapati in substantive ways. Soon after Independence, the government of Bihar mobilized a state-run institution,

[13] The museum consists of a single hall, and displays 'objects associated with the poet'. I could not see the museum when I visited the temple complex in February 2013, as the caretaker of the museum was 'on leave'.

Image 1.3a The Śiva Temple at Vidyapati Dhāma
Source: Author.

Image 1.3b A Jewellery Shop in Vidyapati Dhāma
Source: Author.

Image 1.3c An Eatery in Vidyapati Dhāma
Source: Author.

the Bihar Rāṣṭra Bhāṣā Pariṣad, to find the manuscripts of Vidyapati's writings and make them accessible in print.[14] Another state-aided institution by the name of Maithili Akademi was established in 1975, which also undertook similar initiatives.[15] Manuscripts of some of Vidyapati's compositions had long been in circulation. Many of them were found and published before Independence. However, the post-Independence period saw fresh attempts to produce critical editions of the Brāhmaṇa's works, through a collation of a larger number of extant manuscripts and edited versions. Individual initiatives also played a role in the process. The twentieth century saw the production

[14] Though the Bihar State Legislative Assembly passed an act to establish the Bihar Rāṣṭra Bhāṣā Pariṣad on 11 April 1947, the latter came into being only in March 1957. See Datta, *Encyclopaedia of Indian Literature*, vol. 2, p. 1732.

[15] See Thakur, '*Prakāśakīya Nivedan*'.

of a large number of biographies written by scholars of Hindi and Maithili, as well as by lay admirers from other professions.[16]

It is important to note, however, that the fifteenth-century Brāhmaṇa from Bisfi was far from forgotten in the intervening centuries. References to him can be found in texts composed in the Mithila region since the fifteenth century itself. Even outside of Mithila, he seems to have been known fairly well. At the end of the sixteenth century, Abul Fazl, located far away in the Mughal city of Agra, mentioned Vidyapati in the *Ain-i Akbari* as the composer of *lahcharī* songs.[17] A few decades before that, he was named several times as the poet whose songs moved the famous Vaiṣṇava bhakta of Bengal, Kṛiśṇacaitanya, into ecstasy.[18] Many of these songs figured in the seventeenth-century treatise on music, *Rāgataraṅgiṇī* of Locana Kavi, as illustrations for specific rāgas.[19] Among his Sanskrit works, *Puruṣaparīkṣā* was made available in the nineteenth century by the British to native princes, who were encouraged to study it so as to cultivate ethics. It was even included in the syllabus of the coveted Indian Civil Service examination a little later. An abridged version was prepared early in the twentieth century for use by children in schools. His *Vibhāgasāra* appears to have been used as a reference book for property law at least since the eighteenth century. Probably the most

16 A select list would include Singh, *Vidyapati*; Jha, *Vidyapati*; Thakur, *Mahākavi Vidyapati*; Shrivastav, *Vidyapati: Anuśilan evaṃ Mūlyāṅkan.*

17 While describing 'desi songs' of different regions, the *Ain-i Akbari* noted that 'those in the dialects of Tirhut are called *Lahchāri*, and are the composition of Biddya-pat, and in character highly erotic'. See Abul Fazl Allami, *Ain-i Akbari*, vol. II, p. 266. *Lahchārī*, identifiable with the famous *nacārī* songs dedicated to Lord Śiva, however, were only one of the many genres of songs composed by Vidyapati, and current at least since then in the region. Other popular genres of songs included *sohara, bārahamāsā*, and *chaumāsā*.

18 I have been able to trace at least five references to Vidyapati in Kṛiṣṇadāsa biography of Caitanya. See Kṛiṣṇadāsa Kavirāja, *Caitanya Caritamṛita*, I.13.42; II.2.77; II.10.115; III.15.27; III.17.6.

19 In fact, *Rāgataraṅgiṇī* is an important source for collecting the 'authentic' songs of Vidyapati. The second volume of Vidyapati's *Padāvalī*, published by the Bihar Rāṣṭra Bhāṣā Pariṣad in 2000, carries all the songs attributed to Vidyapati by Locan. See Vidyapati, *Padāvalī*, part 2. Also see Locanapaṇḍita, *Rāgataraṅgiṇī*.

commonly used of his texts, apart from the *Padāvalī*, among the upper-caste Maithils were/are his handbooks for performing rituals for the *navarātra* festival (*Durgābhaktitaraṅgiṇī*), and for worshipping Śiva (*Śaivasarvasvasāra*).[20]

Closer to our own times, the young Rabindranath Tagore compared Vidyapati with Caṇḍīdāsa and noted that Vidyapati's 'verses are filled with rhythm, music and colours; they heave as waves of loveliness, pleasure and enjoyment. They are the euphoria of early youth, displaying nothing but pure bliss and ceaseless melody.'[21] In fact, he was reported to have been so impressed by Vidyapati's songs that he took the pen-name of Bhānu Singh and tried to imitate Vidyapati's style by composing similar songs in the artificial medium of Brajabuli.[22] In 1937, the famous Debaki Bose directed a movie, a biofiction titled *Vidyapati* that starred Pahari Sanyal as the eponymous hero, Kanan Devi as his companion, and Prithviraj Kapoor as Raja Śivasiṃha, the most famous of Vidyapati's many patrons. It was Śivasiṃha who granted the poet's native village Bisapī to him as reported in a copper plate inscription.[23] And it was Śivasiṃha again who honoured the poet with the title of 'Abhinava-Jayadeva', the new Jayadeva.[24]

Of the many types of learned men (*savidya*) that Sage Subuddhi listed in Vidyapati's *Puruṣaparīkṣā*, the most exalted one perhaps was *ubhayavidya*, that is, one who had expertise both in classical lore and folk wisdom. No one would possibly have denied that Vidyapati could rightfully claim to be an ubhayavidya.[25]

20 See Chapter 4 in this volume for details.

21 Tagore, *Ādhunik Sāhitya*, pp. 441–5. I am indebted to Tanika Sarkar for translating the entire text of the essay, including the excerpted lines, from Bangla into English for me.

22 Kaviraj, 'The Two Histories of Literary Culture in Bengal', p. 513. These compositions of Tagore were published as *Bhanusingher Padāvalī* (see Koch, *My Heart Sings*).

23 The full text of the grant-inscription, consisting of about thirty-eight lines in Sanskrit and a translation by Grierson can be accessed in *Indian Antiquary*, vol. XIV, 1885, pp. 191–2.

24 Jha, *Vidyapati*, p. 9.

25 Vidyapati, *Puruṣaparīkṣā*, pp. 122–8.

How did the Brāhmaṇa manage to do this? He might have been born with a creative spark, as they say, but where did he receive his training in the classical tradition of Sanskrit? Did he have a preceptor he was indebted to? What was it like to grow up as a Brāhmaṇa boy in a village in late-fourteenth-century north Bihar? We do not have direct answers to most of these questions. Yet, one can try to make an informed inference by looking at traditions of learning in Mithila, and in the author's own family.

Mithila as a Hub of Elite Learning

Vidyapati belonged to a Brāhmaṇa family of scholars and ministers. Though he rarely gave any information about himself, there are enough references to him and his family in other contemporary texts, pañjī records, and inscriptions to allow scholars to reconstruct the broad contours of his ancestry.

The most prominent of Vidyapati's ancestors, four generations before him, was Devāditya Ṭhakkura. He was probably the first person in the lineage to have achieved public glory. While tracing their lineage, his descendants most commonly identified him as 'the ancestor'. His eldest son Vīreśvara, for example, in his book *Chandopaddhatti*, traced his descent from Devāditya with pride. Bhavasiṃha's *Sugati Sopāna*, a text written for Gaṇeśvara did the same in order to claim an exalted lineage.[26] Devāditya's grandson, Caṇḍeśvara, the famous author of numerous Sanskrit texts, also referred to him several times.

The pañjī records listed Devāditya as a *sāndhivigrahika-mantriratnākara*, that is, a minister of war and peace. This must have been in the court of a Karṇāṭa ruler, probably Harisiṃhadeva. Each of the seven sons of Devāditya Ṭhakkura was noted to have a title signifying a position in the local court. The second son, Dhīreśwara Ṭhakkura, is addressed as a *naibandhika* (from *nibandha*; literally, 'bounded', but usually referred to a piece of prose writing), an official whose charge must have had something to do with writing/

26 *Descriptive Catalogue of Manuscripts in Mithila*, vol. 1, p. 122. Patna: Bihar and Orissa Research Society, n.d.

documentation. Other titles include *sāndhivigrahika* (minister in charge of war and alliances), *mahāsāmantādhipati* (general chief of the landlords), *bhaṇḍāgārika* (minister/officer in charge of the royal stores), *sthānāntarika* (minister/officer in charge of transfers), and *mudrāhastaka* (money changer). Interestingly, all the titles mentioned here figure in Vidyapati's *Likhanāvalī*.[27] In fact, a majority of the descendants of Devāditya up to Vidyapati, and some even after Vidyapati's generation, seem to have held important official positions at the local court. The aforementioned Devāditya Ṭhakkura is mentioned in Caṇḍeśvara's *Kṛityaratnākara* as *Hambīradhvāntabhānuḥ*, signifying that the Brāhmaṇa also participated in a battle, probably in Ala al-Din Muhammad Khalji's (r. 1296–1316) army against Hammīradeva, the famous ruler of Raṇathambhor.

Equally noteworthy is the fact that a number of these men in Vidyapati's lineage appear to be scholars in their own right, if the books (most of them in Sanskrit) attributed to them are anything to go by. Many of these works are extant, and some of them have even been published. The most famous and prolific author in Vidyapati's lineage, apart from himself, was Caṇḍeśvara. A cousin of Vidyapati's grandfather Jayadatta, he flourished in the early fourteenth century. He authored *Rājanītiratnākara*, a treatise on organizing the state.[28] He also wrote a set of seven books, broadly in the tradition of law books, on a range of themes: *Krityaratnākara*, *Dānaratnākara*, *Vyavahāraratnākara*, *Śuddhiratnākara*, *Pūjāratnākara*, *Vivādaratnākara*, and *Gṛihastharatnākara*. Together, these books are referred to as *Saptaratnākara*.

These learned ancestors of Vidyapati were hardly exceptional in Mithila, especially if we consider the scholarly output from the region during this period. In the dharmaśāstra tradition itself, we find an unbroken series of works being composed in Mithila, beginning with those of Ṣrīkara and Gopāla in the eleventh century, Lakṣmīdhara's *Smṛitikalpataru* in the twelfth, Ṣrīdatta's *Ācārādarśa* in the thirteenth–fourteenth, Harinātha's *Smṛitisāra* in the fourteenth, and continuing

[27] See Chapter 3 in this volume.

[28] See Caṇḍeśvara, *Rājanītiratnākara*. For a brief discussion of this work, see Chapter 4 in this volume.

into the fifteenth century with Vidyapati's *Vibhāgasāra*.[29] A few commentaries, like that of Acyut on *Kāvyaprakāśa*, were also produced on literary theory. Another literary luminary was the celebrated Vācaspati Miṣra, a prolific author who is credited with having produced about forty-one volumes, though not all are extant.[30] *Sāṅkhyatattvakaumudī*,[31] *Śūdrācāracintāmaṇi*,[32] *Vivādacintāmaṇi*,[33] *Ācāracintāmaṇi*, and *Candrakaumudī* are some of his better-known works.

No less alive was the emerging trend of writing in the so-called vernacular—the local dialect of what later became Maithili, and the various inflections of Apabhraṃśa and Prakrit. As Chaudhary puts it, 'the period from 1200 A.D. onwards constitutes a landmark in its [Maithili's] history'.[34] Many of Vidyapati's ancestors, including his father Gaṇapati Ṭhakkura, were credited with having composed songs in the local dialect. Chaudhary, in his survey, lists at least fourteen authors who chose to compose in 'Maithili'.[35] A famous contemporary of Vidyapati was Viśṇupuri, who composed the *Bhaktiratnāvalī*, a collection of Maithili songs devoted to the love of Rādhā and Kṛiṣṇa.[36]

In fact, Jyotirīśvara's unique compendium of words, phrases, and appropriate expressions in 'Maithili', aptly titled *Varṇaratnākara*, was meant to be a companion for would-be authors for a wide range of situations. As such it might be indicative of the vibrant industry of 'vernacular' scholarship in the region.

Yet, it was the field of philosophy, in which Mithila, at least during the period from the thirteenth through the fifteenth century, could outshine any other centre of learning in North India. It was here

29 Jha, 'Bhumika', in Vidyapati, *Vibhāgasāra*, pp. 7–9.

30 Jha, 'Bhumika', pp. 17–18. The period during which Vācaspati Miṣra lived is disputed. It is possible that he was a contemporary of Vidyapati. But he might well have lived a century or two earlier.

31 Miṣra, *Sāñkhyatattvakaumudī*.

32 Benke, 'The *Śūdrācāraśiromaṇi* of Kṛṣṇa Śeṣa', pp. 11, 14.

33 Miṣra, *Vivādacintāmaṇi*.

34 Chaudhary, *A Survey of Maithili Literature*, p. 253.

35 Chaudhury, *A Survey of Maithili Literature*, p. 24.

36 Chaudhury, *A Survey of Maithili Literature*, p. 81.

that the foundation of the celebrated *navya-nyāya* system[37] was laid by Gaṅgeśa in the thirteenth century, which was carried forward by Vardhamāna in the fourteenth century, and Yajñapati Upādhyāya and Pakṣadhara Miṣra in the fifteenth. As Pollock remarked, '[f]ew areas in northern India after the fourteenth century, aside from what had become the new frontier zone of Mithilā on the Nepal border, seem to have shown quite the same vitality of Sanskrit literary production as earlier until a revival set in during the early Mughal period...'.[38]

In many ways, it was (and is) this legacy of learning that came to be identified with the geocultural region of Mithila. If Vidyapati has become the modern icon of Maithil identity, he stands in this role not just as himself. As a yugapuruṣa he is burdened with the glorious history of the entire era. In some senses, this legacy has continued in modern times—with a spate of publications by local enthusiasts of Maithil culture on a host of themes in Maithili, Hindi, and occasionally in English too. In its production, preservation, circulation, and probably consumption, the narrow social base of this legacy is obvious but rarely noticed, let alone analysed. In the middle ages, as also largely now, its protagonists were invariably upper-caste (chiefly Brāhmaṇa and Kāyastha) men.

It was the pride of the privileged few, which came to be articulated, in the modern era of identity politics, as the pride of the entire Maithili-speaking population. In a book about language politics in North India in 1974, Paul Brass devoted a long chapter to the fate of the Maithili language in independent India. Contrasting the case of Maithili with some of the more 'successful' languages of modern times, he noted that 'Maithil Brāhmaṇas and Kāyasthas in north Bihar form an elite', who were heavily invested in 'pursuing a policy of caste exclusiveness and adherence to principles of caste hierarchy and orthodoxy'.[39]

[37] Nyāya literally means logic or a set of rules/system. It was also the name of a very famous 'school' of philosophy attributed to Gautam in ancient Sanskrit traditions. The system was revived and made more sophisticated and abstruse in the fourteenth century by several men, the most famous of them being Vacaspati Miśra between the thirteenth and fifteenth centuries. This new (navya) system of logic/philosophy came to be called navya-nyāya.

[38] Pollock, *The Language of the Gods*, p. 492.

[39] Brass, *Language, Religion and Politics in North India*, pp. 114–15.

It is outside the scope of this volume to grapple with the complexity of this politics or the sociology that underlies it. It is interesting to note, however, that the rich traditions of learning in Mithila thrived in a rather narrow social base, and hence the 'richness' of this tradition should not be seen as unqualified.[40] This glorious legacy, in fact, was subject to a geographical differentiation too—another kind of internal layering.

Almost all the medieval authors who contributed to the making of the scholarly traditions of Mithila hailed from its northern parts, that is, the present districts of West and East Champaran, Sitamarhi, Madhubani, Supaul, and the northern parts of Darbhanga and Saharsa. Indeed, the north–south cultural fault line persists as a concept in the lives of many orthodox Maithils even today. In remarking upon the intolerably erudite ways of the northern Maithils, my uncle had pointed to this very long-standing internal cultural differentiation within the region. Even though this divide is rarely acknowledged in formalized discourses, it does appear occasionally in modern fiction in Maithili.[41] While this could become a subject for an independent study, pertinent to note for the purposes of our present discussion is the relatively small world of about a few hundred privileged men in the northern portions of Mithila that constituted the learning milieu of Vidyapati. And yet, many of these men were part of wider subcontinental circuits of textual transmission, some of them probably very well-travelled as well. In its geographical expanse, therefore, Mithila was hardly as 'small' an area as it often appears in modern histories of medieval India.

Geographical Background

The cultural zone known as Mithila today constitutes a major chunk of the modern province of Bihar, north of the Ganga. It is bound by the terai of Nepal and the Himalayas in the north, the state of Uttar

40 For a slightly more detailed discussion of this issue, see Jha, 'Vidyapati: *itihasakāroṃ kī pratīkṣā meṃ*'.

41 For example, in a story entitled 'Pāñc Patra' by Harimohan Jha, an old man, in a letter he writes to his wife, rues the ungainly conduct of his apparently cantankerous daughter-in-law and blames her vices on the fact that she comes from the southern locales, *dakkhinabhar*. The story was probably written in the 1960s. See Harimohan Jha, *Bīchal Kathā*, p. 39.

Pradesh and the district of Gopalganj in the west, the Ganga in the south, and West Bengal in the east.[42] It falls in the latitudes between 25°18' north and 27°37' north. Its longitudinal dimensions lie between 83°48' east and 88°17' east. Roughly, it covers an area close to about 50,000 km^2, with more than 30 million inhabitants at present. It is not possible to estimate the population of this area during the fourteenth and fifteenth centuries, but it was indisputably less than at present, not least of all because a large chunk of land was still under forest cover.

The alluvial plains of north Bihar might be counted among the most fertile areas in the subcontinent. The floods in its numerous rivers annually replenish its loam soil. Indeed, the most striking feature of the landscape of this region is the large number of major and minor rivers, rivulets, and other perennial or seasonal water bodies like ponds. This also meant that moving through the region was never easy, more so during the long rainy season. The average annual rainfall in the region at present varies between 120 cm and 160 cm. The denser forest cover in the middle ages would only have meant higher rainfall in those days. Large portions of the area were densely forested in the fifteenth–sixteenth centuries, especially along the foothills of the Himalayas from the district of East Champaran eastward through a fairly wide but irregular strip up to Purnea.[43]

It is important to note that the region of Mithila never lay on, or even close to, the main transit routes of trade in the subcontinent. North Indian goods bound for Bengal (and vice versa) and further east to the oceans would either pass through the Ganga or take the land route via Patna (Pataliputra/Kusumapura) south of it.[44] Ordinarily,

[42] Going by the current cultural topography, Mithila would thus include the districts of West Champaran, East Champaran, Sheohar, Sitamarhi, Madhubani, Supaul, Madhepura, Saharsa, Khagaria, Begusarai, Samastipur, Darbhanga, Vaishali, and parts of Muzaffarpur, Bhagalpur, and Purnea.

[43] Habib, *An Atlas of the Mughal Empire*, Sheet 10B.

[44] This is reflected in the fact that Vidyapati's *Likhanāvalī* (more fully discussed in the following chapters), which had an entire section on documenting business transactions, did not record even one large-scale mercantile deal.

this would also hold true for military troops, except when strategy demanded otherwise—as when Ghiyas al-Din Tughluq (r. 1320–5) decided to move through this region in order to force the Karṇāṭa chieftain to pay tribute. As Afif recorded in a couple of instances in his *Tarikh-i Firuz Shahi*, and as several stories in *Puruṣaparīkṣā* convey, soldiers from Tirhut did go to distant places in search of military service.[45] Yet, agriculture, one might infer, must have been the chief, if not the only source of livelihood for people in the region for most of the year.

In the geographical representation of Bhāratavarṣa in Varāhamihira's *Bṛihatsaṃhitā* (sixth century), Mithila figured as one of the regions in the east.[46] Śāradātanaya, in his *Bhāvaprakāśana* (twelfth century), listed 'Maithila' as one of the sixty-four janapadas in the southern quarter of Bhāratavarṣa.[47] Though in the mytho-political imagination of epic and Purāṇic tradition, Mithila or Videh or Tirhut/Tīrbhukti figured frequently, we hear of a historical kingdom of Mithila only with the establishment of the Karṇāṭa dynasty in the late-eleventh century.

The Political Setting

The political territory of Bihar during the sultanate period did not encompass Mithila. The latter was an independent principality under the Karṇāṭa dynasty (1097–1320s), founded by Nānyadeva. Like the kings of the Sena dynasty (c. 1097–1223) of Bengal, Nānyadeva and his kin belonged to a warrior lineage that had migrated in the eleventh

[45] See Chapter 4 and Chapter 2 in this volume for relevant references in *Puruṣaparīkṣā* and Afif's *Tarikh-i Firuz Shahi*, respectively. The eastern regions were at the centre of Kolff's study of 'the military labour market' between the fifteenth and nineteenth centuries, though he does not deal with the Mithila region separately. See Kolff, *Naukar, Rajput and Sepoy*.

[46] Pollock, *The Language of the Gods*, p. 196.

[47] Pollock, *The Language of the Gods*, p. 200. It was not simply a 'factual error', to list 'Maithila' in the southern quarter alongside Magadha, Nepal, and Bangāla. Rather, it was a particular time bound ordering of space whereby in the Kaliyuga (the era of Kali), the entire Bhāratavarṣa is shown to be squeezed into the southern most parts of the Indian subcontinent.

century from Karnataka. They constructed a fairly large citadel at Simarāoñ (Simarāoñgarh) in the modern district of East Champaran, close to the border of Nepal.[48] Some reports even suggest that one of its several walls was made of burnt bricks.[49] The circumstances of the 'sudden' appearance of a kingdom where none seems to have existed earlier are obscure.

But we do know that under the Karṇāṭa dynasty, the chieftaincy of Tirhut enjoyed a relatively autonomous position, occasionally perhaps, even full sovereignty.[50] However, Ghiyas al-Din Tughluq (r. 1320–5) brought it under the direct suzerainty of the Delhi Sultanate early in 1324, after removing the last ruler of the dynasty, Harisiṃhadeva (1316–24).[51] A few years later, Muhammad Tughluq put Kāmeśvara Ṭhakkura, a Brāhmaṇa of Oinī village and the erstwhile royal priest (Rājapaṇḍita) of Harisiṃhadeva, in charge.[52] Thus, the second ruling

[48] See Habib, *An Atlas of the Mughal Empire*, Sheet 10 A.

[49] Chaudhary, 'The Karṇāṭa Kingdom of Mithila', p. 111. Dharmasvāmin's account claims that the town of Pata, identified with Simarāoñ, had 600,000 houses, and that it was surrounded by seven walls. This is clearly hyperbole, but a later account of the ruins of Simarāoñ by Hodgson attests to the idea that it was a fairly large establishment, though not made of very durable materials. See *Biography of Dharmasvamin (Chag lo Tsa-ba Chos-rje-dpal)*, deciphered and translated from original Tibetan into English by George Roerich. Patna: K.P. Jayaswal Research Institute, 1959, p. 58.

[50] While almost all historians and scholars of Hindi and Maithili writing on Vidyapati or Tirhut refer to the Karṇāṭa dynasty as sovereign, it appears that at least for some periods, this might not have been the case. Thus, Barani reported that the Raja of Tirhut supplied troops to Sultan 'Ala al-Din Khalaji during the latter's expedition to Tilang in 1302–3. See Jackson, *The Delhi Sultanate*, p. 201. Interestingly, Vidyapati himself portrays a Karnāṭa prince, Narasiṃhadeva, fighting under 'Mahamad', the Lord of the Yavanas, against the '*kāpahara* rājās' in one of his stories; see Vidyapati, *Puruṣaparīkṣā*, pp. 28–32.

[51] Though Barani, surprisingly, does not mention the incident, most other contemporary and near contemporary Persian sources refer to this incident with some level of consistency. These include Ikhtisan's eyewitness account, titled *Basatin ul-Uns* and Isami's *Futuh al-Salatin*, apart from others like Ferishta and Mulla Taqiya. See Askari, 'Historical Value of *Basatin-ul-Uns*'. For details about others, see Ansari, 'End of the Karnata Kingdom'.

[52] Ansari, 'Bihar under Firuz Shah Tughlaq'.

lineage of Mithila, a Brāhmaṇa dynasty, came into being.[53] It came to be known as the Oinivāra dynasty, derived from the name of the village the rulers came from.

In 1371, a Turkish commander, Malik Arsalan (Aslān in Avahaṭṭha), killed the then Oinivāra ruler Raja Gaṇeśvara (or Ganesara), and annexed the territory of Tirhut.[54] Malik Arsalan thus acquired control of the area until two (of the three) sons of Gaṇeśvara (Vīrasiṃha and Kīrttisiṃha) reached maturity, and challenged and defeated Arsalan with the help of the Sharqi ruler, Sultan Ibrahim, sometime in 1401 or 1402. They re-established the reign of the Oinivāra dynasty in the region under the suzerainty of the Sharqis. Vidyapati was friends with, and in the service of, Kīrttisiṃha and Vīrasiṃha. He seems to have visited Jaunpur with the two aspiring rulers to enlist the support of the Sharqi ruler, and reported the whole incident in considerable detail in his *Kīrttilatā*.[55]

It is curious that after the kingdom was restored to the Oinivāra dynasty, it was Kīrttisiṃha, the youngest of the three sons of Raja Ganesara, who ascended the throne (see Figure 1.1). The absence of details regarding the politics and social history of the ruling family makes the succession to high office in this dynasty difficult to fathom. Thus, Kīrttisiṃha was succeeded after his death by his grandfather's cousin, Bhavasiṃha (aka Bhaveśvarasiṃha), who in turn was replaced after his death by his third son (out of four), Devasiṃha. His eldest son, Śivasiṃha, was the most famous of Vidyapati's patrons. His death put his chief queen, Lakhimādevī, on

53 In his *Kīrttilatā*, Vidyapati remarked positively on this uncommon phenomenon. He commended his patron-friend Kīrttisiṃha by rhetorically observing that it was rare for a man to be both *bhūbai* (King, but literally, 'lord of the land') and *bhūdeva* (Brāhmaṇa, but literally, 'god of the land'). See Chapter 5 in this volume.

54 The date of this event is given as the Year 252 of the Lakṣamaṇa Era. The era is named after the Sena ruler, Lakṣmaṇa of Bengal. It was in the court of Lakṣamaṇa Sena that the famous poet Jayadev flourished. A slab fixed in the doorway of Lakṣamaṇa Sena's palace apparently mentioned Jayadev as one of the five gems in the ruler's court. See Grierson, 'Vidyapati and His Contemporaries', p. 183.

55 For a fuller discussion, see Chapter 5 in this volume.

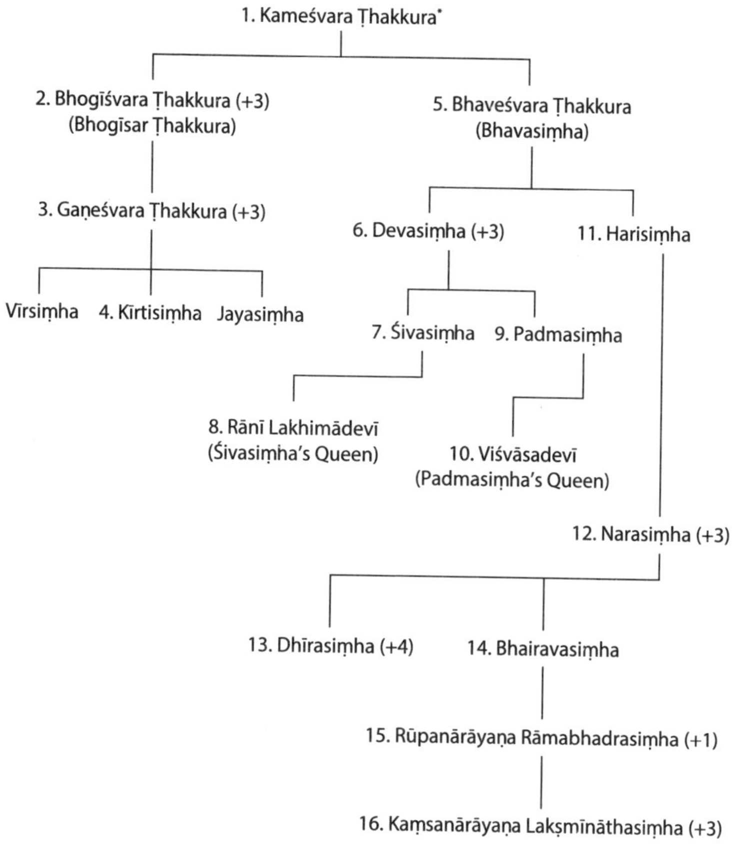

Figure 1.1 Oinivāra Dynasty Succession Chart†

Source: Author's Compilation.

Notes: * The serial numbers before the names signify the order of succession. The numbers in the parentheses indicate the number of brothers each person had. Among brothers, the one on the left is the eldest and the one on the right is the youngest.

† This is based on gleanings from various references to the rulers of the Oinivāra dynasty in Vidyapati's works and those of his contemporary authors from Mithila, as well as some references in Persian chronicles. I have supplemented that data with some of the general histories of Mithila and biographies of Vidyapati. Slightly different genealogy and succession charts of the dynasty are given in Sharmmā, *Mithila kā Itihās*, and Anand and Jha, 'Bhumikā'.

the throne but she soon had to flee to Nepal, probably because of the hostility of one of Śivasiṃha's cousins, Sāmbasiṃha or Rāya Arjuna. She seems to have returned to Mithila after a decade or so, only to rule for a few years before giving way to Padmasiṃha, her husband's youngest brother. Interestingly, another queen (Rani Viśvāsadevī) ruled after Padmasiṃha's death. The names of the rulers of this dynasty up to its last ruler, Kaṃsanārāyaṇa Lakṣmīnāthasiṃha, are given in Figure 1.1.

These details are interesting, and a closer look reveals other patterns. After the fourth ruler, for example, succession shifted from the heirs of Bhogīśvara Ṭhakkura to the collateral cousin lineage of Bhaveśvara Ṭhakkura. There seems to have been some tension between vertical and horizontal lines of succession within the lineage. The former was followed between the fifth ruler, Bhaveśvara, and the eighth ruler, Lakhimādevī. But a contrasting tradition of horizontal succession led to shifts in succession from the lineage of the sixth ruler, Devasiṃha, to the eleventh, Harisiṃha, and again from the thirteenth ruler, Raja Dhīrasiṃha, to the fourteenth, Raja Bhairavasiṃha, before the vertical line of succession reasserted itself again with the fifteenth and the sixteenth, who were, the last two rulers. While intriguing patterns of succession can be deciphered, equally significant are the silences regarding contestation and conflict. We would expect moments of transition from one ruler to the next to have been tumultuous, but whatever few contemporary accounts we have of these moments, fail to notice any such incidence. Sadly, we can only notice these curious details, as there is inadequate evidence to develop them with sufficient rigour.

These problems persist: while we do know the broad sequence in which they followed each other, the period of their reigns cannot be worked out with precision. Since this volume focusses primarily on three of Vidyapati's texts, it is useful for us to know, roughly, the time and sequence in which they were composed. *Kīrttilatā* was dedicated to, and written during the rulership of Kīrttisiṃha, for example, whose reign started in 1401 or 1402 and continued for at least seven or eight years. *Puruṣaparīkṣā* is dedicated to Śivasiṃha, who ruled for not more than five years in the second decade of the fifteenth century. *Likhanāvalī*, the last of the three texts considered here, was composed at the behest of a ruler of a small chieftaincy in Nepal by the name of Purāditya Girinārāyaṇa.[56] Purāditya Girinārāyaṇa is commended by Vidyapati as one who destroyed Arjun since the latter was 'guilty of cruel conduct towards his own kinsmen'.[57] We know that after Śivasiṃha's mysterious disappearance/death, his chief queen Lakhimādevī had to flee and take refuge somewhere in Nepal. It is during this period that Vidyapati, a very close associate and the royal priest of Śivasiṃha, would also have spent time in Nepal. Thus, it may safely be assumed that it must have been after 1418 or so that he would have composed *Likhanāvalī*. This would also go well with the fact that all of the documents in the text are dated to the year 299 of the Lakṣamaṇa Era, which would correspond roughly to 1418 CE.

Apart from the barest outline of the dynastic succession of the Oinivāra rulers, we know very little about the political or institutional developments during this period in the Mithila chieftaincy. Apart from the very few extant inscriptions of the time and occasional references in certain local texts, Vidyapati's own extensive compositions are the chief sources of information for this period. However, the poet, who served seven princes and two queens (see Table 1.1), hardly saw his role as one of merely chronicling the factual details of his immediate patrons. He probably fancied a greater historical role for himself, one that was tied to traditions of scholarship and knowledge production at a much grander level. These traditions were rich and vibrant in Mithila, but they were part of a larger trans-regional network, as we shall see in the next chapter, and in Part 2. Historians, however, have hardly begun to explore these issues. Modern historiography on medieval Mithila, or indeed on Bihar as a whole,[58] has hardly moved beyond the chronicling of the fluctuating fortunes of ruling dynasties, and cultivation of pride in the achievements of local heroes like Vidyapati.

[56] See Chapter 3 in this volume for details.

[57] See Vidyapati, *Likhanāvalī*, p. 63.

[58] Even after Ghiyas al-Din Tughluq brought Mithila (present north Bihar) under the control of the Delhi Sultanate, it did not become part of the Bihar suba. It was only with the establishment of Mughal rule that the Bihar suba came to include Mithila, with Champaran, Tirhut, and Hajipur constituting separate sarkars within it. See Habib, *An Atlas of the Mughal Empire*, p. 39; Sheet 10A.

Historiography

Magadh, the region in and around the ancient city of Pataliputra, was at the centre of much of the historiography of 'Ancient India' as the seat of the powerful Maurya kingdom. The area occupied by the present province of Bihar also included the sites where Buddhism and Jainism were born. However, these areas disappeared from the historian's view a few centuries before the establishment of Delhi Sultanate.[59] Bihar, as we know it today, is an administrative unit, or a region that the geographer Schwartzberg would have identified as 'instituted'.[60] It was the Sultanate chronicler Minhaj-i Siraj al-Din Juzjani in his *Tabaqat-i Nasiri*, who first used the name Bihar for the region, probably because he saw a large number of Buddhist *vihāras*[61] south of the Ganga.[62] Interestingly, it was the township known today as Biharsharif that came to be identified in the thirteenth century as Bihar. In the fourteenth century, the township of Bihar came to be known as Biharsharif in honour of the famous Sufi preacher, Sheikh Sharaf al-Din Ahmad ibn-Yahya Maneri of the Firdausi *silsila* (a chain of preceptor-disciple relationship among sufis, who almost always identified with and took pride in their spiritual lineage), who established his *khanqa* here. Soon the word 'Bihar' came to stand for the whole province though we do not know exactly when or how. Yet, it is clear that the area north of the Ganga was not an integral part of this province. That area, identified as Tīrabhukti or Tirhut, constituted a separate geopolitical and cultural zone until the time of the Mughals. Many would say that this area is culturally and geographically distinct even now. Demands for a separate state of Mithila have variously been made at different moments. Those at the forefront of these demands usually are the upper-caste, Maithili-speaking urban populace of

59 What is meant here is the modern province of Bihar, which consists of both the region of Mithilā/Tirahutā in the northeastern part and the region to the south of the Ganga that was part of the medieval suba of Bihar.

60 Cited in Bhattacharya, 'Reflections on the Concept of Regional History', p. 5.

61 Buddhist vihāras refer to Buddhist monasteries. Vihāra literally means a place to roam around in pleasure. It also meant a Buddhist (or a Jain) monastery. The equivalent of a convent in Buddhism was known as *vihārikā*.

62 Ansari, 'Historical Geography of Bihār'.

north Bihar. Though these demands seem to go back to the 1950s, if not earlier, they have gained some ground since the 1980s.[63] Almost all major political parties, in somewhat perfunctory ways, have pledged their support to the cause, usually on the eve of elections or when new states (Jharkhand in 2000, and Telangana more recently) were carved out.

The Delhi Sultanate's celebrated chroniclers like Minhaj-i Siraj al-Din Juzjani, Ziya al-Din Barani, or Shams-i Siraj Afif offered very little information on the area. This led to the unfortunate consequence that historians writing on the thirteenth or fourteenth centuries tended, with a few exceptions, to forget its existence within the Sultanate realm. To be sure, 'sources' of information were still available for the Sultanate and post-Sultanate period on Bihar. A large corpus of Persian, Sanskrit, and vernacular materials is awaiting the historian's attention.[64] Those few scholars who did take note of these materials only managed to accomplish the basic spadework of research. They put these materials together, with occasional remarks on their immediate contexts. More often, they picked up those pieces of information that helped their own limited agenda of holding aloft the pride of the local Maithil culture, or writing up simplistic dynastic accounts, or studying the peculiarities of the languages used in the area. Prominent among these scholars were George A. Grierson, Paul Jackson, K.P. Jayaswal, H.N. Ansari, S.H. Askari, Qeyamuddin

[63] In 1986, Vijay Kumar Mishra, a Janata Party member of parliament from Darbhanga and son of the Congress Stalwart, Lalit Narayan Mishra, courted arrest with 5,000 supporters, demanding a separate state of Mithilanchal. See *India Today*, 15 February 1986. For earlier, somewhat lukewarm, mobilizations, see Brass, *Language, Religion and Politics*, especially Chapter 2: 'The Maithili Movement in North Bihar', pp. 51–118.

[64] Here is a small sample of published material: Ahmad, *Corpus of Arabic and Persian Inscriptions of Bihar*. A collection of letters written by the famous fourteenth-century Firdausi Sufi Sheikh of Bihar, Sharaf al-Din Ahmad ibn-Yahya Maneri, was translated into English by Bruce Lawrence; see Maneri, *Maktubat-i Sadi or The Hundred Letters*. A *malfuz* (verbatim report on conversation) of Maneri, out of six such extant texts, was translated into English by Paul Jackson. See Arabi, *Khwan-i Pur Ni'mat*. We have already seen how vibrant the Sanskrit, Apabhraṃśa, and local-dialect literary traditions were in Mithila.

Ahmad, Jagdeesh Naryan Sarkar, Radhakrishna Chaudhary, Upendra Thakur, and Hetukar Jha.[65] Limited though their contributions might appear to a later researcher, they did help prepare the basic positivistic ground for further enquiry. Each of these scholars contributed to the process in their own ways, and it is difficult to remark on their individual contributions. Yet, one cannot help but note that in spite of the dissimilarities in their approach, methods, and rigour, most of their contributions are descriptive in orientation, and share certain problematic assumptions. First, all of these scholars, for example, take Mithila as a region as given, one that was mentioned in Mahābhārata and Rāmāyaṇa. They write histories of the glorious rise and unfortunate fall of Mithila, as if it were an integral whole, evenly structured and culturally singular, and as though it had always been so. Second, almost every scholarly work, including the more rigorously researched writings of Radhakrishna Chaudhary and Hetukar Jha, sees the period from the twelfth to the fifteenth century as a period of *crisis* precipitated by 'Islamic military raids'.

That the first autonomous medieval kingdom of the region founded by the Karṇāṭa dynasty (1097–1320s) flourished during this period, or that it is precisely the period between the twelfth and the fifteenth centuries that witnessed a literary efflorescence in both Sanskrit and the vernacular, did not provoke more searching questions about the nature of this assumed crisis. In fact, their writings portray this crisis as social and cultural as well as political.[66] To put it simply, it is not clear as to how social and cultural life is seen to be

[65] A selection of the published works include, Grierson, *Maithilī Chrestomathy*; Chaudhary, *Mithilā in the Age of Vidyāpati*; Chaudhary, *Select Inscriptions of Bihar*; Chaudhary, *History of Muslim Rule in Tirhut*; Thakur, 'Institutions of Slavery in Mithilā'; Aquique, *Economic History of Mithilā*; Sinha, *Mithilā under the Karnāṭas*; Sarkar, *Glimpses of Medieval Bihar Economy*; Ansari, 'Historical Geography of Bihār; Askari, 'A Fifteenth Century Shuttari Sufi Saint of North Bihar'; Askari, 'Bihar in the Time of Akbar'; Askari, *Collected Works*, vol. 1; Thakur and Verma, *India and the Afghans*; Jha, *Man in Indian Tradition*.

[66] Jha, *Man in Indian Tradition*, pp. 12–13. Shivprasad Singh, in what is arguably the most well-researched biography of Vidyāpati, also argues along similar lines. See Singh, *Vidyāpati*, pp. 48–9.

coterminous with dynastic–political fortunes or the interests of the politico-administrative elites. Clearly, if regional political formations suffered simplistic histories, the situation was somewhat worse for the study of 'sub-regional and local' political and social formations, such as the chieftaincy of Mithila/Tirhut.

One reason why historians steered clear of Vidyapati for so long might have to do with what could broadly be understood as the disabling consequence of 'labelling'. Writing his seminal work on the history of Hindi literature in 1929, Ram Chandra Shukla implicitly acknowledged this problem in the interesting way in which he situated Vidyapati, inadvertently linking him with another polymath, the Persian poet and chronicler Amir Khusrau. Shukla divided his history into '*vīragāthā kāl*' (Era of Heroic Poetry, up to 1375), '*bhakti kāl*' (Era of Devotional Literature, up to 1700), '*rīti kāl*' (Era of Tradition, up to 1900), and '*ādhunik kāl*' (Modern Era). Since he could not conveniently assimilate Vidyapati into any of these labels, he created a new one—'*phuṭakal racanāyeṅ*' (literally, loose or occasional compositions)—and discussed Vidyapati together with Khusrau under this curious heading.[67] Almost thirty years later, Shivprasad Singh highlighted the problem more directly when he remarked that 'you can consider Vidyapati as one who gave birth to *rītikālīn* poetry.... On the other hand, you can also call him the first poet of *bhakti kāl*'.[68] Considering the ways in which Vidyapati used *vīra rasa* to great effect in *Kīrttilatā*, Singh might as well have added that Vidyapati was perhaps the last exponent of the vīra rasa as well.[69]

But it was not just the chief thrust of the poet's literary flavour that was under dispute; scholars of Hindi literature could not even agree on his sectarian affiliations. If Shukla and his followers shared the popular perception that Vidyapati was a Śaiva, others like Hazari Prasad Dvivedi and Shivprasad Singh noted that his compositions also displayed a Vaiṣṇava bhakti inclination. Radhakrishna Chaudhary is convinced that Vidyapati was a committed Vaiṣṇava, and tries hard to prove it.[70] The residents of Bisfi, the place of his birth, believe that

67 Shukla, *Hindi Sāhitya kā Itihās*, pp. 37–8.

68 Singh, *Vidyāpati*, p. 16.

69 See Chapter 5 in this volume.

70 Chaudhary, *A Survey of Maithili Literature*, pp. 57–62.

Vidyapati was primarily a devotee of Goddess Bhagavatī,[71] while *also* considering him to be a Śaiva. While such 'confusions' in labelling could have potentially sensitized historians to the limits of such anachronistic usage of familiar terminologies, this did not happen. Instead, in their keenness to write about various eras in the history of literature (or about various shades of devotionalism and other such trends in medieval India), historians selected information that helped to confirm their prefabricated narratives, simply bypassing the fifteenth-century poet, who was much too inconvenient and complex to fit into their categories.

This chapter has tried to trace the broad contours of the familial, social, political, and cultural milieu within Mithila that Vidyapati inhabited and emerged from. The way the 'yugpuruṣa' is glorified and remembered is not the subject of my study. But it is important to understand the contemporary significance of the fifteenth-century poet—both at the scholarly level as well as at the popular level. Taking note of the way in which culture enthusiasts in Mithila have written about Vidyapati and Mithila in recent times constitutes one aspect of it. It is equally important to understand the kind of works that this polyglot might possibly have grown up with in a much broader context. Without that, it would be impossible to excavate the deep histories behind the ones he wrote. At the same time, one has to move beyond the preset sectarian and regional confines and relocate him in the wider world of the creative and political traditions of North India, Bihar, and Bengal in the fifteenth century. I have turned to these questions in the following chapter and mapped the literary cultures of North India in the fifteenth century, before moving on to a more concerted study of some of his compositions and their historical implications in Part 2 of this volume.

71 In his compositions, Vidyapati refers to her as *Ādi Śakti*.

2 *The Literary and the Political in the Fifteenth Century*

The crucial moments for cultural history are not necessarily the great imperial moments, as historians used to think they were, the moments when Alexander dipped his toe into India, or the Guptas built their empire. For some of the richest and most original cultural developments take place when there isn't an empire, in the cracks between the great dynastic periods.[1]

—Wendy Doniger

Fifteenth Century Lost and Found

How does one talk about a century? Is it possible for a historian to talk about *a* century at all? After all, it is merely an arbitrary and arithmetical quantity. As Ivo Schöffer pointed out in the context of European historiography about the seventeenth century, '[t]rends

[1] Doniger, *The Hindus*, p. 20.

and developments do not in fact take 31 December or 1 January into account, and pass unnoticed from the year 99 to 100'. Yet, 'in spite of these rational objections, the desire to treat a century as an era does not seem to die down.'[2] Indeed Schöffer's protest about the historiography of the European seventeenth century is oddly reminiscent of the historiography of the North Indian fifteenth century:

> It sometimes seems as if the seventeenth century, wedged between the sixteenth and eighteenth centuries, has no features of its own. With Renaissance and Reformation on the one side, Enlightenment and Revolution on the other, for the century in between we are left with but vague terms like "transition" and "change" ... for the seventeenth century ... we read only fragmentary treatment, country by country....[3]

The problem of arbitrary arithmetic might, to some extent, be resolved by treating the century, in our case the fifteenth century, in a flexible way, such that it allows us to carve out a more 'meaningful' timespan, broadly encompassing the century. Thus, a recent volume on the fifteenth century envisages it as having started 'after Timur left' in 1398 and ended with the military conquest of North India in 1526 by Babur, a descendant of Timur.[4] This helps frame the century in a conceptual way wherein a common thread may be seen to run through it. Interestingly, this privileging of the regnant political narrative for carving out the slice of time period corresponds too closely to an earlier historiography that the editors of and the contributions to the volume seek to challenge.

While it is important to move beyond the arithmetical cut-off dates of a century on either side, a singular conceptualization of a century, I would like to argue, would still be a problem in some respects. Historical developments in different aspects of life, even those closely related to each other, rarely coincide chronologically. In other words, how far 'the fifteenth century' may stretch on either end should depend on what problem and which place we are talking about. In the

2 Schöffer, 'Did Holland's Golden Age Coincide with a Period of Crisis?', p. 88.

3 Schöffer, 'Did Holland's Golden Age Coincide with a Period of Crisis?', p. 88.

4 Orsini and Sheikh, 'Introduction'.

context of the literary cultures of the Mithila region, for example, it is possible to assert that a text like Caṇḍeśvara's late-thirteenth (or early-fourteenth) century *Rājanītiratnākara* probably belongs more to the fifteenth century inasmuch as a Brāhmaṇa scholar in a tiny local court of north Bihar composed it, far away from any direct influence of the Delhi Sultanate. Including this Sanskrit treatise on politics in the oeuvre of the long fifteenth century, however, is not a factual instrument. Rather, it is an argument that if the fifteenth century embodied the imperium-oriented vitality of local literary elites, such literary expressions could be traced even to the thirteenth and the fourteenth centuries! Similarly, if one is able to demonstrate that many of the Rājapūta lineages who succeeded in consolidating their footholds in their respective domains during the fifteenth century were precisely those who played a critical role in the consolidation of the Mughal dispensation under Akbar, one might say that the shadows of the fifteenth century, if not the fifteenth century itself, loom large even beyond the 1550s! As with the earlier example, however, this too in the end is not a given fact but an argument about the characteristics of the fifteenth century.

Modern historical writing on the fifteenth century might loosely be classified under four heads that only occasionally overlap: (*a*) those that provide histories of 'regional' kingdoms/dynasties; (*b*) those that deal with the development of devotional practices and literatures, mostly 'bhakti' ideas and occasionally Sufi; (*c*) limited explorations on warfare and practices of soldiery including what has been called the 'military labour market'; and (*d*) recent researches (of the last fifteen years or so) on literary cultures and knowledge formations.

Regional History

In the historiography of the regions north of the Vindhyās, the fifteenth century figured for long as 'the period between' the heyday of the Delhi Sultanate and the emergence of the Mughal Empire. K.S. Lal framed the period as the 'twilight of the Sultanate' in 1963, and its historiography has since refused to break out of the mould.[5] The shadow of the Delhi Sultanate still looms large over the fifteenth

[5] Lal, *Twilight of the Sultanate*.

century, with the result that historians are used to noticing only 'signs of decline and disintegration' in this period. If the beginning of the decay was framed by Timur's invasion and sacking of Delhi in 1398, it was deemed to have been reversed with the invasion of Babur in 1526, and the 'consequent' emergence of the Mughal state. This is why the long fifteenth century ended, for Lal and for others following him, in 1526.[6] Indeed this perspective was somewhat relevant for historians interested in the territorial–dynastic fortunes of the Sultanates of Malwa (1401–1562), Jaunpur (1394–1484), or Gujarat (1403–1573), although, even in this limited sense, it carried little salience for historians working on the Sultanate of Bengal (1339–1534) or that of the Bahmanids (1346–1538). For them Timur's invasion was distant and relatively unimportant, and they found points of major historical transitions earlier, in the mid-fourteenth century.[7]

On the face of it, all this appeared 'natural'. There could not be any doubt that the invasions of Timur and Babur were momentous events with significant historical ramifications. Nor is it disputed that the Delhi Sultanate and the Mughal state were the most powerful political entities of their time. The trouble was the presumption, however, that the period that fell between these two formations must be seen only as a 'gap' or as what was left (for example, small regional states constantly squabbling with each other for petty gains) after the Sultanate declined or as the period of 'weak' states incapable of stalling the march of 'foreign' conquerors like Timur and Babur. There was no way to relate the vast corpus of non-Persian or even Persian literary productions of the time, some of which were explicitly political, to this thin historiography.

An assessment of the modern historiography of the fifteenth-century North India presents interesting difficulties. These difficulties are best understood with reference to the uneven ways in which historians have more generally approached the period(s) between the

6 Lal did not call it the 'long' fifteenth century though.

7 Even apart from the establishment of an independent Sultanate, early- and mid-fourteenth century Bengal witnessed far-reaching developments. Sonargaon on the eastern frontier, for example, emerged as a major centre of Islamic/Sufi culture around this time. See Eaton, *Rise of Islam and the Bengal Frontier*; Masumi, 'Sunargaon's Contribution to Islamic Learning'.

seventh and the seventeenth century. Thus, historians perceived the period between the kingdom of Harṣavardhana (death: 647 CE) and the establishment of the Delhi Sultanate (1210/11), as 'early medieval India', a period of local and regional kingdoms. Various models, 'a period of stagnation', 'feudalism', 'integrative', 'segmentary', and so on, cropped up to account for the rise of the 'regions'. With the exception of B.D. Chattopadhyaya and Burton Stein along with those who endorsed/elaborated their views, all others took the 'region' to be the automatic corollary of the disappearance of imperial kingdoms, even as they perceived them in diverse ways. An interesting component of this historiographic mosaic vis-à-vis the early-medieval period was that in the absence of ready-made contemporary histories, most historians engaged with a range of non-chronicler sources–epigraphs and coins, but also literary compositions, dictionaries, Puraṇic literature, travellers' accounts (for example, Hsuan Tsang), genealogies, praise-poems (*praśasti*), and so on–and stitched them together to arrive at an idea of life and livelihood, as well as socio-economic and political systems/processes of the time.

With the establishment of the Delhi Sultanate, the character of historiography changed dramatically. Persian, a relatively new entity on the linguistic map of the subcontinent, emerged for all practical purposes as the Sultanate's language of choice right in the thirteenth century itself. While inscriptions, literary compositions, texts on grammar, aesthetics, and lexicography, as well as philosophy continued to be produced in Sanskrit, alongside the steadily emerging 'regional' languages, historians now had access to an entirely new typology of 'sources': the state-patronized chronicler accounts in Persian that provided a panoramic view of the affairs of the sultanate, especially the activities, preoccupations, and accomplishments of its elite agents. Historians now turned to this new 'archive', mostly to the exclusion of the literary and epigraphic corpus in other languages that was the mainstay of raw materials for them for the earlier period. Predictably, all history for the period after the twelfth century became state-centric, and everything seemed to flow from the government. A range of 'useful' new themes engaged the historians of medieval 'India': reasons for the success of the Turks, nature of the 'nobility', Balban's theory of kingship, market reforms of Ala al-Din Muhammad Khalji, avant-garde projects of Muhammad Shah Tughluq, and the ubiquitous *iqta*[8] as the institutional backbone of a state presumed to be centralized. These themes were served to historians on a platter by their 'primary sources' (read Persian chronicles). Many medievalists referred to these texts as 'authorities' to drive home their ostensible unimpeachability.

As the Sultanate declined, however, the regional kingdoms perforce made a revanche during the long fifteenth century. With different proportions of nationalist sensibilities inevitably inflecting historical reconstructions in the decades just before and after Independence, big imperial kingdoms were easily, though not always explicitly, equated with unity and uniformity of politics and culture. Conversely, the absence of trans-regional polities signified disintegration, disunity, and even a rise in parochial sensibilities. The simplistic binary that this practice imposed on medieval Indian history has been commented upon by scholars at least since the 1970s, and should not hold us back here.[9] Suffice it to say that the trend has not been substantively arrested as yet. The trope of the 'twilight of the Delhi Sultanate' has reappeared in a more sophisticated narrative as the 'epilogue'.[10] When some historians actually started focussing on the fifteenth century, however, they always framed the period in terms of histories of regional polities in a way that took the whole idea of 'regions/regionalism' as natural entities to emerge during periods

[8] Iqta (literally a part/portion) during the sultanate period is widely perceived by modern historians to be a revenue assignment and a military charge usually given by the king to his subordinates in lieu of salary. However, closer readings of Persian literature of the time suggest that it might have been a generic term used in diverse contexts for a selection of administrative/military/revenue charges and more (or less). In fact, the Persian texts of the thirteenth and the fourteenth centuries appear to use the term too loosely for us to allow talking about a singular 'iqta system'.

[9] For the early-medieval context, see Chattopadhyaya, 'Political Processes and Structure of Polity in Early Medieval India', and Chattopadhyaya, 'Introduction'. For a brief comment on the problem in the context of the fifteenth century, see Kumar, '*Bandagī* and *Naukarī*'.

[10] See Jackson, *The Delhi Sultanate*, where the period between 1400 and 1526 is treated in the last chapter as the 'epilogue'.

of non-imperial 'interregnums'.[11] All that such histories typically recorded were dynastic/kingly achievements in terms of territorial victories/losses, court intrigues, and at best, building activities with reference to one or the other 'regional' kingdoms.

Bhakti 'Movement'

Another strand of historiography on the fifteenth century focussed primarily on what came to be regarded as the 'Bhakti Movement'. First noticed by scholars as a new literary current, historians soon started writing about Bhakti as a radical social movement against what was vaguely understood as excesses of the varṇa/jāti order. The bhakti-centred historiography was interesting in as much as it filled up the 'interregnum' of the fifteenth century with an account of meaningful developments in the cultural domain. However, most of these accounts did not bother about the spatial, literary, or material/political contexts of the 'movement'. Cultural history appeared to be an isolated field where radically new ideas, very much like medieval states, appeared to emerge from nowhere in particular. Attempts to provide a historical background to these developments were few and thin. An early attempt was made by Tara Chand, who looked at the Bhakti movement as an outcome of 'the influence of Islam on Indian culture', also the title of his book.[12] It might be seen as a feeble and sweeping attempt to transpose a 'politically correct' Nehruvian ideal anachronistically onto medieval Indian history. Much later, Irfan Habib attempted to explain the monotheistic currents embodied by

[11] A telling example of this trend is the ambitious project, *A Comprehensive History of India*, undertaken and published under the auspices of the Indian History Congress and People's Publishing House. Initiated by a committee of the Indian History Congress in 1943 at Aligarh, the fifth volume of the series had two parts. Curiously, both parts were titled 'The Delhi Sultanate, 1206–1526', even though the first one dealt with the Delhi Sultanate that ran into roughly 750 pages, whereas the second part (in less than 600 pages) dealt with, what Satish Chandra, as secretary to the Editorial Board, called 'the various provincial kingdoms' in his foreword to the second edition of the series in 1992. See Habib and Nizami, *A Comprehensive History of India*.

[12] Tara Chand, *Influence of Islam on Indian Culture*.

sants such as Kabīr, Nānak, and (later) Dādu as a consequence of the policies of the Delhi Sultans. According to Habib, what prepared the ground socially for the monotheistic idealism of the fifteenth–sixteenth centuries were material transitions—the introduction of new technologies and professions, ushered into the subcontinent by the sultanate.[13] This argument fell on the worn out presumption that technology led to the rise of new aspirational professions/groups, and these groups then challenged the existing social and political hierarchies. Yet this was one valiant attempt to link the domain of the literary and the cultural with the domain of the state and the political. It also entailed the diachronic view that what happened in the fifteenth century could have been a result of what transpired in the thirteenth and the fourteenth.

Beginning with the 1990s, however, intimate textual studies of certain Bhakti writings started to emerge. Foremost among these are the works of historians like Charlotte Vaudeville and John Stratton Hawley.[14] These studies marked a new beginning in the study of the Bhakti literary corpus in so far as they paid close attention to the manner in which certain texts were canonized and congealed together long after they were actually 'composed'. Very often they also explored the ideals and literary streams that fed into the texts as well as the ways in which they were remembered and rallied around afterwards. In doing so, they ended up interrogating the very category of the Bhakti Movement, especially the use of the later word to describe this literary–cultural–religious phenomenon. More recently, for example, Hawley has produced a virtual biography of this category in a work marked by extremely rich empirical research. While the early texts and protagonists around whom the idea of the North Indian bhakti movement cohered mostly belonged to the fifteenth or earlier centuries, Hawley argued, it was through a series of textual, performative, and political interventions in the period between the sixteenth and the early twentieth centuries that the taxonomies of the bhakti movement were forcefully articulated and stabilized. Thus, it was a

13 See Habib, 'Kabir: The Historical Setting'. In a social context, a similar argument was put forth by another historian. See Siddiqui, 'Social Mobility in the Delhi Sultanate'.

14 See Vaudeville, *A Weaver Named Kabir*; Hawley, *Three Bhakti Voices.*

network of people, ideas, and canons that distinguished Bhakti as a historical force, according to the author. He noted the crucial role that the Mughal ruling elites and certain Rājapūta chieftains played in this process as both patrons as well as clients of the 'movement'. He also duly acknowledged the parallel and contingent process of literary vernacularization in this context, but did not take it up for detailed treatment.[15]

A recent work by Christian Lee Novetzke focussed on the Marathi vernacular sphere, follows a comparable, if not similar, methodological track. Through an intimate exploration of *Lilacaritra* (c. 1278 CE) and *Jnaneshvari* (c. 1290 CE), the author opens up the world of the premodern Marathi 'public sphere', and argues that 'vernacularization was not an inadvertent consequence of a kind of cultural ecological shift, but rather it was the result of a purposeful and self-aware critique of culture.' It is 'a process of empowerment that negotiated the mores of everyday life', and 'valorized the image of "everyday"'. The 'driving core of vernacularization', he noted, was 'the very quotidian social life it sought to emend'.[16]

Neither of the studies noted above is actually focussed on the fifteenth century as far as the timeline is concerned. However, what makes them relevant for the theme of this volume is the manner in which they posit the process of vernacularization and bhakti religiosity as developments in the sphere of knowledge formation as culturally produced, with significant political patronage (Hawley) or at a remove from state agents (Novetzke). What also distinguishes these works is the attempt to trace the pre-histories and post lives of the texts and taxonomies under their respective scanners.

Indeed, what historians chose to study was an important determinant of the period of their focus. Passing off biographies of the Delhi Sultans as 'Histories of India' was in any case a shaky (though popular) proposition even for the thirteenth and the fourteenth centuries. For the fifteenth century, such a blinkered focus was simply impossible because there were too many sultanates in North India whose territories, like the vernacular languages identified by Pollock, 'did

[15] Hawley, *A Storm of Songs*.

[16] Novetzke, *The Quotidian Revolution*, p. 286.

not travel very far'. As the Delhi Sultanate disintegrated in the fifteenth century, the historiography of medieval India, dutifully tied to its fortunes, also fragmented into telling stories of the 'provincial sultanates'.[17]

Military Labour Market and *Naukarī*

It is hardly surprising that the fifteenth century found its historians among those who steered clear of such dynastic–territorial themes. Interesting interventions in the 1980s came from historians who did not stick to the practice of isolating the fifteenth century in stereotypical frames.[18] Amongst the intrepid few, Dirk H.A. Kolff's work on the novel theme of the 'military labour market' of North India between the fifteenth and the nineteenth centuries was particularly noteworthy. Focussing on peasant–soldiers and their relationship with the state, he attempted to 'acquire a better understanding of the north Indian distributive system, the social history of much of its peasantry and the processes of state formation in *ancien régime* South Asia'.[19]

This was an interesting idea that could open up a range of questions about a whole variety of issues having to do with mobilization of armed power by states and their adversaries, impact of military service on the formation of new social groups, mobility of

[17] This was the scheme followed by a series of ambitious volumes on Indian history edited and overseen by R.C. Majumdar. See Majumdar, *The History and Culture of the Indian People*, Vol. 6. Earlier, Majumdar had collaborated with two other scholars to publish a general volume on history of India. See R.C. Majumdar, H.C. Raychaudhuri, and Kalikinkar Datta, *An Advanced History of India*. Even *Comprehensive History of India*, edited by Habib and Nizami, mentioned above (see footnote 9), followed the same structure. Interestingly, this historiography closely followed Mughal narratives of the Sultanate as well. For an interesting tracing of this historiographic 'continuity', see Kumar, *Emergence of Delhi Sultanate*, pp. 354–60.

[18] Two notable works in this regard are Pollock, 'The Theory of Practice and the Practice of Theory in Indian Intellectual History', and Eaton, 'Approaches to the Study of Conversion to Islam in India'.

[19] Kolff, *Naukar, Rajput, and Sepoy*, p. 2.

peasants, changes in service cultures, and dynamics of political re/alignments. Kolff gathered a tremendous variety of information on the issue from a diverse set of sources. Indeed, his contribution in virtually single-handedly creating a new theme of study cannot be sufficiently emphasized. Many of his insights about the emergence of eastern Rājapūtas as well as about the political possibilities inhering in the existence of a somewhat open-ended military labour market (studied with reference to the rise of Sher Shah Suri) remain practically unchallenged. Yet, his study tended to flatten out the diverse contexts and genres from which these details were drawn. As a consequence, all of pre-modern North India appeared to be populated by an unruly mob of ubiquitously and indiscriminately armed peasantry that underwent little change till the first half of the nineteenth century. The primary challenge for any premodern state in India, according to Kolff, 'was the problem of how to deal with the peasantry at large, how to subject to some manner of control and collect revenue from these *almost ungovernable* tens of millions of people protected by mud forts, jungles and ravines all over the plains of Hindustan and above all by the weapons they were so familiar with'[20] (emphasis added).

Kolff's awareness that 'in the post-orientalist age, Indian history has learned not to venture a formulation of ultimate, irreducible elements which govern South Asian realities' did not stop him from listing the factors that made 'the Indian agro-historical configuration unique':

> They include—in random order, because none of them is autonomous or stands 'at the beginning', but all are interlinked and help to define each other—the demographic factor of the sheer numbers of Indian people, the unpredictable nature of India's monsoon climate and, as a result, of its harvest, the occupational multiplicity and armed mobility of its peasants as they grope for security in the face of local harvest failure and all-India political flux, and the inability of states to collect resources that suffice to bind or demilitarise a significant proportion of India's huge peasant population.[21]

[20] Kolff, *Naukar, Rajput, and Sepoy*, p. 194.

[21] Kolff, *Naukar, Rajput, and Sepoy*, p. 194.

It did not seem to matter that the 'sheer numbers of Indian people' might actually have varied widely in different ecological zones of the subcontinent or that, at different points of time in history, there were large 'no-population' areas that came to be colonized and brought under cultivation for the first time. What is startling about the assertion is the fact that the 'military culture of Indian agro-history' is seen to be timeless and almost beyond history:

> Armed peasant resistance to energetic imperial attempts to establish the sultans' authority was as fierce in the fourteenth century as it was in Akbar's and Jahangir's time. Ibn Battuta's description of Muhammad Tughluq's (1324–51) reign and the reported half a million dead amongst the population as a result of Muhammad Shah Bahmanī's (1358–73) campaigns, do not present stories that are very different from those mentioned at the beginning of this study for the early Mughal period. And Ashoka's Orissa killings and deportations in the third century BC may well have been a very similar affair, a manifestation of the same abiding features of the Indian polity.[22]

The ahistorical hypothesis of innumerable armed peasants as a 'constant' factor in Indian history makes Kolff's line of argument almost completely useless for understanding the historically specific fluidity of the fifteenth century, and the emergence of the Mughal state in the mid-sixteenth century. This was unfortunate since Kolff's chapter on Sher Shah (1540–5) showed how his sudden and extraordinary rise to imperial kingship was made possible by the very unique circumstances that obtained in North India in the long fifteenth century.

Notwithstanding this conceptual short-circuiting of the wealth of material mobilized in the book, the author did successfully demonstrate the need and feasibility of researching themes like those of *naukarī*, service culture, and the 'rajputization' of certain groups of eastern peasants. J.F. Richards rued, more than a decade later, that it did not immediately lead to more focus on the complex issues that it

[22] Kolff, *Naukar, Rajput, and Sepoy*, p. 195.

raised.[23] A recent attempt by Sunil Kumar to trace changing patterns of service culture in North India, builds on and challenges Kolff's largely synchronic account. The more fundamental contribution of Kumar in his study of *bandagī* (from *bandā*, slave; literally, to act/behave like a slave) and naukarī, was to fruitfully link warfare and administrative service in medieval India to changing patterns of normative discourses on the issue, an aspect completely missing from Kolff's work.[24] At another level, Kumar's work also demonstrated the fruits awaiting medievalists who could work simultaneously with Persian and Sanskrit materials.

Historiography of Literary Cultures

Most medieval Indian historians were (and are) trained primarily in Persian, with only the slightest ability to work with Sanskrit or 'vernacular' materials.[25] As a result, histories of medieval literature seldom moved beyond a review of Persian literary genres. For long, historians did not bother with the vibrant range of everyday language

[23] Richards, 'Warriors and the State in Early Modern India'. However, it is to be noted that just before Richards expressed his disappointment, two books appeared on warfare and related socio-political issues in North India, one of them co-edited by Kolff himself. See Gommans and Kolff, *Warfare and Weaponry in South Asia*. Also see Khan, *Gunpowder and Firearms*.

[24] Kumar, '*Bandagī* and *Naukarī*'.

[25] This training had several consequences, especially where the study of North India is concerned. For one, even though from the 1960s, the starting point of the medieval period was pushed back (in the name of early medieval) to the seventh–eighth centuries, few medieval historians possessed the skills to research the pre-Sultanate period. Thus, the major historians of early medieval India continued to be those who were seen as experts on Ancient India, and the effective *break* in the periodization still appeared to be the establishment of the Delhi Sultanate. Second, historians of the Sultanate and post-Sultanate period appeared to be completely oblivious of the large chunk of Sanskrit sources available for the thirteenth through the sixteenth centuries. Those who read and worked on Sanskrit sources were mostly scholars like Chattopadhyaya and Thapar, with no expertise in conventionally conceptualized 'medieval' political formations. See Chattopadhyaya, *Representing the Other?*; Thapar, *Somanātha*.

practices in North India: Hindavi/Hindui, Apabhraṃśa, even Sanskrit, not to mention a host of 'regional' dialects from Gujarati and Marathi to Bengali and Maithili, all seemed to belong only to the realm of colourful ethnography recorded by nineteenth- and early twentieth-century British observers and German ethnographers. Alternatively, local enthusiasts in the respective cultural zones of these languages put together useful surveys of literature produced in them, often composed with a view to articulate regional pride and acquire government patronage. Though largely descriptive, such surveys put a wealth of information together. These proved to be handy to later historians who, mostly from 1990s onwards, tried to grapple with this archive.

In the last fifteen years or so, however, a body of works focussing on a variety of languages and literary practices, and straddling the fifteenth century in interesting ways has appeared. Scholars are now raising a whole variety of new questions about the links between politics, power, and state on the one hand, and cultural objects such as texts and monuments on the other. Moreover, they have often worked with time frames that encompass longer durations in which the fifteenth century figures as a crucial link rather than as a 'twilight' or interregnum.[26] Such histories have moved beyond a description of lives and teachings of great mystics as well as dynastic biographies focussed on territorial expansion/contraction.

They look at the phenomena of knowledge formations, literary cultures, religious processes, textual transmissions, and so on.[27] Even as they investigated the histories of a particular region, they explored the processes through which the region was formed, and the relationship in which they stood with other historical processes of the time. In breaking away from stereotypical dynastic–regional histories, some regions have come to be served better than others. Thus, Gujarat, with its Sultanate having its own chronicles, understandably inspired

[26] A number of such works have appeared in the last fifteen years or so. Some of the most prominent works include Flood, *Objects of Translation*; Alam, *The Languages of Political Islam in India*; Orsini, 'How to Do Multilingual Literary History?'; Kumar, '*Bandagī* and *Naukarī*'.

[27] O'Hanlon and Washbrook, *Religious Cultures in Early Modern India*. Also see Busch, *Poetry of Kings*.

some interesting works—those based on the chronicles as well as those looking beyond to Sufic or other 'unofficial' sources.[28] Bengal and Rajasthan too have attracted historians' attention, though not in equal measure.[29]

Much of this historiography is over-determined as well as charged by Pollock's ambitious millennium-by-millennium paradigm. Though new, it is also beginning to get close critical attention, especially where Pollock's own arguments are concerned. The beginning of this new strand of historiography may be identified with the publication in 1995 of a special issue of the journal *Social Scientist*. Titled *Literary History, Region, and Nation in South Asia*, the issue carried an introductory note and a paper titled 'Literary History, Indian History, World History' by Sheldon Pollock, who also guest-edited it. Pollock's now famous theory of vernacularization of literature and politics in the second millennium of the Christian Era across the Eurasian regions from Java to London received a firmer and more nuanced shape with two other essays published in 1998.[30] He elaborated these views in yet another edited volume in 2003, with contributions focussing on a variety of languages by a range of scholars, not all of whom strictly followed the model he posited.[31] His own primary focus was the Indian subcontinent, though the larger frame was 'comparative', with similar if not identical developments between the Asian and the European world constituting an important aspect of his explorations. Many of these ideas were fine-tuned further in his 2006 monograph on the 'Language of the Gods'.

For all its complexity and rich details, Pollock's thesis is amenable to rather straightforward summarization since the scheme of analysis he uses is rather simple and neat. On the basis of an examination of written compositions in Sanskrit and other languages produced in the subcontinent in the last two thousand years, he broadly

[28] See Sheikh, *Forging a Region*; Simpson and Kapadia, *The Idea of Gujarāt*; Balachandran, 'Texts, Tombs and Memory'.

[29] Eaton, *The Rise of Islam and the Bengal Frontier*; Stewart, 'In Search of Equivalence'; Kapur, *State Formation in Rajasthan*.

[30] Pollock, 'India in the Vernacular Millennium'; Pollock, 'The Cosmopolitan Vernacular'.

[31] Pollock, *Literary Cultures in History*.

categorizes the first thousand years as cosmopolitan, and the following eight centuries or so as a vernacular era. This is so because the first millennium of the Christian Era witnessed the production of literature only or mostly in Sanskrit, a language that is categorized as cosmopolitan. Sanskrit was cosmopolitan because evidently those who used it thought it was cosmopolitan. Moreover, it was understood and its texts could potentially circulate, in a wide area from present-day Afghanistan to Java, and from Kashmir to Sri Lanka. The grammar and syntax of the language did not vary much in this wide area, and the users of the language thought of it as universal and without boundaries. Equally universal, and without boundaries, was the political imagination that the Sanskrit literature reflected. This imperial political imagination appropriately expressed in a cosmopolitan language found its tangible correspondence in the real world, both in terms of widespread endorsement of the ideal of imperium (the idea, for example, of *cakravartin samrāṭa*) as well as the actual existence of imperial kingdoms like those of the Guptas, Colas, or Cālukyas.

Further, he noted that all of this started changing around the turn of the millennium. At the beginning of the eleventh century (or a little before or after, depending upon which region one was talking about), an increasing number of vernacular languages started being visible to historians since they were now being put to writing. The vernaculars were first literized, that is, started getting scripturalized, and then literarized, that is, expressive texts were composed in them. These 'new' languages (Kannada, Telugu, Bengali, and so on) are called vernaculars not only because they 'did not travel far', but also because their users too were aware that they were not understood beyond a known and delimited region. This new literature in the new media also showed a 'forsaking of the universalistic model of imperium'.[32] Their political imaginations were territorially humbler and more bounded, even as their patrons too were rulers of local kingdoms with little aspiration beyond their immediate locality. In the process of being literized and literarized, however, these 'languages of place' (as against the 'universal' Sanskrit) were standardized grammatically and

32 For his elaboration of the idea, see Pollock, 'India in the Vernacular Millennium: Literary Culture and Polity: 1000–1500', p. 56.

syntactically as well as in terms of literary tropes and genres, in relation to, and often imitating, the corresponding structures of Sanskrit. The extent of the cosmopolitan elements in the vernaculars might vary, but its incidence was seminal in the way the vernacular literature (and language itself) evolved. Hence, Pollock noted that '[first] the development of written literature in the languages of Place was hard to imagine without the model of Sanskrit, and, second, that the appropriation of this model was marked, formally and thematically, by sophisticated and variable modes of synthesis'.[33] Pollock regarded this veritable mushrooming of fragmented literary and political sensibilities all across South Asia as primarily diglossic, where the high language (Sanskrit) provided the paradigm for the substantive historical life of several 'low' languages.

Interestingly, nowhere in his extended explorations of the binary of cosmopolitan and vernacular did Pollock imply that Sanskrit works stopped being composed in the second millennium of the Christian Era. In fact, he was one of the first mainstream historians in recent times to highlight what the more 'conventional' Sanskritists had always known: that a larger corpus of Sanskrit compositions from the second millennium of the Christian Era have survived than from the first millennium.[34] It is interesting that the fact did not stop him from giving a 'death certificate' to Sanskrit effectively from around the same time.[35] This was so because for him the provocative phrase, 'the death of Sanskrit' signified that, generally speaking '[w]hat these [Sanskrit] scholars produced was a newness of style without a newness of substance', and in a very precise way, the disappearance of

[33] Pollock, *The Language of the Gods*, p. 395.

[34] Pollock, 'New Intellectuals in Seventeenth Century India'. In fact, in a review symposium of Pollock's edited volume, *Literary Cultures*, David Shulman went to the extent of saying that '[N]o one will deny that, statistically speaking, the great bulk of surviving Sanskrit poetry comes from the second millennium A.D.' See Orsini, Shulman, and Venkatachelapathy, 'A Review Symposium', p. 381.

[35] Note, however, that Shulman, while not in full agreement with the idea of the 'death of Sanskrit', remarked that 'counting texts will not solve the problem Pollock poses' (Orsini, Shulman, and Venkatachelapathy , 'A Review Symposium').

Sanskrit literature from some of the key sites (for example, Kashmir) at particular moments.[36]

As David Shulman remarked, although 'not everyone [would] agree with the terms and parameters of the discussion' as defined by Pollock, yet 'the field ha[d] been irrevocably transformed'.[37] This veritably epic paradigm, deployed to frame the entire range of literary productions of South Asia, and straddling no less than 2,000 years, quickly congealed into an orthodoxy. Like all orthodoxies, it also became a constant point of reference. Several of the finer constituents in Pollock's thesis have been built upon, reformulated, even challenged on occasion. Sumit Guha, for example, in a study of lexical awareness and language use in the Marathi-speaking world during the period 1300–1800 CE, pointed out how the traffic of influence between Sanskrit and the vernacular was not always one way, thus putting a question mark to the idea of diglossia mentioned above.[38] Jesse Knutson's study of *Gītagovinda* provides another counterpoint, wherein, among other things, the lyricism of Jayadeva's Sanskrit songs is seen to be in evident debt to vernacular traditions.[39] In a more recent volume on 'culture and circulation' in North India 'after Timur left', Francesca Orsini and Samira Sheikh offer, without challenging the overarching binary of the cosmopolitan–vernacular, a more complex model to frame the multilinguality of North India: 'While north India was not a homogenous region in political terms, it was a well-connected cultural and linguistic region. Its linguistic economy can be described as one of "multiple diglossias", with several high languages—Arabic, Persian, Sanskrit—and a general spoken vernacular (what we call here Hindavi) written in the Persian, *kaithi*, or *devanagari* scripts'.[40]

36 Pollock, 'The Death of Sanskrit', p. 417.

37 Orsini, Shulman, and Venkatachelapathy, 'A Review Symposium', p. 378.

38 Guha, 'Bad Language and Good Language'. See especially pp. 58, 62. Guha, however, does not directly confront Pollock.

39 Knutson, 'The Consolidation of Literary Registers in the World of the Senas'. See especially, Chapter 3 titled 'The Vernacular Cosmopolitan: Jayadeva's *Gītagovinda*', pp. 115–39.

40 Orsini and Sheikh, 'Introduction', p. 7.

While multiple diglossias might help us account for the influence of cosmopolitan languages other than Sanskrit, especially Persian, on the making of the so-called regional languages and literatures, the frame still fails to account for the traffic of 'influence' between the cosmopolitan languages themselves ('Persian genres' like *insha*, for example, being emulated by Vidyapati's *Likhanāvalī*, discussed in Chapter 3 in this volume). Even more common are the cases wherein Sanskrit and Persian themselves carry traces of 'regional' linguistic practices and sensibilities as evidenced in Sumit Guha's study of Marathi lexicography or Jesse Knutson's study of Sanskrit lyrics. Orsini's own views on the idea of diglossia and multiple diglossias in her earlier piece on 'How to Do Multilingual Literary History' provided for a more complex reading than the Introduction to the volume, *After Timur Left*.[41]

To be sure, there is one sense in which the diglossia, especially between Sanskrit and the North Indian vernaculars, cannot possibly be denied: almost all of the medieval authors—whether of Sanskrit or of the vernaculars—themselves believed that the vernaculars could not but be diglossically related to Sanskrit. They believed this in the general sense in which all languages other than Sanskrit (for example, even the other cosmopolitan languages like Prakrit or Apabhraṃśa) were always already mere derivatives of the language of the gods. But they also seem to have believed this in the specific sense of a particular language at a particular moment of history being indebted to Sanskrit and Sanskrit alone for its very existence. This is evident, for example, from the assertions of scholars like Hemacandra about Apabhraṃśa. His grammar of Apabhraṃśa (composed in Sanskrit) is clearly based on the presumption of its diglossic relations with Sanskrit.[42] The very etymology of Apabhraṃśa, literally, 'corrupt', and practically coming to mean 'the corrupt form of Sanskrit', indicates how embedded the

[41] Orsini, 'How to Do Multilingual Literary History'. See especially, pp. 230–2.

[42] Hemacandra wrote grammars primarily of Sanskrit and Prakrit but also dealt in detail with Apabhraṃśa in his compendium of grammars. He was the only medieval scholar to have done so. See Hemacandra, *Shri Siddhahemacandraśabdānuśāsanam*. For an interesting discussion of it, see Ollett, *Language of the Snakes*, pp. 134–5.

idea of it being a derivative of Sanskrit must have been. The question that is still to be probed is whether claims like these (based at least in part on claims of the divine origin of Sanskrit) might be taken at their face value, and accepted without further ado.

The problems posed by such formulations, however, are not confined to their exclusion of an admittedly limited number of instances of emulations, some of which I have noted above. First, the binary of cosmopolitan/universal on the one hand, and local/vernacular on the other, fails to account for the fact that the languages and dialects of North India existed in a continuum, often without a dramatic break line, a fact that gave much wider reach to alleged 'vernaculars' that Pollock had thought, 'did not travel far'. How else do we account for the peculiar phenomenon of inter-intelligibility between Avadhī, Brajabhāṣā, western Gujarati, Śaurseni, and Hindavī, that effectively constituted almost the whole of North India into a single socio-textual community? As I have argued in Chapter 5 in this volume, the written oeuvre in each of these languages appears to be indebted to Sanskrit, Persian, Prakrit, Apabhraṃśa, and each other, in crisscrossing and uneven ways.[43]

Second, it is true that increasing levels of 'vernacularization', as witnessed in the literization and literarization of hitherto 'indeterminate' oral dialects one after the other, is a major historical phenomenon beginning in the ninth–tenth centuries all across South Asia. Evident in the second millennium is an incremental insistence on putting more and more matter to writing as well as a wider 'spread' of manuscript culture in 'local' languages. Yet, the theory of vernacularization implying a corresponding decline both of the Sanskrit cosmopolis and of the political imagination of imperium (as reflected in literary expression) is simply not tenable. Indeed, any attempt to theorize the second millennium of the Christian Era, and that is my third point, if such a theorization is at all desirable, is useless from the perspective

[43] This is not to suggest that all languages and literatures, even notionally, were equal, and rivalled each other in a free for all. Rather, the attempt here is to highlight the need to first disaggregate specific issues subsumed unidentifiably in the tempting rush to fix a whole millennium in one sweeping judgement, howsoever compelling that judgement might appear at first look.

of a historian of medieval India if it does not factor in that fount of cosmopolitan culture called the Mughal state. (We leave aside the courts of the Delhi Sultanate and the Vijayanagara kingdom for the moment.) One does not have to be in agreement with any of the disputed propositions about the extent of centralization commanded by the Mughal state to see that it was just too big territorially, too powerful financially, and too diverse in its cultural–ideological engagements to be reduced to a footnote or two in any narrative about the literary cultures of the time.

Even a century before the Mughals, there flourished a number of 'regional' states—the sultanates of Jaunpur, the Bahamanids, Bengal, Malwa, and Gujarat being only the more prominent ones—that simultaneously patronized several languages, both cosmopolitan and vernacular, and deployed them in diverse ways. Thus, right in the middle of the fifteenth century, Udayarāja could call the Gujarati Sultan, Mahmud Begada, a truly *cakravartin suratrāṇa*, 'universal ruler', in a Sanskrit text that also shows signs of localization as far as its language is concerned.[44] The political idealism of Tulsidas as expressed in his magnum opus *Rāmacaritamānasa*—written primarily in Avadhī but peppered with Sanskrit ślokas, and probably emulating the styles and metaphors of the earlier Sufi texts in that 'dialect'[45]—was nothing if not a reworked and theologized model of the universal kingdom seeped in the classical tradition of Sanskrit. A Sanskrit treatise on politics (*rājanīti*), duly entitled *Rājanītiratnākara* and composed by Caṇḍeśvara in the tiny chieftaincy of the Karṇāṭas in Mithila, 'incorrectly' invoked Nārada to state that there were three kinds of kings, *rājā trividhaḥ*: emperor, tax-paying, and non-taxpaying, *samrāṭa sakaro-akaraśca*. It went on to designate the *samrāṭa* (paramount sovereign) as the one who collects taxes from other kings and

[44] See Udayarāja, *Rājavinodamahākāvyam*. For an interesting discussion of the Sanskrit text as a panegyric to the 'Muslim' sultan, see Kapadia, 'The Last *Cakravartin*?'.

[45] 'Yet few people know that the Avadhī *Rāmacaritamānasa* is preceded by three centuries of Muslim Sufi writing in the same language. In a very real sense, these Sufis shape the poetic, metrical, and narrative conventions that Tulasī uses so skillfully', wrote Aditya Behl. See Behl, 'Presence and Absence in *Bhakti*'.

asserted that such a king was a *cakravartin*.[46] More significantly, over sixteen carefully delineated sections (*taraṅgas*) of the text, the author described the various components of the only true state, namely, the imperial state—replete with ministers, priests, jurists, courtiers, forts, a treasury, an army, a network of spies, and so on.

Examples like the ones cited above can be multiplied. Clearly, networks of state and non-state patronage cut through a multiplicity of languages, genres, and a range of imaginative literary conceptualizations of power. Any easy correspondence between the 'size' of a kingdom and the political imagination of its literary elite would be misleading. Equally misleading would be any attempt to establish a direct correlation between the supposed narrow/wide reach of a language and the limits/scope of its politico-ideological sensibilities. In short, the millennium-by-millennium binary grid of cosmopolitan–vernacular permits too many nuances to pass unnoticed and unremarked. I find it more useful to work with the broad idea of a dynamic multilingualism. My work has a narrower temporal focus though, limited as it is to the fifteenth century, and to Mithila and Vidyapati, with North India as a general backdrop. This allows me to situate the texts under analysis in their deep histories, both in terms of their multilingual inter-textualities as well as in terms of their meaningful interventions in an ongoing political discourse.

Multilingualism

One has to carefully historicize multilingualism itself, and trace its dynamic, continuous histories as well as uneven temporalities. In some senses, most, if not all, languages, insofar as they are historical entities, are constituted multilingually. Either they partake in the speech, scripts, words, and forms existing already, whether in writing or orally, or, more commonly, they grow together with other languages in a shared cultural idiom, tapping into commonly available forms of communication. Since most premodern cultures put a premium on the perceived purity of a language, the more powerful ones tended to

46 *Sarvebhyaḥ kṣitipālebhyo nityaṃ gṛhyāti vai karam/Sa samrāḍiti vijñeyaścakravartī*. See Caṇḍeśvara, *Rājanītiratnākara*, p. 5.

obliterate their histories more successfully than others. Such indeed is the case of Sanskrit and Arabic, and to a lesser extent, Latin. Thus, the scholarly tradition within Sanskrit insisted that it was a primordially pure language, and refused to relate it to an identifiable place or to acknowledge its worldly debts.[47] Though it is impossible to situate Sanskrit in its early bounded temporality, one should still be wary of its claims to be the font from which *all* other Indic languages were derived just 'because Sanskrit won the race to the archives and was first to be written down and preserved'.[48] This is not to suggest that a language, say Apabhraṃśa, did not 'borrow' a whole range of forms and structures from Sanskrit. It is instead necessary to acknowledge that both Apabhraṃśa and Sanskrit, flourishing in the same geo-cultural zone, must have tapped into common oral resources current in a spectrum of speech and expressive practices.[49]

If we keep the contours of this lost, if vague and commonsensical, history in mind, it makes sense to think of multilingualism in the long fifteenth century as existing in several registers, forms, and locations: those that were manifest in a 'borrowed' vocabulary; those that we witness in the bending of verb endings or verse metres; those that surfaced in the adaptation or interpenetration of genres

[47] Thus '[t]he sociolinguistic biography of Sanskrit was entirely different. The historical record does not enable us to attribute to it any local roots at all. Whereas some regional languages such as New Persian achieved transregionality through merit, and others such as Latin had it thrust upon them through military conquests, Sanskrit seems to have almost been born transregional; it was at home everywhere—and perhaps, in a sense, at home nowhere. In respect to everyday discourse, Sanskrit was, from a very early date—indeed probably from its very beginnings—marked by distance and distinction. In general its relationship with actual local speech types was hyperglossic, as it has here been named, something to which the distance between Latin and its 'earth-bound' register, a classic diglossic situation, bears no comparison.' See Pollock, *The Language of the Gods*, p. 262.

[48] Doniger, *The Hindus*, p. 16.

[49] Working with the broadest definition of *a* language, I am not engaging here with the debate about the distinctions to be made between a dialect and a language. That taxonomy itself is an indication of the hierarchization prevalent within the language domain—the politics of which is what interests me more.

across languages; and those that existed 'outside of the texts'. The same author writing in different languages, though only occasionally practiced, also constituted a different order of multilingualism as did the use of unexpected or 'foreign' scripts for compositions in Indic languages or vice versa.

Shared words, with or without phonetic and spelling adaptations, were probably the most common, if elusively simple, form of multilingualism. The problem for historians is compounded since very few languages were literized or even named. Communicative practices, even stable ones, existed within language continuums, where they often remained without names. Take the example of a 'unique' text like the thirteenth-century *Varṇaratnākara* by Jyotirīśvara. Most modern scholars agree that this compendium of words, phrases, and expressions frequently used in literary compositions was itself composed in Maithili. Yet, we hardly hear of Maithili as a language before the early nineteenth century.[50] Indeed, the intense debate about the origin/history of the Maithili language itself is a telling example of the problems in ascribing modern names to early and unnamed language practices. If Subhadra Jha rigorously attributed the genesis of all of Maithili's lexical and syntactic resources to Sanskrit alone, De Vreese argued that the influence of Santhālī on Maithili was equally, if not more important.[51] Both the scholars buttressed their arguments with examples. The problem lay in the scholars' refusal to acknowledge the existence of an undocumented world of oral practices, where lines were fuzzy and rarely identified.

In some instances, especially after the sixteenth century, we do have contemporary accounts of such intermixture. Thus, Bhikharidas noted that Brajbhāṣa was interesting because it was constituted by borrowings from six different languages.[52] It is also easier to see words shared between languages with a relatively stable stock of vocabulary and syntax. It is easy to see, for example, that Avahaṭṭha, the language

50 Yadav, 'Maithili Phonetics and Phonology'. See especially, the 'Introduction'.

51 See Jha, *The Formation of the Maithilī Language*. Also see De Vreese, 'Review of the Formation of the Maithilī Language', pp. 402–6.

52 *Brajabhāṣā bhāṣā rucira kahai sumati sab koi/Milai Sanskrit Pārasihuñ pai ati pragaṭa ju hoi/Braja Māgadhī milai amara nāga javana bhākhāni/Sahaj*

in which Vidyapati composed his *Kīrttilatā* in the fifteenth century, and Abdul Rahmān composed his *Sandeśarāsaka* a century earlier, carried a large number of both Sanskrit and Persian words, unlike the Apabhraṃśa texts of an earlier era.

In some cases, such borrowings were not only easily identifiable; they also indexed a deeper historical appropriation. An interesting instance is the topical deployment of the Persian word *kafir* in a story about a truthful hero in Vidyapati's Sanskrit composition, *Puruṣaparīkṣā*. The story relates how two Rājapūta princes served a 'Yavana' ruler of Delhi and helped him save his kingdom against a concerted attempt by some envious *kāpahara* rājās. The term *kāpahara* for the Sultan's enemies was shorn of its sectarian connotation in this retelling, but it was used only in the context of the 'Yavana' king's enemies and never before or after in the text.[53] Words could thus carry a whole cultural world into another language, but also, in the process, be affected in its meaning by such relocation! Better still, such relocations may also indicate the limits of our modern labels and boundaries.

The more easily visible, if not frequently practiced, form of multilingualism was witnessed when an author had mastery of, and composed in, more than one language. Of the latter, we do not have too many extant instances, though not as few as generally believed either. Among the few exceptions to the general Sanskrit monolinguality, Pollock cites Vedantadeśika in Tamil and Sṛināthа in Telugu, apart from Vidyapati.[54] Of the other claims (by King Harṣa of Kashmir and Viśvanātha of Orissa), he is dismissive in the absence of actual surviving work. Surprisingly, he misses Tulsidas. If one was to look beyond the world of Sanskrit, examples might be given of

---

Phārasī hū milai ṣaṭa vidhi kahata bakhāni (Brajabhāṣā is a delectable language, so say all the right-thinking men/Where Sansakrit and Parsi are present together/Braja and Māgadhī blends with Amaranāga and the language of the Greeks/Easy Persian also merge with these, thus it gets extended in six different ways). Cited in Singh, *Kīrttilatā aur Avahaṭṭha Bhāṣā*, p. 20.

53 See Vidyapati, *Puruṣaparīkṣā*.

54 See, Pollock, 'Introduction', p. 68, footnote 65.

Amir Khusrau and a few others who composed in both Hindavi and Persian.[55]

It is interesting, in spite of the limited number of examples cited above, that the ideal of mastery over more than one language was respected. Viśvanātha's *Sāhityadarpaṇa* mentioned a separate category of composition, *karambhakaṃ* (besides the standard genres such as *kathā* [fictional story], *ākhyāyikā* [celebratory biography], and *campū* [text consisting of both prose and poem]), that he defined as one that was 'made of different languages', *bhāṣābhirvividhābhirvini rmitam.*[56] He gave the following instructions to playwrights in this regard:

> For educated men, and for men of superior and middling stature, Sanskrit should be used. If a man, albeit educated, is of inferior status, Sanskrit is not used for him. Similarly, for educated women and women of high stature, Śaurasenī should be used. Use Mahārāṣṭrī for women's tales. The attendants inside the Rājā's household [*antaḥpuracāriṇām*] should speak Māgadhī. Use Ardhamāgadhī for servants/slaves [*ceṭānāṃ*], Rājapūta, and tradesmen [*śreṣṭhināṃ*]. Prācya for comedians, the language of Avantī for the cunning [*dhūrtas*]. For warriors, city-dwellers, and sportspersons, dākṣiṇātyā should be used. Śābarī should be used for the Śabaras and the Śakas. For the inhabitants of the north, Bāhalika bhāṣā and Drāviḍa for the Draviḍas. Ābhīrī should be used for the Abhīras, and Cāṇḍālī for the Cāṇḍālas. Ābhīrī and Cāṇḍālī should be used also for those earning their livelihood from wood and leaves [*kāṣṭhapatropajīviṣu*]. The same should be used for leather-workers, iron-smiths, and so on. Paiśācī is for the Piśācas, and Śaurasenī should be used for maidservants of superior and middling stature. For boys, eunuchs, and lowly astrologers, the

[55] A few examples are also cited in a review article; see Tieken, 'The Process of Vernacularization', p. 367.

[56] Viśvanātha Kavirāja, *Sāhityadarapaṇaḥ*, VI: 337, p. 327. He also gave the example of his own work titled *Praśastiratnāvalī* that he claimed was composed in sixteen languages, *ṣoḍaśabhāṣāmayī*. No such work seems to have survived, prompting Pollock to say that '[w]hen such claims are not simply expressions of scholarly (and not creative) mastery or mere bragging, they represent limited experiments'. See Pollock, 'Sanskrit Literary Culture from the Inside Out', p. 68, footnote 65.

> intoxicated and the impatient, Śaurasenī mixed with Sanskrit should be used. Prakrit should be used for those high on opulence, those suffering from penury, beggars and those carrying phloem. Sanskrit should also be used for Buddhist nuns and for high-born women. Some people say that Sanskrit should also be used for queens, daughters of ministers, and prostitutes. For other characters of low stature, the language of the respective region (*taddeśyaṃ tasya bhāṣitam*) should be deployed.[57]

To be sure, we do not have a single extant work that followed this advice even halfway through. The tenor and the overlaps/repetition of categories also suggest a degree of laboured stretching of language choices, if not pure hyperbole. Yet, it would be difficult to deny that the passage denotes a degree of insistence on a pattern in the division of labour among languages. Several plays from the period deployed two or three languages simultaneously. Vidyapati's *Gorakṣavijaya*, composed in Prakrit and Sanskrit, for example, carried Maithilī songs.[58] Even more telling is the fact that in several places, the play simply indicates that a song should be sung without actually providing any, presumably with the tacit understanding that a song in a local language would be included at the time of performance, depending on the place of its performance. This was also the case in his first Sanskrit play, *Maṇimañjarīnāṭikā*.

A different form of multilingualism is countenanced, though only occasionally, wherein some kind of a 'nonce-language' was forged, in sixteenth-century Bengal. Thus, Sudipta Kaviraj draws attention to the fact that

> the linguistic texture of the *Caitanyacaritamṛta* shows that the traditional structure of linguistic practice, in which individuals knew and used several languages, especially Sanskrit and Bangla, continued.

[57] Viśvanātha Kavirāja, *Sāhityadarapaṇaḥ*, VI: 158–69, p. 204. All translations are mine.

[58] See Vidyapati, *Gorakṣavijaya*. It is interesting that this was probably not exceptional. In fact, the twelfth-century poet Śaradātanaya in his *Bhāvaprakāśana* recommended that the local language should be used in songs, and the gestures typical of the locale should be used in dance. See Pollock, *The Language of the Gods*, p. 199.

> Associated with these movements was the creation of a kind of bridge language, a form of Sanskrit that could be read from both sides. Accessibility from the Sanskrit side ensured that these compositions would have a wide circulation and make sense to those who understood Sanskrit or neighboring vernacular languages; accessibility to Bangla meant that the works could also circulate among Bengalis who knew little or no Sanskrit.[59]

Kaviraj goes on to note that many popular hymns such as those by Tulsidas and Vallabhacharya also had the same status. Clearly, these 'improvisations' as well as the multilingualities of other kinds, if we may call them that, indicate the messy state of affairs outside of text, in the sphere of everyday communication, especially in the cities.

Many authors, probably because of their training, would be loath to admit of these 'influences', whose sources were quotidian and sub-elitist. As I have tried to demonstrate in Chapter 3 in this volume, Vidyapati's *Likhanāvalī* too seems to have taken a leaf or two from the Persian insha tradition without explicitly acknowledging it. In some cases, 'deliberate' elisions were a result of an entirely different anxiety. In the case of Avadhī Sufi romances, for example, Simon Digby pointed out,

> [t]he verse literature produced in the qaṣbās and *dargāhs* of the region of Awadh from the end of the fourteenth century onwards is in a different dialect if not in a different language from the current speech of the urban population of Dehli. It is a fully developed form of eastern Hindi with different terminations in the tenses of the verbs, and different forms of the postpositions; and a vocabulary which appears consciously to exclude Persian and Arabic loanwords. This conceals—one may argue deliberately—the obvious source of inspiration for the new romantic narrative poems with tinges of mystical sentiment. This is not Sanskritic but derived from the Persian poetic tradition so greatly loved by Sufis, and particularly from the romantic mathnawis of the pattern set by Niẓami of Ganja and imitated in Dehli by Amir Khusraw. The sophisticated strategy that was adopted by these poets in Awadh was a deliberate bilingualism designed to propagate a world-view, a

59 Kaviraj, 'The Two Histories of Literary Culture in Bengal', p. 520.

climate of sensibility and a theology that would enhance the influence, power and acceptability of the immigrants in this particular Indian environment.[60]

Elsewhere, Aditya Behl had also remarked on the impact of the mathnawi tradition on Sufi *premākhyānas*, though the written corpus assiduously avoided any mention of such 'influence'.[61] In some cases, historians can trace such forms of embedded multilinguality through a careful exploration of the intertextuality of extant compositions. In other cases, it is important to 'extrapolate', as realistically as possible, life outside of the text.

It is pertinent to note that actual learning for most young scholars and creative writers was probably single track: they would usually be groomed, so far as North India was concerned, in one of the classical traditions, either in Sanskrit or in the Perso-Arabic tradition. In real life, however, they had to contend with a variety of historical factors: the pervasive presence of Persian[62] (especially its simplified speech variety that Bhikhārīdāsa called *sahaj Phārasī* [easy Persian]), the activities of trans-regional states like the Sultanate of Delhi (to some extent even others like those of Jaunpur and Gujarat, and later, the Mughal state), the effects of more intensified military rivalries, and the movement of soldiers, mystics, and itinerant traders.[63] Many of the sultanates, most

[60] Digby, 'Before Timur Came', pp. 340–1.

[61] See Behl, 'Presence and Absence in Bhakti'.

[62] Already by the mid-fourteenth century, Alam and Subhrahmanyam noted, 'as Persian grew in significance as a language of communication, even the court-centres that were outside the direct influence of the Sultanate of Delhi testify to its use, at least for some limited purposes'. See Alam and Subrahmanyam, *Indo-Persian Travels*, p. 47.

[63] It would be interesting to imagine how troops drawn from distant places and placed together communicated with each other. Late in the fourteenth century, for instance, when Firuz Shah Tughluq was camping in Sind to invade Thatta, he got reinforcements of 'troops from Badaun, Qanauj, Sandila, Awadh, Bihar, Mahoba, Eraj, Chanderi, Dhar, the interior and exterior of Doab, Samana, Multan and Lahore'. See Afif, *Tarikh-i Firuz Shahi*, trans. Jauhri, p. 142.

notably Gujarat[64] and Malwa,[65] patronized a whole variety of languages and literatures.[66] These must have added to the diversity of (at the least) lexical choices available to writers of expressive compositions.

Among the 'languages' that gained from these contingencies were sub-elite entities that seemed to have currency and intelligibility all over North India: Hindavi, Avadhī, various inflections of Apabhraṃśa, and to a lesser extent, the simplified Persian referred to above. Available sources do not permit a comprehensive reconstruction of these practices, but those that can be accessed appear fairly revealing. Thus, Shams-i Siraj Afif tells us that during Firuz Shah Tughluq's protracted seize of the fort of Iqdala in Bengal, one Malik Qabul was sent as an emissary to the stranded Bengal sultan with an offer of a truce. After Malik Qabul had offered gifts to Sultan Sikandar, the latter asked Qabul his name. 'Malik Qabul', reports Afif, '*replied in Hindavī* that "the slave was called Torabanda" (emphasis added). The context of the narrative suggests that speaking in Hindavī was a gesture of informality, and probably signalled simple-minded trust.[67]

The example above alerts us to the world of oral communications and the multiple choices available to people in that world. On the other hand, the appropriation of the Rāmāyaṇa narrative by authors of Sufi *premākhyānas* (Daud, *Qutban* and *Jayasi*), attests to a pool of cultural idioms and metaphors shared among languages and their

64 The Gujarati Sultans 'patronized scholarship and literature in Arabic, Persian, and Sanskrit. During sultanate rule in the fifteenth century, scholars and poets began to write in early Gujarati and Gūjarī, a Gujarati-inflected version of early Urdu'. See Sheikh, *Forging a Region*, p. 6.

65 A number of Sanskrit inscriptions from the Malwa domain indicate that the language flourished under the sultanate during this period. Particularly noteworthy is the Lalitpur Stone Inscription of 1424 recording the consecration of the images of Padmanandi and Damavasanta. See Prasad, *Sanskrit Inscriptions of Delhi Sultanate*, pp. 185–91.

66 Even in the Jaunpur court, Vidyapati noted, princes gathered from different regions, and each spoke in his own language, *ni-a bhāsā*. See *Kīrttilatā*, p. 91.

67 Afif, *Tarikh-i Firuz Shahi*, trans. Jauhri, p. 107.

users, belonging to varied religious traditions.[68] What it certainly signifies is the shift towards more intensely interactive and reflective/reflexive idioms, languages, texts, and genres. Equally, it also gestures to increasingly greater interactions, and greater possibility of such interactions, among peoples, places, and performative practices attached to 'a locality'.

Even more unmistakable is the fact that roughly from the fourteenth century onwards, we see an unprecedented and massive rise in the number of texts composed in North India, indeed in the entire subcontinent. After all, not only do we have a greater number of Sanskrit compositions in this period, we also witness local-language texts mushrooming all over, as well as a whole new world of literary production in the Perso-Arabic tradition. The process only intensified further in the fifteenth and sixteenth centuries.[69]

What would some of the long-term historical implications of the extraordinary literary efflorescence, its multilingual (or polyglossic) forms, and its rich repository of trans-regional trans-confessional idioms that we countenance in the long fifteenth century be? A response to that question must start with an exploration of the more general theoretical–historical problematic: the relationship between literature and history, or in a related way, the complex links between politics and reigning forms of knowledge. Embedded in that general formulation are questions of socialization into ideals of conduct, processes that lay down a lexical grid for talking about politics both among those in positions of power and those who 'did not matter', in short all the tangibles and intangibles that go into defining the character, expanse, and limits of politico-cultural discourse. That discourse, however, is produced within a field of power and history, through what one may broadly call 'literature'.

68 I deliberately refrain from using labels like 'syncretism' to avoid short-circuiting the study of this complex process. For a very useful discussion of the problems in using the 'descriptive' paradigm of syncretism, see Stewart, 'In Search of Equivalence', pp. 261–3, 269–74.

69 For a detailed discussion of the issue, see Jha, 'Literary Conduits for "Consent"', especially pp. 330–5.

Literature, History, Power

Any reflection on the links between literature, history, and power must begin with an acknowledgement that these are dynamic categories. What they refer to depends as much on the time, place, and context of their usage as on who is using them. The problem is compounded by the fact that these are English words. While using them in the context of medieval India, one also has to account for the 'gaps' vis-à-vis the relevant equivalent terms.

I intend to start with a quick mapping of the meanings of each of these terms—by no means a comprehensive mapping—with a view to flag the sense(s) in which I would be using them as also to illuminate the particular senses in which they are relevant for my study. Let me start with 'literature'. The present popular view of literature holds it to mean text compositions with a strong element of the 'imaginative'. Thus, short stories, novels, and poetry are seen as hard-core literature in a way that a newspaper report or even a book of history is not. The latter's claim to only stitch together a set of facts in a neutral way rules it out of the purview of literature. This understanding of literature depends on a neat distinction between fact and fiction, between memory and imagination, and between objective reports and subjective/fictional narratives. It thus fails to take cognizance of the complexity of relationship and the overlaps within the pairs listed in the last sentence. Another disadvantage of using this definition of literature is that it has little space to factor in the role of readers (the consumers of literature) in the entire exercise. For, it is perfectly possible that the same piece might be read as literature by one person and non-literature by another.

Of the scores of attempts to define literature in the modern period, the one by Terry Eagleton that, following John Ellis, compares it to a weed, is probably the most useful for a historian:

> There is no 'essence' of literature whatsoever. Any bit of writing may be read 'non-pragmatically', if that is what reading a text as literature means, just as any writing may be read 'poetically' … . John M. Ellis has argued that the term 'literature' operates rather like the word 'weed': weeds are not particular kinds of plant, but just any kind of plant which for some reason or another a gardener does not want around. Perhaps 'literature' means something like the opposite: any kind of writing

> which for some reason or another somebody values highly. As the philosophers might say, 'literature' and 'weed' are functional rather than ontological terms: they tell us about what we do, not about the fixed being of things. They tell us about the role of a text or a thistle in a social context, its relations with and differences from its surroundings, the ways it behaves, the purposes it may be put to and the human practices clustered around it. 'Literature' is in this sense a purely formal, empty sort of definition.[70]

A historian reading 'literature' composed in the past may turn this empty definition of literature 'inside out' by determining how exactly contemporaries defined and read literature. Or, she might fill it by placing herself as a modern reader of literature. Both appear to be useful exercises, and may complement each other.

Of the several languages in which scholars produced what might be considered to be included in literature, at least one, namely, Sanskrit, had a long and rigorous tradition of theorizing the literary. This tradition started with Bhāmaha and Daṇḍin in the seventh century and continued for almost a thousand years. Three different words corresponding to three different approaches to the literary are available in this tradition: *vāṅmaya, sāhityaṃ*, and *kāvya*. Etymologically, Vāṅmaya refers to simply anything made of words or language with an implicit sense of that consisting of 'spoken words';[71] Sāhityaṃ stands for an association or combination (of words and meanings) with the implicit sense of composition;[72] Kāvya on the other hand refers to a description or one that is fit to be described/praised by a wise man (*kavi*).[73] While vāṅmaya is clearly the largest and most inclusive category, the etymologies do not help much in distinguishing between kāvya and sāhityaṃ.

Among the Sanskrit works on the science of literature, Bhoja's *Ṣṛiṅgāraprakāśa* (tenth century) probably carries the most explicit

70 Eagleton, *Literary Theory*, p. 8.

71 The root is *vāc*—a word, sound, or expression; alternatively it stands for language or speech. See Apte, *Sanskrit–English Dictionary*, p. 840.

72 Apte, *Sanskrit–English Dictionary*, p. 985.

73 *Kav*, an *atmanepad*, is to describe, praise, or compose, whereas *kavi* was a man of wisdom and intelligence. See Apte, *Sanskrit–English Dictionary*, p. 344.

elaboration of each of these categories.[74] Bhoja, while admitting that it was the unity (*sāhitya*) of words with their meanings that constitutes kāvya, denoted twelve different types of words as well as of meanings and compositions. However, like his predecessors, he gave elaborate rules which kāvya must adhere to. These included deployment of *guṇas* (merit/traits),[75] adornment with *alaṅkāras* (literary tropes), inclusion of *rasas* (production/experience of [pure/assorted] emotions), and avoidance of errors.

In fact, medieval theorists in Sanskrit show almost no disagreement with the idea that kāvya was the privileged medium of organized expression, even though it was always defined in terms of its linguistic organization, and never in terms of thematic or philosophical distinctiveness. It could be either in prose or in verse or in a mix of the two, but it could be composed only in Sanskrit, Prakrit, or Apabhraṃśa. This of course was an extraordinary claim to power and exclusion that reduced compositions in other languages to the status of non-kāvya, even as their existence was not only acknowledged by the theorists but also commented upon. Songs were composed mostly in the *deśabhāṣā* (with a few exceptions, the most prominent being *Gītagovinda*), and singers were expected to learn theory as well as become 'master of the place-languages', *deśabhāṣāviśārad*.[76]

Also pertinent is the fact that from Daṇḍin (late seventh century) onwards, the distinction between the fictive kāvya (kathā) and the 'factual' narrative (ākhyāyikā) was 'annulled'. This is not to say that the distinction between fact, fiction, and mythology disappeared altogether in theory. Rather, it meant that this distinction was not the basis of distinction for genres, and that all were accorded equal status as kāvya. As historians in the twenty-first century, we must, of course, take note of these claims made by the Sanskrit theorists.

Yet, nothing prevents us from going beyond and reading non-kāvya compositions as 'literature', as part of the field that we must

74 Bhoja, *Śṛṅgāraprakāśa*.

75 *Guṇa* also refers to one of the three qualities that were supposedly found in all things created: *satva*, *rajas*, and *tamas*, or it could refer to one of the five senses, namely, *rūpa*, *rasa*, *gandha*, *sparśa*, and *śabda*.

76 *Mānasollāsa*, 4.120–21, vol. 3.12, cited in Pollock, *The Language of the Gods*, p. 300.

reckon into our reading as literary. If part of the substance of 'literary' inheres in ways of reading it, may we not, as historians, read the non-literary too as literature?[77] *Vāṅmaya*, things made of words or language, would appear more useful to us as a category but with the full cognizance that this did not exclude oral compositions. After all, it was in the interplay of all forms of composition—expressive and informative, oral and written, factual and fictive, mythological and historical, theoretical and pragmatic, private readings and public performances—that the wider field of literary culture could be said to have been cultivated.

It is another matter that the domain of literary culture, like so much else, was not a homogenous one. It was marked by internal hierarchies so widely respected, that even the poets who chose to compose in a 'regional' language felt obliged to explain why they were not writing in Sanskrit.[78] The field was further complicated by the impressive and unavoidable presence of Persianate culture right from the thirteenth century onwards, as I have tried to indicate above, and as the following chapters (especially Chapters 3 and 5 in this volume) demonstrate further.[79]

The question remains as to how we may read this literature to enrich history, not just histories of literature or literary cultures but also the so-called mainstream history. If the study of literary cultures is not to suffer the isolation of comparable fields like art history, it

[77] 'If I pore over the railway timetable not to discover a train connection but to stimulate in myself general reflections on the speed and complexity of modern existence, then I might be said to be reading it as literature', wrote Terry Eagleton. See Eagleton, *Literary Theory*, p. 8.

[78] Among many others, this was the case with Vidyapati in the fifteenth century, Tulsidas (*Rāmacaritamānasa*) in the sixteenth, and Keśavadāsa in the seventeenth. See Chapter 5 in this volumc.

[79] It is curious that Pollock acknowledges the influence of Persian on the subcontinental literary culture only *after* the sixteenth century. Thus he states: 'Vernacular beginnings were tentative in a literary space entirely dominated by Sanskrit. The semiotics of socioideological registers used in literary texts shows the same complexity as elsewhere in South Asia, and the competition between them shows the same intensity, though both were made yet more complex and intense by the presence of Persianate culture after the sixteenth century.' See Pollock, 'Introduction', *Literary Cultures in History*, p. 17.

must flourish in full and intimate engagement with history 'proper' whatever that phrase might mean. After all, this 'isolation' is merely a euphemism for an uncritical and presumptive endorsement (or rejection) of whatever the other histories have tried to establish. If this sounds a little ambivalent, it is because modern academics use the English word 'history' in several overlapping senses, often without bothering to make a distinction between them.

In everyday parlance, history simply refers to information about the past, of an event, monument, practice, and so on. We may call it the quizmaster's view of history, and denote it within quotes, as 'history', to distinguish it from academically more grounded connotations of history. When a guide apprises visiting tourists of the 'history' of the Taj Mahal, giving them information about who built it, when, and why, he uses the general non-specialist sense of the word. While facts about the past are important ingredients of what the specialists might call history, facts in themselves do not constitute history.[80]

A very distinct sense in which the word 'history' is deployed, mostly in academic circles, relates to a particular way of seeing things, both present and past. It is true that there are wide disagreements among academics about what exactly is historical or (in a more specific way) what a historicized attitude towards the past and present might mean. Yet, it is generally accepted that a keen sensitivity towards change and continuity, understood along the co-ordinates of time, space, and human agency, constitute the vital ingredients of such an attitude. Historians might disagree about how best to practice this particular perspective in their craft or how much flexibility the discipline of history should be allowed, but usually they would accept the significance of these ingredients of historical thinking. The tangible manifestation of this attitude is to be found in the rigours of research that the academic discipline of history, varied though it might be in its orientation, stands for. Thus, if a historian declares that the ancient narrative

80 For a substantive discussion on the complex links between facts and history, see Rao, Shulman, and Subrahmanyam, *Textures of Time*, pp. 11–19. Elsewhere in the text, they point out, evocatively: 'Facts are not so hard to come by; *purānas* have them, folktales may have them, even newspapers sometimes have them. It is always a matter of what one does with them—or means to do' (Rao, Shulman, and Subrahmanyam, *Textures of Time*, p. 263).

tradition of *itihāsa* is not history, this is the sense in which the term is employed.[81]

The differences among modern historians are even more pronounced on the issue of what tools and techniques of analysis are more effective in recapturing and narrativizing the complex patterns of change and continuity. A number of works in the tradition of 'What is History?' actually grapple with this issue.[82] In doing so, they engage more with the craft of professional history writing rather than with what history is in an ontological sense.

There exists a third meaning of history—linked to the other two but functionally separable. History stands, in a related but distinct way, for the force or burden of the past as we are obliged to feel it in our present. In the comment, 'sex is biology but gender is history', the word History (with a capital 'H') is used to invoke this sense. The relationship between the academic discipline of history on the one hand, and History as a socio-politico-ideological force on the other, is both complementary and contradictory. What History, as a burden of the past, may present as natural, universal, unchanging, and hence, unchallengeable (for example, gender), is often shown to be changing, contingent, and hence, challengeable by the discipline of history. If the academic pursuit of history is dynamic, the force of History is also subject to change through the continuing politics of knowledge. Historians' reinterpretations of the past, after all, are also an attempt to intervene actively in the moving course of how the burden of the past is felt, and dealt with, by human agents in the present.

These taxonomic distinctions between 'history' within quotes, history as an academic pursuit, and History as a naturalizing force, are vital for laying out the precise terms in which to denote a set of possible relationships between literatures and histories. It is equally important to keep in mind the varied meanings to which the term 'literature' itself is subject. The modern discipline of history has a lot to learn from the discipline of literary studies and vice versa. However, I am not concerned with this dimension of the relationship

81 Ray, 'What Ought to be History'.

82 See for example, Carr, *What is History?*; also see Bloch, *The Historian's Craft*.

between history and literature right now. My interest lies in unravelling the ways in which the literary compositions of fifteenth-century North India attempted to intervene in the course of History as they encountered them then. Such an endeavour essentially sees the act of composing a text as primarily a political act—not in the narrow sense in which a court poet might help carry out royal propaganda, but in more fundamental and profound ways.

What were these 'other' ways in which literary compositions could affect the course of History? Before we begin to answer that question, it is important for us to imagine, in a historically informed way, the place of literature in the order of things in premodern societies. Literature, especially its more 'popular' forms that could circulate freely in an oral culture (stories and versified/reciteable poems and songs) must have performed a whole range of functions including those we would today associate with electronic media, print media, and even cultural products (namely, cinema, plays, music).[83] More than disseminating 'information', literary composition could help people acquire the elementary vocabulary in which to make sense of the world around them. In doing so, literature would 'naturally' set up the scope and limits of the ways in which the world could be meaningfully referenced in ordinary conversation or scholarly discourse. Litterateurs would of course play on the existing vocabulary of other comparable literary compositions of the past, and simultaneously draw upon a personally acquired knowledge through institutional interactions and everyday observations.

It was through literature that a larger number of people in ever-wider circuits of communication would thus be socialized into specific idioms and overarching archives (I do not use the word 'archive' here

83 Let us not forget that unlike Christian Europe, where the weekly mass was an extraordinary source of information for people about what was going on in the world around them, there was no comparable institution in South Asia. Royal courts, itinerant merchants, peasant–soldiers returning home after earning some extra money fighting for unknown or known patrons were some of the agents who helped in the dissemination of information. But most important perhaps were the cultural products like literature and music, especially those that could be remembered easily and retold or recited over and over again.

to denote the physically bounded space where government files and records are stored and systematically indexed). In the context of the modern state—whether western, colonial, postcolonial, or its numerous variants—it is almost a truism to say now that scholars 'need to move away from archive-as-source to archive-as-subject'.[84] The idea that archives are no innocuous stores of information waiting to be mined has caught on especially from the 1980s onwards among anthropologists, literary theorists, and historians alike. Early statements on this might be traced back to the 1970s, if not earlier.[85] Thus, way back in 1972, Foucault proposed that archives are 'systems of statements':

> By this term I do not mean the sum of all the texts that a culture has kept upon its person as documents attesting to its own past, or as evidence of a continuing identity; nor do I mean the institutions, which, in a given society, make it possible to record and preserve those discourses that one wishes to remember and keep in circulation. On the contrary, it is rather the reason why so many things, said by so many men, for so long, ... are born in accordance with specific regularities; ... The archive is first the law of what can be said, the system that governs the appearance of statements as unique events ... it is that which defines at the outset *the system of its enunciability*.[86] (emphasis in original)

It is 'systems of statements' or archives as described above that determine the limits of what one can, or cannot, imagine/think/say in a given age. That is, for any age, a concrete manifestation of the burden of History. Is it possible to recover in such archives an ecosystem of conceptual vocabularies instituted in the public imagination through expressive forms? That brings us to the question of how history as a discipline may deal with literature as its raw material for working out insights into the past. Should we always look at literature as a 'reflection' of something more tangible? Should we not consider it also as an argument that sought to articulate a view on whatever it talked about? That argument of course would be intelligible in the context of

84 Stoler, 'Colonial Archives and the Arts of Governance', p. 93.
85 Certeau, 'The Historiographic Operation'.
86 Foucault, *The Archaeology of Knowledge*, pp. 128–9.

other similar/contesting arguments in response to which the literary text constructed its own. To the extent that we can reconstruct this intertextual dynamic, and relate it to issues of ethics, knowledge, and power, we might meaningfully relate literature and history as well as literature and power.

As with literature and history, there is no singular meaning that we can attribute to the idea of 'power'. In the last hundred years or so, scholars have intensely deliberated over the character of power as a political phenomenon, and the usefulness of 'power' as a conceptual category of analysis in a range of disciplines from philosophy and political science to history and critical theory. It is not possible to engage with all hues of arguments on the issue of power here. In any case, much of this debate was carried on in terms of philosophical abstractions with only indirect bearing for disciplines like history, and even less so where premodern historiography is concerned.

Social scientists often see power variously as the authority that a state and its integral or adjunct institutions exercise over their subjects and as the 'influence' that is wielded over people by community leaders, mystics, or traditionally respected institutions like caste associations and village bodies. This is the most visible form of power in which two distinct but overlapping meanings of power are clubbed together—the brute physical force that the state and other armed institutions wield on the one hand, and the might of ideological constructs that both validate the state's power as well as create myriad 'independent' ideologues and stakeholders in the reigning dispensation. This is the more conventional, if still relevant, meaning of power.

Postmodernist thinkers like Foucault, infamous for their 'near-obsessive concern with power', posit it in a very different and far more complex sense. 'Extended to realms far beyond authoritarian rule or class exploitation, the two forms prioritized in conventional liberal and Marxist criticism, power is seen to be all-pervasive and yet decentred. It penetrates to the very pores of everyday life, can become deeply internalized, and is all but irresistible, since "effective" resistance tends to produce new forms of power.'[87] Power in this formulation is seen as a discursive field, almost coextensive with 'forms

[87] Sarkar, 'Post-modernism and the Writing of History', p. 294.

of knowledge', and embodied in the Foucauldian notion of archive referred to above. We may denote this sense of the word with a capital 'P' (Power as against the power exercised directly by the state over its subjects, men over women, and so on).

These ideas are grounded firmly in very complex, distinct, and controversial theories of postmodernism. Yet, one does not have to uncritically buy into the entire Foucauldian paradigm to see the obvious and commonsensical takeaway: that forms of knowledge, the terms of its enunciation, the lexical grid in which it is couched (and which it helps create), are critical vectors that any form of power—whether of state, or of caste, gender, ethics, or religion—must contend with. In the context of the histories of literary cultures, this conception of (a knowledge-wedded form of) Power helps me describe the ways in which literature ('things made of language') as a primary field of knowledge production can be seen as a vital constituent of both History and Power. The state and other agents, both in the exercise of power and in an attempt to resist it, must contend with History and Power as constituted through the discursive field of literature.

* * *

In one of his early attempts at theorizing the vernacularization of politics and literature in South Asia, Sheldon Pollock noted:

> We must attempt to reconceptualize the key terms of the problematic, culture and power, from within our empirical materials, resisting at once the preconcepts of nationalized, colonialized, and orientalized thinking, and even perhaps normal social science. It is typical of such science, as the common sense of modernity and capitalism, to reduce one of these terms (culture) to the other (power)—a reduction often embodied in the use of the concept of legitimation of power. There is no reason to assume that legitimation is applicable throughout all human history, yet it remains the dominant analytic in explaining the work of culture in studies of early South and Southeast Asia.[88]

He went on to suggest that 'in earlier epochs the grounds for social change, even radical change, might ... be located in some more

[88] Pollock, 'India in the Vernacular Millennium', p. 44.

autonomous aesthetic imperative, for example, such as a new desire for vernacular style'.[89]

Now, there can be no doubt that the dominant modes of modern historiography on medieval South Asia have only too often used the idea of 'legitimation' to short-circuit all possibilities of a sustained study of cultural productions, textual or otherwise, in their own terms and in a historicized manner. Historians have tended to see genealogies, land-grants, the construction of temples, performance of rituals, composition of historical narratives, retellings of mythological tales, and much else as mere instruments for legitimation of state power. While Pollock's objection to the scourge of legitimation is valid, it is curious that he gives no reason why he privileges, or even what he means by, 'some more autonomous aesthetic imperative'. A 'new desire for vernacular style' as an imperative simply begs the question.

The problem, it would appear, lies not so much in the idea of legitimation per se (one might in fact ask how power could survive without validating itself, unless one puts it beyond history). A state in the pre-modern, pre-nation era also had to contend with society at large before the former could exercise power over the latter. However, it would never be enough for it to construct a suitable genealogy or a fancy theory and let it loose on a presumably unsuspecting mass of people. Such a readymade 'plug and play' conceptualization of legitimation of power makes no distinction between what linguists call the code and the message.

The codes of politico-ideological discourse, the terms in which the good and bad are talked about, traditions within which the ability to discern the ethical from the unethical is cultivated are all bequeathed to an age by earlier generations through History. These codes germinate over a long period, and are encrusted into the very language that is used to 'create' literature.[90] That is why the discipline of history

[89] Pollock, 'India in the Vernacular Millennium', p. 44.

[90] 'We are within language as within our body', wrote Sartre, '[w]e feel it spontaneously while going beyond it towards other ends, as we feel our hands and our feet; we perceive it when it is someone else who is using it, as we perceive the limbs of others'. See Sartre, *What is Literature? and Other Essays*, p. 35.

needs to ground itself in philological excavation, so as to recover the vestiges of prejudgement from within language. This makes the philological exercise into a politically charged act of historical analysis. For it helps expose the inbuilt, hidden, and unexamined judgements in narratives that claim only to provide an objective description. In the subsequent chapters, I have tried to ground my reading of the texts at hand in a philological exercise that extends into possible prehistories of terms, idioms, genres, and layers of meaning.

Indeed, what we need to excavate and systematically explore is the layered and charged field of already existing literary discourses into which an aspiring/fledgling regime plugs in order to communicate with (or reassure) its future (or uncertain) 'subjects'. One might say that the conditions for converting ordinary people into 'subjects of power' are created much before that power is actually exercised. To put it differently, an analysis of the long-term rhythms of literary production is a prerequisite for understanding legitimation for what it was often in the premodern era—a protracted, messy, and continuous process. This concept of legitimation as a diffused and long-term process helps us analyse literature in all its multifarious dimensions and relate it to diverse visions of power in the narrative about uneven temporalities of History.

In his essay on the 'Vernacular Millennium', Pollock asserted that the Sanskrit ecumene of the second millennium was 'restricted to the expressive and divorced from the documentary', which made its 'relation to power far more aesthetic than instrumental, a "poetry of power," perhaps, in an aesthetic state'.[91] It is not clear as to what is meant here by 'an aesthetic state' though it sounds vaguely plausible. On the other hand, what would a 'poetry of power' consist of if not a literary technology that seeks to camouflage the inherent inequities of power, and present it as beautiful and natural, and hence just, ethical, and acceptable? To put it from the other end, the study of 'knowledge formations' must be relocated as a vital component of political histories. This can be done only by diachronically linking the literary imagination with political possibilities, and hence reworking the relationship between literature and politics.

[91] Pollock, 'India in the Vernacular Millennium', p. 48.

Our discussion in the earlier sections of the chapter tried to demonstrate how the fifteenth century witnessed an unprecedented growth in the sheer volume and range of literary productions. While the literary cultures of the time were evidently multilingual, they were also multivalent in their ideological orientation and diverse in their cultural projects in a way that cannot fully be explained in terms of the immediate imperatives of governance, rulership, or states. This is evident in all the three texts of Vidyapati that I take up for closer analysis in the chapters in Part 2.

Part II

Texts

3 *Writing State and Order*

Sometime in the second or perhaps the third decade of the fifteenth century, a small chieftain in the semi-autonomous principality of Droṇāvāra in Nepal (bordering north Bihar but part of the politico-cultural zone of Mithila) made what must have been an unusual (if not unprecedented) request to a reputed scholar of the region. The chieftain was Purāditya Girinārāyaṇa, the scholar was the prolific Brāhmaṇa poet, Vidyapati, and the request was to produce a ready manual for writing, an aid for scribes. The result was the composition of a truly extraordinary text in Sanskrit entitled *Likhanāvalī*. The author duly noted in the text, not once but twice, that the manual was prepared on the orders of Purāditya. Immediately after paying obeisance to Lord Gaṇeśa, 'whose lotus like feet are worshipped with the crown jewels of those gods and demons who desire opulence [and] with whose pleasure all goals can be achieved', Vidyapati noted:

> Following the command of the son of Sarvāditya and king of Droṇāvara, Purāditya Girinārāyaṇa, I compose *Likhanāvalī* for the instruction of

> the ignorant, for the recreation of the informed, and for the affection of gentlemen. [I am] writing the rules about how to write to those above, those below, and those who are at the same level [in the social hierarchy] as also about [how to frame documents regarding] regulations and conduct.[1]

The author restated the role of his patron once again at the end, this time with some additional information: 'Defeating hordes of enemies and distributing their wealth among supplicants, having established his royal authority over the territory of Saptarī [area cannot be identified] with the might of his arms, and [having] killed Rāya Arjuna [since the latter was] guilty of cruel conduct towards his own kinsmen, Raja Purāditya got this *Likhanāvalī* composed'.[2]

To the extent that I can ascertain, it would appear that there was hardly any precedent in Sanskrit literature for writing the kind of manual that *Likhanāvalī* turned out to be. We have no means to know if this 'original' idea was his patron's or his own. In any case, that should not hold us long. It is probably more pertinent that such a book was written and became important enough to survive in at least one copy for more than 500 years or so. In what follows, we will try to describe and analyse the structure of this text, its language, and its contents. It would be useful to investigate what exactly the poet, a courtier already having acquired a reputation for learning and probably wisdom, tried to accomplish with the enterprise at hand. What could have been the possible 'inspiration' behind the idea of such a text is another question worth consideration.

The obvious question that would strike a student of history in general, and a student of fifteenth-century 'India' in particular, is this: what was the need, of all things, to have a book about how to write letters and frame documents? An answer to that big question might have to wait for further research, and discoveries of new manuscripts and recovery of new information. As of now, we might actually

[1] *Alpaśrutopadeśāya, kautukāya bahuṣrutām/Vidyapatissatāṃ prītyai karoti likhanāvalīm*. See Vidyapati, *Likhānavalī* (henceforth, *Likhanāvalī*), p. 1. All the excerpts from the book refer to page numbers in this printed Sanskrit text. All translations are mine unless otherwise indicated.

[2] *Likhanāvalī*, p. 63.

disaggregate that big question into smaller but equally important ones: where did the idea of writing such a manual come from? If there did not exist a tradition of producing such manuals in Sanskrit that Vidyapati might have been familiar with, could he have taken a clue from a non-Sanskrit source, such as the Persian tradition of insha? Does such a composition indicate the growing importance of scribes in the fifteenth century? Equally, if Vidyapati was not familiar with an already existing tradition (if any) of such a genre in Sanskrit, what extant literary conventions from within the world of Sanskrit could/did he draw upon to compose *Likhanāvalī*? Should this development be read as an indication of the emergence of a new kind of state, one that was far more diligently engaged in producing written documents and inscribing all communications in more durable formats? We will deal with these and other related questions in this chapter. Before that, let us first take a look at the way the text is organized and structured. A consideration of the framing strategies deployed and the literary devices used by him should help us reconstruct aspects of the literary world(s) that he inhabited.

Organizing the Text

Writing about the pitfalls of working with medieval texts in the context of thirteenth-century France, Gabriel Spiegel underlined the significance of the structure of the text in helping the historian recover the perceptual grids with which medieval writers worked.[3] Spiegel is only one of the many scholars who in the last two decades have commented on the problems in using a text merely for picking

[3] 'For, just as history, being transparent, was susceptible to invasion by fictions circulating in the chronicler's sources, so also was it receptive to being shaped by structures already residing in the social reality which the historian perceived as the focus of his narrative. And, in keeping with my metaphors of perception, I would like to call these structures "perceptual grids," which directed the historian's glance at relatively fixed categories of human experience and governed both the nature of his perceptions and the manner in which he transmitted them.' See Spiegel, 'Genealogy: Form and Function in Medieval History Narrative', p. 46.

up 'relevant' pieces of information, without first accounting for the 'wholeness' of a text, its specific rhythms and unique structure, and so forth. Let us start then by taking a look at how the text is organized.

Likhanāvalī is divided into four, or rather three plus one parts. The first three parts consist of model letters written to one's superiors, inferiors, and equals, respectively.[4] The fourth part carries model documents that primarily record details of what may broadly be termed 'business transactions'. The first part carries eighteen letters, and the second has twenty-eight. The third part that illustrates how to write to one's equals puts together only seven letters, understandable for a society where relationships were mostly framed within formal hierarchies and very few ties of equality existed. The section on documents, the fourth part, entitled *vyavahāralikhanāni*, literally, 'Writing Conduct', carries thirty-one entries. None of the letters in the first three sections are dated. But almost all of the documents in the fourth section are duly dated in the Lakṣamaṇa Era.[5]

Tables 3.1 to 3.4 below give the details of each of the four sections:

Table 3.1 Model Letters to Those with Higher Status

Receiver/Sender	Letter Number(s)	Total	Theme/Remarks
To Guru from Disciple	1, 2	2	(i) Requesting for books (ii) Sending *guru-dakshiṇa* to honour the knowledge gained from the guru
To Teacher–Ascetic of Varanasi from a Ruler	3	1	Alms in return for blessings securing various things for the realm (Very interesting mapping of all that is required for the smooth functioning of the state)

[4] *Uccaiḥkakṣalikhanāni*, *adhaḥkakṣalikhanāni*, and *samakakṣalikhanāni*, respectively.

[5] The Lakṣamaṇa Era in all probability started in 1119. For a discussion for and against this calculation, see Chapter 1 in this volume.

To Teacher–Ascetic of Kashi from a rich man (landholder/trader)	4	1	Alms sent in return for blessings securing health, wealth, and sons
To Father from Son	5	1	Task completed, coming back home
To Mother from Son	6	1	Quality of food
To Brother from Younger Brother	7	1	Freeing a fettered śūdra
To King from Army Chief	8, 9	2	(i) Reporting victory after initial retreat (ii) Reporting on Yavaneśvara's march
To King from Chieftain	10	1	Rehabilitating deserted lands
To King from Minister of Peace	11	1	Performance of rites for victory in battle
To Chief Minister from a local Tax Superintendent	12, 13	2	(i) Reporting non-payment of taxes by some (ii) Tax as per the previous years is unfair; measurement requested
To Minister of War and Peace from a Sāmanta	14	1	King upset, Sāmanta wants amnesty
To Minister of War and Peace from Army Chief	15	1	Mobilizing *Rāutas* and soldiers
To King from Chief Counsel	16	1	Officials and criminals who owed fines have paid up to the end of their capacity
To a Judge* from Village Man (Headman?)	17	1	Requesting a judgement in a dispute
Chief Priest from a Village Brāhmaṇa	18	1	Alms for sons from court

Source: Adapted from *Likhanāvalī*.

Note: *The word used in Sanskrit is *dharmādhikaraṇik* (literally, one who is authorized by dharma/ethics), an arbiter of disputes.

Table 3.2 Model Letters to Those with Lower Status

Sender/Receiver	Letter Numbers	Total	Themes/Remarks
From King to Chieftain	19, 20	2	(i) For tribute and attendance of son or brother and threat of invasion (ii) Similar but specifying the contents of the tribute
From Chief Justice to Rāuta	21	1	Summons and order for return of slaves captured
From Chief Minister to a Chieftain	22	1	Tax dues
From Chief Minister to an Accountant	23	1	Directions to investigate revenue embezzlement by Choudhary
From Chief Minister to a Choudhary*	24	1	Amnesty issued, and Choudhary asked to rehabilitate the village, give up his immoral disposition, and submit to the royal order and appear in court
From Chief Minister to Protocol Officer	25	1	To arrest the thief and produce him along with the stolen goods
From Minister of War and Peace to Travel Officer	26	1	Bring the army commander who defected from the enemy king with due honour
From King to entire population of a village	27	1	Notice about the whole village being granted to someone as a *brahmottara* (a village whose tax revenue was granted to a Brāhmaṇa by the state)
From King to Choudhary	28	1	To make sure that the grantees of a village get the possession as per the grant
From Chief Minister to Traders (of a locality)	29	1	Subscription for commerce granted to a Kshatriya Ṭhakkura at 2,80,000 (currency not mentioned)

From Chief Minister to all those dependent on *haṭṭs* and *ghāṭs* for livelihood	30	1	All haṭṭs (markets) and ghāṭs (river banks) given to a Vaṇik trader for 10,000 (currency not mentioned)
From City Superintendent to Fishermen	31	1	Waterbodies have been given to the Sāhani for 1,000 (currency not mentioned)
From Army Chief to Area Commander	32	1	Seeks information in writing about absentee and present Rāutas and soldiers
From Chief Minister to Superintendent†	33	1	Pay subsistence dues to a Cauhāna Rāuta out of fines paid
From a Village Headman to the Karmāntika (one assigned with a particular task, in this case, cultivating land)	34	1	Seeks information about seed varieties in writing, asks Karmāntika to send some samples, and gives instructions for how to go about cultivation
Father to Son	35, 37	2	(i) Asking for everyday expenses, and suggestions for augmenting income like reporting about fallen folks‡ and expanding the size of armed contingent (ii) Sermonizing about the duties of a Kāyastha and state official
Mother to Daughter	36	1	Heard about your ill-repute, quarrels with sister-in-law and co-wife; lesson on virtuosity, humility, and devotion to husband and elders
From a Father to Son-in-Law	38	1	Informs about and invites for daughter's marriage; sending someone to request his parents' permission to send our daughter
From Chief Documentation Officer (*pāñjika*) to a Clerk	39	1	Complaining about a mismatch in tax register and asking the clerk to come and correct

(*Cont'd*)

Table 3.2 (*Cont'd*)

Sender/Receiver	Letter Numbers	Total	Themes/Remarks
From Head Chef to a Subordinate Chef	40	1	I am going on leave for my daughter's marriage, so you will be responsible
Official in Charge of Betel Leaves to Store Keeper of king's sister	41	1	You went to fetch betel leaves but have been away for a month now. Return as soon as possible
Officer in Charge of Water to a Potter	42	1	Make large number of pitchers. Also buy aromatic stuff from traders
From Chief Intelligence Officer to a Spy	43	1	You [are] sitting at home. Do not delay work [assigned to you] even by a day
Naibandhika Ṭhakkura (Writer) to Accountant	44	1	Overstayed your leave, return immediately since you are the one in the know of details about soldiers
Chief Priest to Florist	45	1	Overstayed your leave, return since there is an issue with flowers at the time of royal worship
Chief of Treasury to Keeper of the Seals	46	1	When you were sent for some work, you carried the seals too, send the seals as soon as possible

Source: Adapted from *Likhanāvalī*.

Notes: *A Choudhary could be a headman, but the word was also frequently used as an epithet for a land-owning man with a high degree of social status.

† The Sanskrit word used is *kāryyi*, literally, 'a deputy'. The context suggests that this man might have been a superintendent of accounts.

‡ The expression used by Vidyapati is *patitajīvasaṃkhyā*, literally, 'the number (*saṃkhyā*) of fallen (*patita*) creatures (*jīva*)'. The word patita probably referred to those who were morally corrupt and who had forfeited their rank/position/caste. It is more likely that the author used the word to refer to those who have fallen from royal grace and might be considered rebels. From the context in which 'patitajīvasaṃkhyā' occurs, it would appear that reporting on the 'morally corrupt' or 'politically rebellious' was supposed to bring material rewards from the authorities.

Table 3.3 Model Letters to Those with Equal Status

Sender/Receiver	Letter Nos.	Total	Themes/Remarks
From King to another King	47	1	Army of Yavaneśvara moving towards your territory. As a friend, I can help with gifts if you want to compromise, or I can send my army if you want to fight
Minister of War and Peace to his counterpart in another kingdom	48	1	We are friends, so stop encroachment by relatives of the King. Kings are independent by nature, in case of problem in relationship, people will blame you and me. Also issues a veiled threat
Father of a girl to her father-in-law	49	1	Let my daughter's misery remain hidden, and you behave as per your exalted station
Trader to some eminent person	50	1	Had a successful business trip on account of your advice; please accept four pearls we have brought for you
A Prince to another Prince	51	1	You have gone away after a squabble with the King; please come back, the King is apologetic. Invokes loyalty to King and collegiality of princes
From a Cultivator to a Merchant–Agriculturalist	52	1	Enquiring about some variety of paddy seeds, and sending some other variety in response (presumably) to an earlier letter by the addressee
From a Chief Minister to another of a different kingdom	53	1	The King no longer listens to you; a subtle and guarded invitation to defect after homilies on virtues of loyalty and propriety

Source: Adapted from *Likhanāvalī*.

Table 3.4 Model Records of Business Transactions and Affidavits

Subject	Document No.	Total	Themes/Remarks
Debt Repayment Dispute Case Judgement	54	1	Decree awarded on the strength of witnesses' depositions
Sale Deed for sale of slaves	55, 56, 60	3	(i) Invokes the realm of Sultan Shah (recipient of the grace of *Khuda*) and his subordinate ruler (Nārāyaṇa-like for his *Kaṃsa* enemies!) before giving details of the transaction. Slaves referred to as Śūdra and Śūdrī (ii) A śūdra sells himself for 2 *ṭaṅka*, mistakenly referred to once as a Rāuta (iii) Both (letter nos. 55 and 56) specify work that the slave will have to perform, both sales are forever, and that they will be brought back to slavery with this deed as legitimate claim (even if he is hiding beneath the Royal Throne!) (iv) A Śūdrī (daughter of boatman Śūdra) is sold here by a Kāyastha to an Upādhyāya. But the Śūdrī is being acquired through a process of marriage to a Śūdra boy, presumably already a slave of the Upādhyāya
Buying human labour on mortgage	57, 58, 59	3	(i) Mortgaged persons' tasks are specified as that of carrying loads like the Śūdras did, but with the option of relief from work if the fine is paid (6 *kākinīs*). No obligation as to food or cloth is mentioned on the part of the purchaser of the mortgage (ii) Mortgaged person also to get a man-meal (meal sufficient for an adult male) daily, and a jute and a cotton cloth annually. His work is specified too (iii) Mortgaged on a four-days-a-week basis

Debt Bond	61 68 69 70 71 75 76 77 78 79 also see below 72, 73, 81	9	(i) The duration after which 25 per cent becomes due is not specified, and guarantor for each of the three debtors has different terms and conditions. For one, he is security guarantor, for another he is appearance guarantor, and for the third, he is payment guarantor. Each term is explicated (ii) For four months only by an accountant to an Upadhyāya, with the condition that after the due date, interest on interest will also be charged 'as per convention'. No guarantor, only witnesses (iii) Sāhu gives the debt bond; 100 *purāṇa kapardaka* taken at 25 per cent rate of interest. No guarantor, only witnesses (iv) Sāhu gives the debt bond to a Ṭhakkura; Sāhu takes loan for daughter's marriage; monthly interest rate of 6 *paṇa*s for each ṭaṅka, but in words it says only 2 paṇas for each ṭaṅka. No guarantor, only witnesses (v) Wholesaler gives debt bond to Ṭhakkura; loan of 15 ṭaṅkas, and interest promised trip-wise. After every trip Śivākṣa to be paid to creditor. No guarantor, only witnesses (vi) Nāyaka gives deed to Sāhu, after pawning 10 *tolaks* (measure of weight approximately equal to 10 grams) of gold and borrowing 30 ṭaṅkas with the interest fixed at 4 paṇas per month (vii) Rāuta borrows 3 ṭaṅkas from Sāhu, and pawns a milch cow with its calf as well as a bull 'deft at ploughing'. Interest payment will be in the form of cow's milk and bull's ploughing

(*Cont'd*)

Table 3.4 (*Cont'd*)

Subject	Document No.	Total	Themes/Remarks
			(viii) Vanik chief borrows 20 ṭaṅkas from Kāyastha Ṭhakkura with the interest fixed at 1 paṇa for each ṭaṅka, 'for fear of royal punishment and oppression by state officers' (to pay tax?) (ix) Boatman borrows 10 *khārīs* (a heap that a pack animal may carry usually equal to 16 *droṇas* [where a *droṇa* stands for approximately 30 kilograms] or roughly about 180 kilograms) of paddy from a Vaiśya Vanik under 'one and a half times settlement' payable at the time of harvest (x) A Sāhu gives a settlement deed to his Kāyastha creditor for an existing debt, through which he notes what he has already paid back, as well as the value of the remaining amount. He also puts in terms under which the interest will be paid on the remaining amount
Deed of Separation among four brothers	62	1	Eldest one gets his due before equal share distributed among each (but leaving aside the women's share)
Revenue receipt	63, 64	2	(i) Probably the shortest document. Just acknowledges payment (ii) Rāuta pays tribute to the King
A Royal order	65	1	*Could be part of the second section. A *muqaddam* (a village chief, also known as *mukhia*) reminded that the Rāuta's payment made to him is actually the property of the King and should be paid up duly. One of few in this section that is not dated

Exoneration Deed	66	1	A certain Śrīśarmā gives the deed to a Nāyaka after the latter is forced to pay double the principal amount by the Village Council
Manumission Deed	67	1	*Owner relinquishes all rights over the slave or over his property. 'Dharma itself is witness'
Settlement Deed for future sale of harvest	72, 73	2	(i) A householder takes 10 ṭaṅkas from a Sāhu and promises to give 10 khārīs of paddy for each ṭaṅka at the time of the harvest. The system is called *molāvyavasthā* (ii) Householder takes 2 ṭaṅkas from a Sāhu. Two ṭaṅkas will be payable at the time of the harvest along with an interest of 8 *mānīs* of paddy, that is, 4 mānīs per ṭaṅka
Settlement Deed exchanged among four traders	74	1	Four traders pledge to do business together after borrowing from a patron. After the transactions, they will return the principal to the patron, and divide the profit equally amongst themselves
Deed for renting a boat	80	1	A fisherman rents a boat from a Rāuta with the rent fixed at 2 ṭaṅkas. Under the settlement, if the boat is destroyed due to the fisherman's carelessness or accident, he will 'pay the price fixed by the village council'
Letter pledging to pay the debt and not run away	81	1	*Ṭhakkura gives pledge to another Ṭhakkura: 'I owe 200 purāṇas to you; I will not go away without paying. May misfortune fall my way if I do. May it be written in legible handwriting.' No witnesses mentioned

(Cont'd)

Table 3.4 (*Cont'd*)

Subject	Document No.	Total	Themes/Remarks
Affidavit by a man about not having had sex with a particular woman. Woman too makes a similar declaration. Both are identified by name	82	1	*Devadatta declares that I have not moistened Śrīpadma's vagina with my semen, and Padma declares my vagina has not been moistened with semen. There is another sample of a declaration under water immersion oath by a certain Vishṇumitra that he has repaid a loan. And a śloka is invoked that 'Dharma knows men's manner of thinking'. Includes advice that this śloka should be written in the affidavit, and also specifies particular months for particular types of oaths
Pledge to end animosity between two Rāutas	83	1	Two Rāutas pledge to give up animosity and be good to each other, and so on, and 'not indulge in territorial transgression'. Third Rāuta becomes intermediary for the purpose, and pledges that if he is not able to accomplish this, then may he incur the sin of an ungrateful person
Sample of a witness's declaration	84	1	'I know that the Kāyastha sold a Śūdra and his wife to the Upādhyāya's father', and so on, followed by four lines in verse that end with 'A witness ends up among the enemy if he does not speak what he knows'. Interestingly, the verse starts with the following line: 'Even thousands of horse sacrifices cannot stand against the truth!'

Source: Adapted from *Likhanāvalī*.

Note: *Not dated.

A quick look through the content of the texts as tabulated above leaves no doubt that the work we are dealing with was probably much more than a mere manual for writing. The practice of consigning long-distance messages, courtly or business transactions, and sundry information to writing, especially at the behest of the state, was at least 1,800 years old by the time of Vidyapati, as we will see below. A sculpture from the second century of the Christian Era at Nagarjunakonda shows a scribe taking notes in a royal court. Writing as a full-time profession, and scribes as a distinct community with unique characteristics, emerged very early, at least by the middle of the first millennium of the Christian Era, if not earlier.[6] As Daud Ali noted, 'sustained and influential discourses about scribes are attributable to the first half of the second millennium.'[7] Yet there are very few texts in Sanskrit—at any rate we do not know of too many—that gave lessons exclusively on the craft of writing. One such text, apart from *Likhanāvalī*, was *Lekhapaddhati*, also composed in all probability in the fifteenth century.

Comparing *Likhanāvalī* with *Lekhapaddhati*

We would be in a better position to appreciate the historical specificity of the structure and content of *Likhanāvalī*, if we compared it with another text of roughly the same genre, one that is chronologically close as well. Unfortunately, *Likhanāvalī* did not record when precisely it was compiled. However, it is possible to broadly identify the time of its compilation. The documents in the fourth section titled '*Vyavahāralikhanāni*' are dated 299 in the Lakṣamaṇa Era, that is to say c. 1418 CE. One may reasonably infer then, that the text might first have been composed in, or a few years around, that time. Was it a first-of-its-kind text in Sanskrit? I have not been able to trace any other treatise in Sanskrit on 'writing' that could be dated even close to the time of the composition of *Likhanāvalī*. Considering, however, that a large number of Sanskrit manuscripts from this period, probably

6 For an extremely interesting and substantive account of how scribes as a professional community were perceived and described during the early-medieval and medieval period, see Ali, 'The Image of the Scribe'.

7 Ali, 'The Image of the Scribe', p. 170.

thousands, lie buried in numerous libraries, archives, museums, and private collections in India and abroad, one may only say that this must have been one of the earliest attempts to provide a ready reference book for Sanskrit scribes of the time.

Interestingly, a Sanskrit treatise that analysed everyday speech, the 'corrupted' (Apabhraṃśa) dialects of ordinary folks, entitled *Uktivyaktiprakaraṇa*, composed in the twelfth century, also had two chapters on writing. Titled '*Lekhalikhanavidhi*' and '*Vyāvahārika-lekha-patra-likhana-krama*', these chapters are unfortunately missing from the single extant manuscript of the treatise.[8] The only other Sanskrit work resembling *Likhanāvalī*, that may possibly be dated to the (late) fifteenth century, is the more famous *Lekhapaddhati* from Gujarat. It might then be interesting to compare these two texts.

Lekhapaddhati is probably the best-known Sanskrit text of its kind from the middle ages in the Indian subcontinent, owing largely to the fact that it was published as early as 1925 by Gaekwad's Oriental Series. C.D. Dalal, the editor, used all the four extant manuscripts to put together a critical edition of the text.[9] It got further attention from scholars when, more recently, another annotated critical edition with an English translation appeared.[10] *Lekhapaddhati*, also entitled in two of its manuscripts as *Lekhapañcāsikā*, is a compilation of Sanskrit documents and letters composed in Gujarat between 744 CE (the date of the earliest dated document) and 1475–6 CE (the date of the latest dated document). One of the manuscripts notes at the end that 'Śrī Rām wrote this *Lekhapañcāsikā* for his own study and satisfaction during the victorious reign of Rāṇā Śrī Jagamala Haridas'[11] in Vikram Saṃvat 1533. It is not clear however, if Śrī Rām was the 'original' compiler of the text, or, as is more likely, a mere transcriber. His manuscript carries only thirty-eight documents while two other manuscripts carry a much larger number (sixty-one and fifty-four, respectively). This is interesting even if we make discounts for the

[8] See the editor Vijay Muni's 'Introduction' in Dāmodar, *Uktivyaktiprakaraṇa*, p. 8.

[9] Dalal, *Lekhapaddhati*.

[10] Prasad, *Lekhapaddhati: Documents of State and Everyday Life from Ancient and Early Medieval Gujarat*.

[11] Prasad, 'Introduction', *Lekhapaddhati*, p. 34.

fact that two leaves are missing from this manuscript. While two of the extant manuscripts are dated in the 1470s (Vikram Saṃvat 1475–6 and 1478–9, respectively), the other two are not dated. Considering, however, that the last dated document is from 1475–6, and that one of the manuscripts is also dated around the same time, it is very likely that the text was put together during that time. The only other possibility could be that one version was compiled earlier, but other compilers kept adding newer documents to it in the later transcripts. Some of these even carry names of the authors of the individual documents. Someone at a later date must have put them together in the form of a single text. This indicates a complex and long-drawn trajectory for the composition of *Lekhapaddhati*, both in terms of the published critical edition of the text (based on several recensions), as well as with regard to the extant individual manuscripts.

In contrast, *Likhanāvalī* seems to have been composed *and* compiled by the same person, and 'in one go', so to say. Moreover, unlike *Lekhapaddhati*, whose authors mostly, though perhaps not always, put together preexisting drafts of documents from different moments roughly across seven centuries, Vidyapati appears to have himself composed each of the documents in *Likhanāvalī*. He put forth these documents as model templates, and made no bones about the fact that they were all fictitious. He never named any major or minor historical character in ways that anyone could identify them. Instead, he left the space for names practically blank with the formulaic expression 'so and so'.[12] The fact that all the letters and documents in the text are evidently fictitious means that the author would have had to first imagine an entire world, somewhat like a modern novelist, in which to set these communications. He populated that world with kingdoms and kings, chieftaincies and princelings, ministers and soldiers, peasants and traders, along with fathers, mothers, sons, and daughters as also slaves and their owners, disciples and their preceptors, and so on. He also cast networks of political, familial, social, and

[12] '*Amuka*' is the word by which he always referred to kings, ministers, priests, and other dignitaries. The author did, however, occasionally name kingdoms like those of Dillī, Gauḍa, Tirhut, and so on. In some instances, when *Lekhapaddhati* left the names of characters/places blank, it also used the word 'amuka'; see for example, Dalal, *Lekhapaddhati*, pp. 2, 6, 7, 9.

affective relationships, both in idealistic and not-so-idealistic moulds, to animate that world. This may be compared to the 'factual' grid of *Lekhapaddhati*, which historians may profitably use to string together the whole genealogy of the Cālukya dynasty, among other things.[13]

However, the Gujarat text is divided into two parts. The critical edition that put together the materials from the overlapping contents of the four manuscripts contains seventy-eight documents in the first part, and twenty-three in the second. None of the documents in the second section can be said to have this factual grid. The first part contains mostly state documents, records of business transactions, or juridical judgements. Most of them are dated with the year, lunar month, fortnight, day, and date clearly indicated. The second part carries private correspondence between individuals. These are letters exchanged between preceptors and disciples, between brothers, between husbands and wives, lovers and beloved, and even between sons-in-law and fathers-in-law/mothers-in-law. The content suggests that these letters are fictitious rather than transcribed from actual drafts of correspondence. None of the documents in the second part are dated. One may say that broadly, the first three sections of *Likhanāvalī* with private communications between individuals (including state actors) correspond with the second part of *Lekhapaddhati*, whereas the fourth part of *Likhanāvalī* may be comparable to the first part of the Gujarat manual.

A second point of comparison between these two texts could be the manner in which their respective compilers articulated their own ideas about what they were doing and trying to achieve with their respective works. We have already seen how Vidyapati unambiguously stated that he wrote *Likhanāvalī* under instructions from his patron–chieftain, Purāditya Girinārāyaṇa. In the same vein, he also noted that this was 'for the instruction of the ignorant, for the pleasure of the informed, and for the affection of gentlemen'. The way the text was organized into four strictly defined compartments was clearly envisaged at the very beginning with the declaration that it contained 'the rules about

13 Pushpa Prasad has actually undertaken such an exercise with great precision in his 'Introduction' to the text. See Prasad, 'Introduction', *Lekhapaddhati*, p. 5. He also compared the data in the text with those gleaned from contemporary inscriptions and found that they match.

how to write to those above, those below, and those who are at the same level [in the social hierarchy] as also about [how to frame documents regarding] regulations and conduct'.[14] Before spelling out all of these issues, at the very beginning, Vidyapati was also careful to pay his obeisance, following standard convention, to Lord Gaṇeśa.

Many of these marks of a typical Sanskrit text composed in the middle ages were missing in the opening stanzas of *Lekhapaddhati*. It starts on a somewhat bland note and rather vaguely: 'Having received instructions of the teacher, and following the advice of learned scholars, for knowledge of things that one is ignorant of, I am putting down here the models of documents'.[15] It goes on to list, however, more than thirty-five different types of documents, models of which are given in the body of the text, without any attempt at classifying them. The list includes expected types of documents such as *Rājādeśa* (Order of the King), *Śāsana pattalā* (Royal Charter), *Deśottāra* (Permit or Passport), and *Grāma pattalā* (Village Charter) on the one hand, and interesting sounding documents such as *Ṭippanakaṁ yathā* (Certificate), *Ḍohalikā mukti yathā* (land of which the ownership is doubted and hence taken by the government), and *Ḍhaukaṇa patra* (Presentation Letter [for divorce and remarriage]), on the other. Curiously, *Lekhapaddhati* also lists out in its prologue, the 'main departments' of the state, thus underlining the state-centric character of the project.[16] It is not surprising then that almost all of the seventy-eight documents in the first part of the text, and even some of those in the second part, are directly related to the work of one or the other department of the government.

A third point of comparison, somewhat clumsier, could be the language and style of the two texts. Written in two somewhat different registers of Sanskrit prose, the language of *Likhanāvalī* is heavily

[14] It may be noted that the author never actually laid out any rules as such. He only provided model documents that were supposed to illustrate rules that were presumed rather than spelt out.

[15] Prasad, *Lekhapaddhati*, p. 49; Dalal, *Lekhapaddhati*, p. 1.

[16] This includes: 'Chief Secretariat; the accounts department; king [that is, the royal department]; department of justice; department of collecting *śulk* [taxes]; department of harbours [*veākula*], roads, and waterways; department of building [related to education]; and the mint'. See Prasad, *Lekhapaddhati*, p. 49; Dalal, *Lekhapaddhati*, p. 1.

stylized in some parts, whereas other parts are composed more simplistically, without the burden of elaborate metaphors. Typically, the first part in the letters that praises the addressee is couched in a pedantic vocabulary with elaborate aestheticization, using such *alaṅkāras*/tropes as *upamā* (metaphor), *rūpaka* (simile), *atiśayokti* (hyperbole), and occasionally even *anuprāsa* (alliteration), and so on. The same is also true of a large number of documents that record transactions, wherein the actual transactions are often described after invoking the reigning ruler, the feudatory, and the respective dynasties, along with their patron gods. The workman-like, business-related parts, on the other hand, are written in very simple language, occasionally using vernacular and even Perso-Arabic words.

A large number of documents in *Lekhapaddhati* too, display identical characteristics so far as the two different registers of Sanskrit are concerned. This may be a result of the fact that both probably drew heavily from the established conventions of framing inscriptions, especially copper plate inscriptions. In fact, the Gujarat text, containing actual historical documents as it does, includes at least one such copper plate inscription dated (Vikram) Saṃvat 1288 (1230–1 CE) that is clearly identified as *Tāmra Śāsana Yathā* (Copper Plate Charter).[17] Interestingly, this is true as much of the documents from the eighth century, as it is for those belonging to the thirteenth or the fifteenth century.

As for the use of 'vernacular' words, *Lekhapaddhati* employs Sanskrit forms of several Gujarati terms.[18] Instances of certain Marathi words in their Sanskritized form can also be found, though not with equal regularity. Indeed, in comparison with *Likhanāvalī*, vernacular terms occur with even more regularity in *Lekhapaddhati*. Again, some formulaic expressions were commonly used by both texts, the most recurring example being that of *svasti* (may it be well), a word with which most communications/letters, but not records of transactions, began. Both texts were primarily composed in prose

[17] Prasad, *Lekhapaddhati*, pp. 58–60; Dalal, *Lekhapaddhati*, p. 5.

[18] As Pushpa Prasad points out, terms such as '*avalagā*' (Guj. *olaga*), '*kriyāṇakāni*' (Guj. *kariyanu*), '*khashcā*' (Guj. *khānca*), *caṭāpaka* (Guj. *chaḍhābo*), *pottaka* (Guj. *pottuṃ*), *pocila* (Guj. *poci*), and so on are only some examples. See Prasad, 'Introduction', *Lekhapaddhati*, p. 9.

with occasional verses in between. In fact, a few verses are to be found in both texts with minor variations.[19] A *śāsana patra* (royal charter) in *Lekhapaddhati* declared:

> He who confiscates the land given by himself or others, becomes a worm in the excrement of a dog and sinks [into hell] with his parents.
>
> The donor of the land enjoys bliss in heaven for sixty thousand years, and he who destroys [or resumes] it or who abets the destruction dwells in hell for the same period.[20]

In almost identical terms, the twenty-seventh document in *Likhanāvalī* too, expresses the same sentiments:

> One who gives and one who accepts land in dāna,
> Both doers of good deeds surely go to heaven.
> One who captures land, donated by self or by another,
> Becomes a worm and lives in shit with his father.[21]

It is noteworthy that both texts show remarkable concern about a later ruler of the same or another house reclaiming land having once been donated. A number of verses were quoted by both texts to pre-empt such an eventuality, a practice that they may have borrowed from the land-grant inscriptions of an earlier period.

One may also note that most of the verses in the second part (one that carries private correspondence) of *Lekhapaddhati* are composed,

[19] This should not be interpreted to mean that the author of one of them had necessarily consulted the other text. It is more likely that both were drawing upon an existing stock of '*subhāsita*' literature, a freely floating compendium of verses, supposedly carrying a classical rendering of folk wisdom. On subhāsita, see Ali, 'The *Subhāṣita* as an Artifact of Ethical Life in Medieval India'; also see Jha, 'Beyond the Local and the Universal', especially pp. 32–3.

[20] *Bahubhirvasudhā bhuktā rājabhiḥ sagarādibhiḥ/Yasya yasya yadābhūmistasya tasya tadā phalam/Svadattaṃ paradattaṃ vā you harenca vasundharam/Sa viṣṭhāyāṃ kṛimirbhūtvā pitṛibhiḥ sah majjati.* See Dalal, *Lekhapaddhati*, p. 3; Prasad, *Lekhapaddhati*, document no. 2, p. 54.

The same verse, with minor changes in the vocabulary, occurs again in the next document; see Prasad, *Lekhapaddhati*, document no. 3, p. 60; Dalal, *Lekhapaddhati*, pp. 4–5.

[21] *Likhanāvalī*, document no. 27, p. 22.

intriguingly, in Jain Prakrit.[22] No parallel for such a practice exists in *Likhanāvalī*. Another unique feature of the Gujarat compilation is the fact that the private letters in the second part invariably identify an individual, both addressee as well as addressor, with a place name. The state documents in the first part too, often though not always, associate the listed individuals with an area or a territory. Thus, 'a letter of an angry wife to her husband [*saṁrushṭa bhāryā bhartṛilekho yathā*]' starts with, 'From place A, X [wife] sends the message to [her] respected husband Y of place B thus:...'.[23] Similarly 'a letter of a happy wife to her husband [*prasanna bhāryā bhartṛilekhaṃ prasthāpayati yathā*]' starts as follows: 'From place A, always obedient X [wife] with love, with eagerness, and with modesty communicates to her respected husband Y of this same place...'.[24] The letters in *Likhanāvalī* do not identify the place of origin or residence of the recipient or writer as frequently as *Lekhapaddhati*. Rather, every time a state official is mentioned, whether the sovereign, or a subordinate ruler, or a minister, or a military commander, his position is immediately marked as having been established with all the due procedures. The Sanskrit phrase '*samastaprakriyāvirājamāna*' (literally, 'all due procedures present') and some of its minor variations are probably the most frequently occurring set of expressions in the text.

It should be noted too, that the occasional use of words of Perso-Arabic stock, especially for administrative or commerce-related practices is more marked in Vidyapati's text, with the use of words like *paikār*[25] for a wholesaler, *pariganā*,[26] for a sub-provincial

22 It is not immediately clear as to why this was done. Might we conclude that Sanskrit was used only for formal and official communication, and that people preferred to use Prakrit, another literary language, for personal and intimate communication?

23 Prasad, *Lekhapaddhati*, document no. 10, part II, p. 206; Dalal, *Lekhapaddhati*, p. 63.

24 Prasad, *Lekhapaddhati*, document no. 9, part II, p. 205; Dalal, *Lekhapaddhati*, p. 62.

25 *Likhanāvalī*, document no. 71, p. 54.

26 This is a Sanskritized version of the common Persian term for an administrative division, 'pargana', rendered in Devanāgarī as '*pariganā*'; see *Likhanāvalī*, document no. 23, p. 20 and document no. 27, p. 22. Other notable

revenue unit, or *pot* for a boat. Vernacular words appear with slightly greater frequency in the text: *khepī, gaḍhavāra, gonḍhi, ṭeḍhi,* and so on are some examples. In any case, the world that Vidyapati imagined for composing his text was certainly more diversified than the world we encounter in *Lekhapaddhati*, even though the latter spanned a much greater period of more than seven centuries. The composition from Mithila reflects the myriad colours of the social, cultural, and political ferment of the fifteenth century far more faithfully, at least in terms of its disparate practices. The fact that a large number of the documents in the Gujarat text were drawn from the period before the fourteenth century might possibly be the reason why it does not take cognizance of the Persianate courts and cultures.

One of the documents in *Likhanāvalī*, for example, referred to the suzerainty of a king (*suratrāṇasāha*),[27] blessed by 'Khoda'[28] in the same breath as a subordinate chieftain who was committed to the

---

non-Sanskrit terms are *khārī* (a measure/unit of weight), *khepī* (a trip/or a load that one person is able to carry), and *molāvyavasthā*, a hybrid between *mola* (Pers.) and *vyavasthā* (Sans.).

[27] The word 'suratrāṇasāha' was an extremely interesting spin-off from the Turko-Persianate term, Sultan. For, apart from the fact that it invoked the title (Sultan) adopted by most of the Turkish rulers of North India from the thirteenth century onwards, it also carried the additional connotation in Sanskrit of one who protects (*trāṇa*) god (*sura*). Vidyapati was definitely not the first person to have used this term in Sanskrit for a Sultan. Examples of the practice are to be found in earlier Sanskrit renderings of the Turkish title. See for instance, the 'Pālama gāoñ inscription', in Prasad, *Sanskrit Inscriptions of Delhi Sultanate*, pp. 3–15. An example from a place closer to Vidyapati's abode is the fourteenth-century stone inscription from Rajgir near Patna in Bihar; see 'Rajgir Jain Inscription of the 14th Century A.D.', in Choudhary, *Select Inscriptions of Bihar*, p. 119. Probably the best known example is the Sanskrit epic poem (*mahākāvya*) *Śrīmahamūdasuratrāṇacaritra* by the Gujarat poet, Udayarāja, in praise of the famous ruler Mahmud Begada (1458–1511). This text also had an alternative title, *Rājavinodamahākāvyam*. See Udayarāja, *Rājavinodamahākāvyam*.

[28] '*Khodāyavaralabdha ... mahāsuratrāṇasāhi*'. See *Likhanāvalī*, document no. 55, pp. 42–3.

devotion of the Brāhmaṇic god, Lord Śiva. It would appear in fact that the link with the Persianate literary culture might go a little deeper so far as the very idea of composing *Likhanāvalī* was concerned. How exactly that 'link' may actually be identified and described, appears, prima facie, to be a rather complex question. But before we explore that aspect, let us try and see what the rich resources of the Sanskrit literary world had in store for the scribes of Sanskrit in the fifteenth century.

Mining the Sanskrit Epistolary Conventions

It would not be implausible to assume, as Oskar Von Hinüber does, that 'as soon as the script was introduced in India the art of writing letters may have been practiced', even though 'this is not known directly from any surviving correspondence'.[29] As with so many other aspects relating to the state and administration, it was *Arthaśāstra* of Kautilya that provided the first detailed reflections on the art of writing state writs and framing documents. The section titled '*śāsanādhikāraḥ*' ([Framing] Royal Writs) in Book II of *Arthaśāstra* gave a blueprint for use by scribes. It is clearly stated at the outset that this is a crucial part of state-building: '*śāsane śāsanamityācakṣate. śāsanapradhānā hi rājānaḥ, tanmūlatvāt sandhivigrahayoḥ* ... [Experts say that a command is a state writ. Writs are crucial to rulers as (these are) the cause of (both) alliance and enmity]'. The qualities required of a person to be appointed as a scribe (*lekhaka*) are enumerated pointedly: that he should have qualifications like those of a chief minister (*amātyasampadopetaḥ*); be learned about all times,[30] adept in composition, and capable of clear writing and precise reading (*sarvasamayavidāśugranthaścārvakṣaro lekhawacanasamartho*).[31] Somewhat like the authors of insha manuals in Persian more than a thousand years later, Kautilya too reminded

[29] Hinüber, 'Did Hellenistic Kings Send Letters to Aśoka?', p. 261.

[30] This was probably a euphemism for being familiar with existing traditions.

[31] Kauṭilya, *Arthaśāstra*, p. 167.

future scribes to be mindful of the relative social/political station of the addressee:

> *Jātiṃ kulaṃ sthānavayaśṣrutāni karmardhiśīlānyath deśakālau*
> *Yaunānubandhaṃ ca samīkṣya kārye lekhaṃ vidadhyāt puruṣānurūpam*[32]

> (After having considered the caste, lineage, position, age, learning, work/occupation, character, time, place, and blood-kinship [*yaunānubandha*] of the man [that is, the addressee], the writ should be committed to writing accordingly.)

Such a piece of writing should have the qualities, Kautilya declared, of systematic arrangement (*arthakramaḥ*), relevance (*sambandhaḥ*), completeness (*paripūrṇatā*), sweetness (*mādhuryam*), munificence (*audārya*), and lucidity (*spaṣṭatvam*). The passages following this defined each of these qualities. What followed next, however, was even more interesting, as the purposes, thirteen in all, for framing writs were enumerated, probably for emphasis, in verse:

> *Nindā praśaṃsā pṛicchā ca tathākhyānamathārthanā*
> *Pratyākhyānamupālambhaḥ pratiṣedho-ath codanā*
> *Sāntvamabhyavapattiśca bhartsanānunayau tathā*
> *Eteṣvarthāḥ pravartante trayodaśasu lekhajaḥ*[33]

As noted in these lines, the thirteen purposes for which a writ could be framed were: reproach, commendation, enquiry, narration, request, counter-narration,[34] censure, prohibition, command, pacification, holding out a promise, threat, and polite persuasion (*anunaya*). A line or two describing each category of writs followed this. After the explanations, certain other purposes of writs are also mentioned—information, order, gift, remission, licence, guidance,

[32] Kauṭilya, *Arthaśāstra*, p. 168.

[33] Kauṭilya, *Arthaśāstra*, p. 172.

[34] The word used in Sanskrit is '*pratyākhyānam*', literally narrating something as a counter (or parallel) to an existing narrative. A state might have resorted to it where it wanted to put out its own version of an incidence/tradition/episode, where a popular version might already be doing the rounds.

reply, as well as a general proclamation (*sarvatragaśceti*)—extending the total number of the recommended types of writs to twenty-one.[35]

It may be noted that Vidyapati's *Likhanāvalī* actually carried all the above-mentioned categories of letters and more. Several letters exhibit overlapping intents too: letter no. 24 condemns, threatens, and offers conditional amnesty to the addressee at the same time; letter nos. 21 and 25 condemn and command the recipient in equal measure, and so on. Occasionally, examples of a closer linkage between the ancient prescription and the medieval text may be found. The most striking case is that of a letter in the Mithila manual supposedly written by a prime minister to conciliate and win over his counterpart in a neighbouring kingdom. Here is the text of the letter in translation:

> May it be well. Humbly and affectionately, this is a letter laced with the nectar of utmost cordiality for the prime minister with all due procedures, Ṭhakkura Śrī so and so, mastermind of blameless politics, most famous for maintaining moral propriety as per dharma, and of pure heart. All is well here. We wish that all is well there too. The purpose of this letter is that we have heard that the Honourable King conducts the business of the state without regard to Śrī so and so.[36] [He] does not any longer have affinity with you. For this we have a grudge [against the king]. We have affinity with you, [and] he is the King. It behoves the high born to serve one's king with one's heart, deeds, and speech. Whatever the kings might do, you should not [ideally] let go of propriety. Still, if you do let go of it, we will remain committed to you. We have our property and life, and you should covet our possessions (*asmākaṃ dhanāni prāṇāśca vidyante tatoasmākamāyatte vastunyāsaktiḥ kartavyā*). When you give instructions, those will indisputably be followed. Whose soul mate is who in times of affluence? [that is, everyone professes loyalty to you when you are affluent]. Friendship can be measured only when the occasion comes [that is, when you have fallen into bad times]. What more? The name is written on the outside.[37]

[35] Kauṭilya, *Arthaśāstra*, p. 173.

[36] 'Śrī so and so' refers here to the addressee of the letter, an established way (in Sanskrit as well as in many North Indian vernaculars) of respectfully referring to the addressee not in the second but in the third person.

[37] *Likhanāvalī*, letter no. 53, pp. 39–40.

In the course of its cryptic explanation for each of the thirteen categories of letters, the *Arthaśāstra* noted that 'to say "what I am so you are, what belongs to me is yours is [the way to] conciliation" (*yoahaṃ sabhavān, mam yaddravyaṃ tad bhavataḥ ityupagrahaḥ sāntvaṃ*)'.[38] It is difficult to miss the distinct similarity in the tone as well as substance of this instruction in the highlighted part of the letter cited above. In fact, the fit between the two texts goes deeper not just in this instance but in certain other cases too.

Kautilya mentioned, for example, four types of strategies (presumably for the well-being of a state and the sustained exercise of its power vis-à-vis other states): negotiation, material inducement, sowing dissension, and invasion (*sāmopapradānabhedadaṇḍāḥ*), and here is how he explained the five ways of negotiation—praising the qualities, describing the bonding, invoking mutual interests, showing future prospects, and identity of interests (*guṇasaṅkīrtanaṃ sambandhopākhyānaṃ parasparopakārasandarśanamāyati-pradarśanamātmopanidhānamiti*) —precisely what Vidyapati's fictitious minister was trying to do with his counterpart in the letter cited above as well as in another. The following letter, supposedly written by a minister of war and peace to his counterpart in a neighbouring kingdom, makes for interesting reading in the light of Kautilya's advice excerpted above:

> May it be well. Sanctified by [expertise in] alliance, war, friendship, charity, and all other enterprises worth initiating, the learned Minister of War and Peace with due procedures, Ṭhakkura Śrī so and so, whose glory is as seductive as the fragrant pollen of the Kevarā[39] flower, [sends] this letter with utmost affection and good wishes for Śrī so and so. Be satisfied that all is well here. Give us joy by sending the news of your well-being. Earlier, having seen your king's friendly conduct and desire for friendliness, we encouraged our own king to have a friendly relationship [with your king]. Here, the King—great soul that he is—has worked to maintain [the friendly relations] in such a way that people on both sides of the frontier live and pursue agriculture peacefully. Currently, your king's relatives are indulging

[38] Kauṭilya, *Arthaśāstra*, p. 173.

[39] The Umbrella tree, also known as the Screw plant (Botanical name: *Pandanus odoratissmus*) famous for its sweet fragrance.

> in intrigues in certain places. If [our] king comes to know about these intrigues, he will not tolerate anything untoward and will be angry. Who will douse the fire of his rage then? You are the minister in that kingdom and I am close to the king in this one. If there is a problem in our friendliness, then we will be exposing ourselves. Kings are independent by nature [*sahajasvatantrāḥ*];[40] they act as per their own wishes. People will blame the ministers only, [you] know this, so do not encourage these individuals, [rather] evict the jealous, [and] stop the encroachment of land. You are [yourself] clever, so say what should be said. As such, our friendship will stay for a long time to come. The name is written on the outside.[41]

A broader comparison of the prescriptions of *Arthaśāstra* with what we find in *Likhanāvalī* suggests, however, that while the letters and documents of the latter broadly appear to be following the spirit of the ancient treatise, the world of scribes had probably become far more complex by the fifteenth century, as a quick look at the variety of letters and documents, as well as the diversity of writers, recipients, and subjects in Tables 3.1–3.4 would suggest.

If the improbability of a direct transmission of the prescriptives of *Arthaśāstra* to Vidyapati must be demonstrated beyond historical common sense, here is a set of interesting, if contradictory, facts. First, *Arthaśāstra* was written a millennium and a half before *Likhanāvalī*, and hence the 'influence' should not simply be presumed.[42] Second, even though the largest number of manuscripts of Kautilya's magnum opus was found south of the Vindhyas, the text was certainly well known among the Sanskrit literati of ancient and medieval North India.[43] That it was probably well known in Mithila as well is attested by the fact that just a century before Vidyapati, Caṇḍeśvara in Mithila

40 The word may also be translated as 'naturally autocratic' or 'sovereign by nature'.

41 *Likhanāvalī*, document no. 48, pp. 34–5.

42 *Arthaśāstra* might have been composed anytime around the beginning of the Christian Era, two centuries before or three centuries after. For a diligent attempt at dating the text by analysing linguistic evidence, see Trautmann, *Kautilya and the Arthaśāstra*.

43 Rao and Subrahmanyam, 'Notes on Political Thought in Medieval and Early Modern South India', especially p. 182.

quoted passages from it in his *Rājanītiratnākara*.[44] Third, it was not necessary for a Sanskrit scholar to actually read *Arthaśāstra* in order to be familiar with or imbibe the spirit of that text. Passages from it were quoted verbatim by almost every other nīti (political ethics) and even *smriti* (literally '[based on] memory'. This genre referred to the *dharmaśāstras* like *Mānavadharmaśāstra* [popularly known as *Manusmriti*], *Nāradasmriti*, and so on) texts throughout the 1500 or so years that separated Vidyapati from Kautilya. The intertextuality between *Arthaśāstra* and *Manusmriti*, one of the better-circulated and oft-cited texts in Sanskrit, has been commented upon extensively.[45] In the same spirit, one may suggest that the ideas in the 'Royal Writ Section' of *Arthaśāstra* may have worked their way into common knowledge for Sanskrit scribes (with due modifications as per changing requirements) in subsequent centuries. This would be true as much for the secretaries writing letters and framing documents in early India as for others who would be composing the thousands of copper plate and rock inscriptions from that period.

Several letters in *Likhanāvalī* used formulaic expressions in their *praśasti*-like first parts that were very similar to and occasionally identical with those used in the inscriptions from the seventh century onwards. Apart from stock expressions like *Mahārājādhirāja* and *Paramabhaṭṭāraka*, we also have instances of recurrence in *Likhanāvalī* of laboured expressions commonly found in the early-medieval epigraphs from North India including those from the eastern regions. Thus, if several letters in the Mithila compilation often refer to the king with epithets such as 'Destroyer of darkness like enemy with his powerful solar majesty [*prabalatarapratāpārkkani-rastariputimira saṃhāra*]'[46] or some similar sounding title, we come across numerous expressions with a similar sense but worded differently in the inscriptions from the eastern regions. Compare, for example, the abovementioned title with the epithet used for Śrī Harṣagupta in the Aphsad Stone Inscription of the seventh century CE: '*yasyāsaṅkhyaripu*

[44] Caṇḍeśvara, *Rājanītiratnākara*. For the nature and frequency of such citations, see Jayaswal, 'Introduction', *Rājanītiratnākara*, especially p. 37.

[45] Olivelle, 'Manu and the *Arthaśāstra*'.

[46] Letter no. 9, *Likhanāvalī*, p. 7.

pratāpajayinā doṣṇā mṛigendrāyitam sakalaḥ kalaṅkarahitaḥ kṣatatimira stoyadyeḥ śaśāṅka iva'.[47]

It may also be pointed out that the dating era (Lakṣamaṇasena saṃvat) and style used by Vidyapati was almost certainly following the inscriptions of the region in the immediately preceding period. Probably the earliest example of dating in the Lakṣamaṇasena saṃvat in the Mithila region is to be found in the Janibighā stone inscription of Jayasena found in the Gaya district. It is dated to the eighty-third year of the era named after the Sena ruler of Bengal, and starting with the 1119th year of the Christian Era.[48]

As for literary compositions proper, we do come across references to letters (being written, sent, received, read, and replied to) 'occasionally in Sanskrit dramas, mostly in passing, and in Buddhist literature, frequently, particularly in the Jatakas'.[49] But an instance where a letter was actually excerpted was rare. One such example comes from the *Mudrārākṣasam*, an early medieval play by Viśākhadatta revolving around the characters of Chāṇakya and Rākṣasa. Two letters figure in the play: one was an intelligence report by a spy, and the other a fake one authenticated with a stolen seal. Like several letters in *Lekhapaddhati* and almost all the letters in the first three sections of *Likhanāvalī*, these two letters start with the formulaic expression '*svasti*' (May it be well).[50] In one instance, the learned minister, while giving instructions about the content of the letter to be written, tells his aide to frame a letter in which 'the [writer's] name was not written outside (*adattavāhyanāmānam*)'.[51] It is interesting that all the letters written to one's equals in *Likhanāvalī* (the third section) end with the phrase 'the name is

47 Here, the king is compared to a lion (mṛigendra) who with his glorious might obtains victory over uncountable number of enemies ('Aphsad Stone Inscription of Adityasena', in Choudhary, *Select Inscriptions of Bihar*, p. 26).

48 'The Janibigha Stone Inscription of Jayasena', in Sahai, *The Inscriptions of Bihar*, p. 142.

49 Hinüber, 'Did Hellenistic Kings Send Letters to Aśoka?', p. 261. As Hinüber points out, the word used in Pali for a letter was *paṇṇa*.

50 See Viśākhādatta, *Mudrārākṣasam*, pp. 178, 270.

51 Viśākhādatta, *Mudrārākṣasam*, p. 50.

written on the outside (*bahirnāmalikhanam*)', though worded a little differently.[52]

It should be clear from the survey of available evidence above that the author of *Likhanāvalī*, or for that matter that of *Lekhapaddhati*, could and did use many of the extant epistolary conventions already current in Sanskrit. They also expectedly deployed the literary techniques, aesthetic devices, and figures of speech respected within Sanskrit *kāvya* tradition. Yet, the idea of compiling a compendium of model letters in Sanskrit, whether actual or fictitious, was certainly novel in the fifteenth century. It may help to look at the other major cosmopolitan literary culture of the time, that is, Persian.

The Insha Connection

Likhanāvalī may or may not have been a first-of-its-kind text in Sanskrit. Even if it was not, a text on 'how to write letters and frame documents' was certainly not common in Sanskrit literature, classical or otherwise. In Arabic and Persian, however, compiling model documents/letters into a text or composing a manual for scribes was already a literary achievement to be proud of, even by the thirteenth century, if not earlier.[53] Such compositions were known as insha, and their most 'representative form' in Persian came to be regarded as *rasail* (literally, letters). In classical Arabic, the word insha simply meant 'creation'/'construction'. At an indeterminate time in the early middle ages, however, the word came to connote 'prose composition, letters, documents and state papers'.[54] A parallel tradition of Persian

[52] *Likhanāvalī*, letter nos. 47–53, pp. 34–40.

[53] Storey actually provides a list of such texts, ostensibly not comprehensive; yet even a cursory look at it suggests that a large number of such texts were composed in and prior to the fifteenth century in the subcontinent. Between the thirteenth and the sixteenth century itself, Storey lists more than forty texts in the insha/rasail genre or one closely related. See Storey, *Persian Literature*. Relevant for the theme discussed here is the section titled 'Ornate Prose', especially, pp. 240–71.

[54] Zilli, 'Development of *Insha*' Literature till the End of Akbar's Reign', pp. 309–10.

letter writing, *maktubat*, flourished among the Sufis in the subcontinent. These letters, however, were neither administrative/political nor personal. Sufi preceptors mostly wrote them like essays that sought to inscribe instruction in metaphysical and everyday aspects of religious belief and practice.[55] Addressed to a chosen disciple, these were often written in the hope that they would be circulated more widely.[56] This body of literature is not directly relevant for our purposes, and we will not discuss it here.

That framing of letters, state writs, and documents 'properly' became a crucial part of politics and administration by the turn of the Christian millennium, if not earlier, is fairly well documented. In his famous seventh-century magic tale *Kādambarī*, Bāṇabhaṭṭa described the palace of the fictitious prince Chandrapīḍa as a place where 'thousands of royal orders were being written down by court scribes (lekhaka) who knew the names of all the villages and cities and who looked upon the whole world as if it were a single house'.[57] In the eleventh and twelfth centuries, scribes appear in 'staggering variety in various Kashmiri literary works'.[58]

The increasing significance attached by states to the work of documentation is even more evident in the case of states invested in the Perso-Arabic languages. By the eleventh century, most of the Persianate–Islamicate states came to have a separate department, *Diwan-i Rasail*, headed by a senior minister. It was common, as William L. Hanaway pointed out, for the head of the Chancellery to be promoted to the post of the highest authority after the king, Vizier. Such indeed was the case with Abu' Nasr Mushkan and Abu al-Hasan Maymandi, two of the famous heads of the *Diwan-i Rasail* (the Chancellery) under Sultan Mahmud of Ghazni early in the eleventh century. Such was

55 One of the most important collections of such letters was written by the fourteenth-century Firdausi Sufi sheikh, Sharaf al-Din ibn-Yahya Maneri of Bihar. See Maneri, *Maktubat-i Sadi*.

56 In one of his letters to Qazi Husam al-Din, Sheikh Maneri advised the former to borrow his *Hundred Letters* from 'somebody' and get a copy made for himself. For a discussion of this collection of letters, see Jha, 'A Table Laden with Good Things'.

57 Cited in Ali, 'The Image of the Scribe', p. 167.

58 Ali, 'The Image of the Scribe', p. 170.

also the case with the famous Seljuqid statesman and author of *Siyasat Nama*, Abu Ali Hasan Nizam al-Mulk (1019–1091).[59]

Equally, established conventions of insha compositions became so complicated that soon it also developed as a separate branch of learning in its own right. Texts were composed not just to directly guide the amateur scribe, but also to provide for additional aids for writers. A treatise composed in the twelfth century, *Irshad al-kuttab*, was 'a vocabulary of Arabic words of ordinary occurrence in composition with Persian explanations'.[60] Similarly, the late thirteenth-century work, *Nuzhat al-kuttab wa-tuhfat al-ahbab*, was a 'collection of passages suitable for quotation in letters and other prose compositions'.[61] Even in the tenth century, when Abu Abd Allah Muhammad bin Yusuf al-Katib of Khwarazm wrote the Arabic treatise *Mafatih al-Ulum* on the sciences, he devoted a full chapter to *kitabat* (writing), in which he prescribed prose styles for secretaries and provided technical terminology for use in the Chancellery.[62] Abu al-Bayhaqi, the author of *Tarikh-i Masudi* and a famous luminary in the Ghaznavid court in the mid-eleventh century, too, was appointed chief of the *Diwan-i Rasail* for some time. Pertinent for our purposes is the fact that Bayhaqi also wrote *Zinat al-Kuttab*, a guidebook for writing letters.[63] Clearly, insha was already a distinct genre in Persian literature by the thirteenth century, when that language came to the Indian subcontinent.

The ability to compose an insha text soon came to be seen among the finest achievements of a Persian litterateur. It was no coincidence perhaps that Amir Khusrau, the poet who Ram Chandra Shukla inadvertently clubbed together with Vidyapati under the label '*phuṭakal racanāyeñ* [occasional compositions]',[64] was also the proud composer of a Persian text in that genre entitled *Ijaz-i Khusaravi*.

It is tempting to infer that Vidyapati may have got the idea of composing a manual for amateur scribes from the mature tradition of insha in Persian. In fact, there are signs that may point in that

59 Hanaway, 'Secretaries, Poets, and the Literary Language'.

60 Storey, *Persian Literature*, p. 241.

61 Storey, *Persian Literature*, p. 242.

62 Hanaway, 'Secretaries, Poets, and the Literary Language', p. 105.

63 Hanaway, 'Secretaries, Poets, and the Literary Language', p. 106.

64 Shukla, *Hindi Sāhitya ka Itihās*, pp. 37–8.

direction. Consider, for example, the fact, that writing about the conventions of composing a *rasail* in the early-sixteenth century, Muhammad Yusuf Yusufi observed that it is classified according to the nature of the relationship between the writer and the addressee. Separate conventions were prescribed for three different eventualities, depending upon whether the addressee is superior in status to the writer, or inferior, or equal.[65] Yusuf Yusufi's own text in that genre entitled *Badai al-Insha* was a compilation of model letters 'arranged according to the rank and class of the persons addressed, and, in the later part, according to subjects'.[66] Let us recall, as noted above, that Vidyapati also structured his *Likhanāvalī* exactly along these lines, with three separate sections, each devoted to letters addressed to one's superiors, inferiors, and equals, respectively, and a separate section on documenting transactions that was organized thematically.

There are other details pointing to the same direction of 'influence'. In a well-researched thesis on the career and historical context of Chandar Bhān Brāhmaṇa, head of chancellery under the Mughal emperor Shah Jahan, Rajiv Kumar Kinra noted,

> [T]he 'Abbasid *inshā'* style began to emphasize *elaborate titles and forms of address*, in an attempt to emulate ancient Persian grandeur. This epistolary sub-convention eventually evolved into a full-blown literary style, referred to as *tarassul*, or 'deliberate writing'—a high-flown literary style that became so fashionable that it eventually came to dominate Arabic prose, so much so that it was often referred to simply as the 'classical' style, contrasted by literary historians with the earlier, less elaborate prose style under the Umayyads. Proper implementation of *tarassul involved a number of literary techniques*, many of which became standard practice over time, such as the *use of rhymed prose* [*saj'*]....[67] (emphasis added)

As we noted above, both *Likhanāvalī* as well as *Lekhapaddhati* furnished extremely elaborate titles for rulers and even ministers, writing or receiving letters. Witness too, by way of an example of

65 Zilli, 'Development of *Insha*' Literature till the End of Akbar's Reign', p. 310 and f.n. 8.

66 Storey, *Persian Literature*, p. 270.

67 Kinra, 'Secretary–Poets in Mughal India and the Ethos of Persian', p. 96.

'deliberate writing', the first part of a typical letter from *Likhanāvalī*, written incidentally not to a sovereign, but by a sovereign to a priest in Varanasi:

> May it be well. In the Vīreśvara temple at Varanasi, the one whose inner being has been purified with the ultimate wisdom of the Vedic doctrines; who has overpowered all his senses with the yogic practice of the eight *aṅgas* [namely], the five moral commands, śāstric regulations, physical exercises, prostration before the Sun, diet control, contemplation, concentration, and deep absorption; to Him, of the three punishments, to that teacher–renouncer Śrī so and so is this letter sent [as a mark of] hundred prostrations from the Ruler Śrī so and so from [his] capital. With the grace of Your feet and by the blessings sent [by you], we are all well....[68]

While the wilful effort with which this prose is crafted is perhaps obvious, the use of 'rhymed prose', known to Persian scholars as *saj'*, is lost in translation. Here is how it could sound in Sanskrit, with words broken at places, for those not familiar with Sanskrit to appreciate the way in which the words were supposed to echo each other's sound, creating a crackling staccato if read out aloud:

> *Svasti. Vārāṇasyāṃ Śrīvīreśvaramaṭheṣu vedānta-siddhānta-śuddhāntaḥ-karaṇavṛittiṣu yama-niyama-āsana-prāṇāyama-pratyāhāra-dhyāna-dhāraṇā-samādhī....*[69]

The usage of such 'decorative' devices was not pioneered by Vidyapati. The Persian *saj'* and other comparable figures of speech were already available in the Sanskrit kāvya tradition so meticulously codified by scholars starting with Daṇḍin and Bhāmaha during the early-medieval period, and continuing beyond Viśvanātha Kavirāja in the fourteenth century. What is remarkable about their appearance in *Likhanāvalī* is the fact that it seemed to coincide with the epistolary practices established within the Persian tradition.

Could it be a mere coincidence that Vidyapati appeared to be following, in a Sanskrit composition, at least some of the conventions

68 *Likhanāvalī*, letter no. 3, p. 3.
69 *Likhanāvalī*, letter no. 3, p. 3.

commonly prescribed and practiced in the Persian tradition? What were the limits of this commonality seen here between two of the most vibrant cosmopolitan languages in the medieval world?

Vidyapati did occasionally use certain Persian words in *Likhanāvalī* as also in some of his other Sanskrit and Avahaṭṭha texts, most notably in *Puruṣaparīkṣā* and *Kīrttīlatā*, as we will see in the following chapters. However, unlike *Likhanāvalī*, the typical insha (or *rasail*) text in Persian carried only the occasional document crafted by the author/compiler: most of the letters/documents in the Persian tradition were actual/'authentic' official documents simply transcribed into the text. The best example from the North Indian tradition would be *Insha-i- Mahru* from the fifteenth century.[70] (One must concede though that texts wherein most of the documents were fictitious and framed by the author himself were also known in Persian, the famous *Ijaz-i Khusravi*, also known as *Rasail ul-Ijaz*, of Amir Khusrau being a prominent example.) Further, if the Persian texts on letter writing, such as those by Bayhaqi in the eleventh century or Yusuf Yusufi in the sixteenth, prescribed strict rules on how to address the recipient, how to start a letter, how to codify the message, or how to conclude, an examination of *Likhanāvalī* documents in that light suggests that Vidyapati did not follow these elaborate rules at all. Finally, there is no evidence to suggest that Vidyapati knew enough Persian to be able to read a text in that language. Does that piece of fact rule out his being 'influenced' by the insha traditions?

With this question in mind, let us examine Vidyapati's temporal co-ordinates a little more closely in order to explore the apparent confluence of two 'parallel' literary traditions in his writing about writing.

Limitations of Boundaries

In the impressive and diverse corpus of compositions that Vidyapati left behind, he provided very little information about his personal life. There are very few things about him that we can say with any degree of certainty. These include the fact that he was a scholar, poet, and

70 See Abdur Rashid, *Insha-i Mahru*.

lyricist who could compose with equal facility in Sanskrit, Prakrit, Avahaṭṭha, and Maithili. That he was also a successful courtier meant that he was very well networked too. We need to remind ourselves that as a scholar, he was only one among many in the region of Mithila and the larger cultural zone of Eastern India. There were Sanskrit and even vernacular scholars of equal, if not greater repute within the Mithila region, two centuries before as well as after him, as we noted in Chapter 1 in this volume. Yet, if he became an icon probably in his lifetime itself, it was because he inhabited several worlds, all at the same time. We have already noted how prolific he was. An author and a statesman, Vidyapati responded to the needs and anxieties of people of all hues. In short, we may safely say that he was a man very closely tuned into his time. And he surely lived in exciting times.

By the time Vidyapati started writing at the beginning of the fifteenth century, the Delhi Sultanate was already reduced to being one, surely not the most powerful, among many sultanates in North India. As Simon Digby demonstrated over a decade ago, with the mushrooming of multiple sultanates all over North India even before Timur came, there did not appear to have been a serious problem of mutual intelligibility between those who spoke or wrote in the easterly vernacular 'Awadhi and the speakers of the western "proto-Urdu" dialects of the capital city or the Deccan'.[71] Such mutual intelligibility among apparently distinct linguistic groups also facilitated the rise of an increasingly more cosmopolitan class of secretaries and accountants. The careers of several such successful men in the mid- and late-fourteenth century indicate an interesting phenomenon: professionals trained in accountancy and mathematics (*siyaq* and *hisab*) in a Sanskritic or vernacular milieu of a local chieftaincy could smoothly move to the Persian-dominated court in Delhi and make a successful career, rising in some cases to occupy the highest position possible for such a professional. Such was the case, among others, of Kannu, who from being a trusted courtier of a local Raja in the Deccan rose to the position of deputy vizier under Muhammad Tughluq, and vizier under Firuz Tughluq. Afif, in his biography of Kannu in *Tarikh-i Firuz Shahi*, indicated that even though the latter lacked writing skills

[71] Digby, 'Before Timur Came', p. 346.

in Persian, he was very wise and very adept at his work because of his administrative experience.[72] As Sunil Kumar points out,

> there were other non-Muslim literati whose suspect Persian skills, not to speak of their infidel backgrounds (at least in the eyes of Baranī), did not hamper the flow of Sultanate patronage [for them]. There was Ratan the fiscal administrator of Sindh who was 'skilled in calculation and writing', Bhiran, the auditor (*mutasarrif*) at Gulbarga, Samara the governor of Telangana and Dhara the deputy vizier at Daulatabad.[73]

It would appear that men like Kannu or Ratan could smoothly transit across linguistic–literary boundaries because the professional expertise required of them did not change much as they flitted between courts. Scribal and secretarial practices in the Persian, Sanskritic, or vernacular courts of South Asia drew from a shared pool of images and symbols, words and metaphors, textual genres, and aesthetic sensibilities. As Aditya Behl argued in a similar vein, Awadhi idiom could be made to articulate, already in the fourteenth century, both Sufi and Bhakti religiosities with the identical move of turning *sṛingāra rasa* into *prema* or *bhakti rasas* with an overlapping set of literary vignettes.[74]

It is pertinent to note here that much of what Behl refers to in the case of the shared world of Sufi *premākhyāna* and later *saguna bhakti*[75] literary productions actually took shape in the heart of the Sharqi domains, the political circle in which Vidyapati moved. It would be reasonable to assume then that our author was not immediately or directly beholden, in any simple way, either to Sanskrit conventions of letter-writing codified early by *Arthaśāstra*, or to the Persian insha tradition. These erudite traditions had already been somewhat quotidianized and probably sublimated by the fourteenth and fifteenth century into a richer, more complex, and more accessible pool of literary resources, cutting across linguistic boundaries.

72 Afif, *Tarikh-i Firuz Shahi*, pp. 394–430.

73 See Kumar, '*Bandagī* and *Naukarī*'.

74 Behl, 'Presence and Absence in *Bhakti*', pp. 319–24.

75 Saguna bhakti referred to the tradition of devotion to a god with attributes as opposed to *nirguna bhakti* that referred to 'devotion to the God without attributes'.

The rarefied world of fictitious letters and documents, and of imagined characters and situations, that Vidyapati conjured up in *Likhanāvalī* represented this reality more than any 'historical' text could. Talking about the fictitious documents in insha collections, Zilli remarked that

> the fabricated documents, are not altogether useless for a student of history. The general principles and norms of political and social behaviour projected in them could be of immense help to a historian studying the social and political processes of an age. Sometimes a fabricated document would be of great historical interest even for the motives for which it was manufactured by the compiler.[76]

In order to be useful to aspiring scribes, a collection of 'fabricated' documents must not set itself in a fanciful world. Rather, it would tend to presume frequently occurring situations and realistic contingencies in which to place the imagined recipient as well as the sender of a message. Would that also mean that a look at the contents of the letters of *Likhanāvalī* and the contingencies that the text provided for might give us slices of the politico-social 'realities' of Vidyapati's world? To say that, however, would amount to anachronistically projecting our contemporary obsession with utility-oriented education onto the fifteenth century.[77] There is no reason for us to believe that the contours of the 'imagined reality' of *Likhanāvalī* would be entirely bounded by the given temporal context of the Mithila chieftaincy alone. The manual for educating aspiring secretaries and assistants must also be placed within a more diachronic frame of scribal culture, the long and patchy history of which, across different languages, was traced earlier in the chapter.

We have noted some of the striking stylistic continuities as well as occasional differences of *Likhanāvalī* with political-textual (*Arthaśāstra*), literary (*Mudrārākṣasam*), epigraphic (copper plate),

[76] Zilli, 'Development of *Insha*' Literature till the End of Akbar's Reign', p. 312.

[77] Such a method on a historian's part reverts to the old maxim that 'literature is a mirror of society', an idea that we briefly examined in Chapter 2 in this volume.

and epistolary (insha/rasail and *Lekhapaddhati*) conventions in the longue durée. Without forgetting the imperative force of that History, let us turn to the content of the documents that our author 'fabricated'.

It is interesting to look at some of the concerns of state and society that Vidyapati presumed and played upon in his text. What dynamics of state-society, its fiscal apparatus, administrative function, military organization, or its sexual economies did he conjure up to make his epistles and the record of transactions meaningful, even possibly topical (or topically possible)? In the context of a 'variety of reflections on the question of statecraft in medieval and early modern India', Rao, Shulman, and Subrahmanyam recently noted that 'these reflections are in fact as diverse as the states in the region and range from grandiose imperial ideological statements to recipes for the survival of small kingdoms that are squeezed between massive rivals'.[78] Within this wide spectrum of political formations, one might 'naturally' expect *Likhanāvalī* to fall in the latter category of texts. A couple of letters indeed seem to meet that expectation. Take the following letter, for example, by an Army Chief (*senāpati*) to the king:

> May it be well. To the Destroyer of darkness like enemy with his powerful solar majesty, the navigator of the river of clean politics, the ocean of moral propriety, subjugator of herds of kings,[79] Kṛiṣṇa ensconced in his heart, Nārāyaṇa for Kaṃsa-like enemies, steady in his devotion to Śiva, and victorious in the battlefield, Mahārājādhirāj Śrī so and so Deva's lotus feet, goes this letter of salutation from Chief of the Army, so and so from village so and so with head bowed before the lion-throne. All is well here with the ascent of Your Majesty. The special matter is that I received the letter [written with your] own hands with due reverence, carefully understood the meaning therein, and am acting accordingly.

[78] Rao, Shulman, and Subrahmanyam, 'A New Imperial Idiom in the Sixteenth Century', pp. 69–70.

[79] The expression I have translated as 'subjugator of herds of kings' is actually a long, and what must have been, even by the standards of Sanskrit, a laboured expression: *saṅgrāma sīmādurvvāra aneka rājacūḍālaṅkāramaṇimayūkhamañjarīpiñjarīkṛita caraṇāravinda*. Literally this should translate as '[one who] in the battlefield, paints his lotus feet yellow with the rays of light emanating from the jewels in the crowns of herds of difficult kings'!

> Submitting that the Lord of the Yavanas has started from Dillī with the Lord of Gauḍa as [his] target, as reported by four men who came [to me]. The Lord of Gauḍa too is anxious about repairing forts and mobilizing the army. It is not known if he will fight or compromise. I will write when [that is] known. Presently, please give instructions for whatever is appropriate and whatever needs to be done. What more.[80]

Not all letters are so easy to place within the territorial limits of an anxious and insecure chieftaincy sandwiched between the Delhi and Bengal Sultanates. A larger number of the communications as well as the records of transactions in the fourth section actually defy such easy contextual emplacement. Here is a letter to the superintendent of the court (Śrīkaraṇa) by a revenue collector raising an issue and suggesting a solution, both of which, if we trust the dominant historiography, were the stuff of which an imperial formation alone, such as the Mughal state, was made:

> May it be well. To The Superintendent of the Court, adorned with expertise in judicial administration, having Caṇakya-like tact in the business of the state, complete with all [other] due procedures, the Great Chief of the Sāmantas, the Chief Minister, Great Ṭhakkura Śrī so and so's lotus feet goes this letter of salutations with eight parts of the body from the Revenue Collector[81] on such and such subject. With the ascent of Your Majesty, all is well here. Particular matter is that the official here is demanding tax from people according to the previous years' [assessment] register. However, here, some villages are settled and some are deserted. Hence, if tax this year was collected in this country after measuring land [*bhūmimāpanaṃ kṛitvā rājakaro gṛihyate*], then the full proceeds may be collected and the weak would not suffer either. But officials cannot do this without the King's order. So, I am conveying it clearly. Hence, I will act [as per] whatever orders are given. What more.[82]

Clearly, the state ideal of 'appropriation of the entire agrarian surplus' based on measurement of cultivated land (leaving aside

80 *Likhanāvalī*, letter no. 9, p. 7.

81 *Osathi*.

82 *Likhanāvalī*, letter no. 13, pp. 11–12.

the issue of actual practice under the Mughals, let alone in the pre-Mughal era), could be formulated and articulated without much fuss in the fifteenth century within a Sanskritic ecumene. Nor was such micromanagement of people, resources, and productive processes confined only to the fiscal sphere so far as Vidyapati's presumed world is concerned. Imagine with the letter below a (hypothetical) situation, wherein a sovereign ruler, clearly not a local chieftain, tries to bring a recalcitrant chief under control through means that one would associate with the armoury of an imperial state:

> May it be well. From so and so city, the victorious and venerable King of kings so and so, adorned with a raised sceptre, silk crown, lion-throne, white *chatra* and *cāmara*, and complete with all procedures of royalty, [one] whose nails shine with the rays emanating from the jewels of numerous kings' thrones, [who is] a lion for his elephant-like enemies, [one] in the light of whose glory bloom water lilies, from Him goes this message to king so and so with shining character. Currently, you are not providing the kind of service that you should; you are not paying tax [to the extent] that you should; [and] your conduct is indifferent. What is this? Even now, if you want [to protect] your own interest, then submit each year's due tax in the court, [and] send your son or brother in attendance along with an army. If you do not act this way, then go away to a place where you can live [that is, remain alive]. Or else, we will invade and with the force of elephants, cavalry, and infantry, we will reduce your fortress to dust and also send you to Yamapur [that is, kill you] with the blows of arrows from crores of our warriors. That's it.[83]

We may note that the appearance of this letter in *Likhanāvalī* could not have been incidental, especially when there is another, the very next one, carrying almost an identical message from an imperial overlord to another local chief.[84] In fact, a whole range of letters and documents were focussed on the fiscal, military, or territorial concerns of what

[83] *Likhanāvalī*, letter no. 19, p. 17.

[84] See *Likhanāvalī*, letter no. 20, pp. 17–18. The principle that Vidyapati probably followed in the text was to provide for a diverse set of contingencies, and present a whole variety of prototypes of documents. One may presume that he would repeat a particular prototype only when he thought it was more important than others.

clearly appears to be a supra-local political outfit, if not an expansive imperial state. Thus, a military commander reported the mobilization 'from this country and others [*svadeśīyā videśīyā*]' of many 'Surukī, Cauhāna, Caṇḍela, and other warriors [who were] courageous, high born, loyal, trained in wielding different kinds of weapons, [and who had] earned glories in several battles'.[85] Yet another from a prime minister (*mahāmattaka*) to an accountant/secretary (*lekhi*) purported to enquire about the progress made by the latter in an inquiry instituted into a case of possible embezzlement. The letter gave specific instructions to send a written report 'on the basis of the evidence available there, as to how much was taken, embezzled, or ignored by the Chaudhary,[86] how much was lost on account of the negligence of the clerk,[87] [and] what amount of revenue all of it added up to'. Thereafter, the accountant was to 'bring the official and his registers with himself [to the court] so that [they could] calculate and collect the dues after tallying [the figures] with those in [the] registers'.[88] In a similar vein, letter no. 26 gave elaborate instructions on how to welcome, reinstate, and reward a resourceful army commander, who had defected from a hostile neighbouring kingdom.[89]

The envisaged investment of the court in the improvement of agrarian production and productivity (and hence, tax paying ability) was no less striking. This is reflected in several writs sent to subordinate officials. One of these, written by a chief of the princes (*rāutapati*), referred to a (royal) 'instruction to rehabilitate the deserted land (*ujjaṭabhūmivāsārtha*)', and reported the successful accomplishment of the task with the 'arrival of people from outside (*videśādāgatya*)'.[90] Two other letters talk at length about the variety of paddy seeds, and possibilities of procuring and using better seeds.[91]

[85] *Likhanāvalī*, letter no. 15, p. 13.

[86] A village headman who often was practically the revenue collector for a village/group of villages.

[87] *Pañjikār*, literally, a registrar.

[88] *Likhanāvalī*, letter no. 23, p. 20.

[89] *Likhanāvalī*, letter no. 26, p. 21.

[90] *Likhanāvalī*, letter no. 10, p. 8.

[91] *Likhanāvalī*, letter nos. 34 and 52, pp. 26, 39. The seed varieties mentioned are: *keralī, gaḍhavāra, magahī, tulasī*, and *golā*.

The exalted position of the sovereign's household, not so much as a private domain, but more as the extension of royal privileges, is underlined through several letters. It is worth citing one of these:

> May it be well. From the betel store, the Chief Official in charge of betel-leaves, complete with all due procedures, Ṭhakkura Śrī so and so sends this message to Śrī so and so, the store-keeper for the king's sister. Here, in the royal sister's stores, the betel leaves have become unusable and putrid with white and black [spots]. You were sent to fetch ripe white betel leaves. You have been there for a month now. No betel leaves suitable for the sister of the king are [left] here, so you will come here with white leaves at the earliest. Get *Bhīmasenī*[92] camphor worth a thousand ṭaṅkas too. Look [also] for *Nāgara-khaṇḍa*[93] leaves and red betel nuts. Take these too if you get them. That's it.[94]

Other letters centring around the household related to an order for earthen pitchers, handing over of charge of the royal kitchen, and obtaining a regular supply of flowers for use by the king for worship. The obsession with 'due procedures' in these letters, even for minor officials of the royal kitchen, gestures towards an elaborately laid out and meticulously graded administrative hierarchy that insisted on 'bureaucratic' protocols for every single official. Readers would also have noticed in Table 3.2 above, that three letters (nos. 29, 30, 31) attest to how the state was supposed to lease out commercial rights over trading, including mining water bodies, to private players for a price. Letter nos. 35 to 38 and letter no. 49, on the other hand, underlined the importance of patriarchal values in the maintenance of 'order' within families. While these communications highlighted the role of the male elder in the maintenance of familial order, the state's possible (or actual) role in the micromanagement of a moral–sexual economy (and the patriarchal family as an institution) is evidenced by the striking 'affidavits' recorded in another document. The explicit language used in the document, and the rarity of such

[92] It appears that '*Bhīmsenī*' was a variety of camphor used with betel leaves.

[93] Again, '*Nāgara-khaṇḍa*' appears to be a variety of betel leaf.

[94] *Likhanāvalī*, letter no. 41, p. 31.

documents in the middle ages, makes this one truly extraordinary for historians:

> Śrī Devadatta does solemnly declare in affliction and solicitous desire [*taptamārgākarṣaṇadivye*][95]—I have not moistened [*siktim*] Śrīpadmā's vagina with my semen and that is the truth. At the same time, Padmā too does solemnly declare—my vagina has not been moistened with semen and that is the truth. Śrī Viśṇumitra takes the water-immersion oath [*jalamajjanadivye*] to solemnly declare—I have repaid the loan that I had taken from Śrī Śivadāsa and that is the truth. That which is written in the verse is payable by me:[96]
>
> Moon, Air, Fire and the Sun,
> Sky, Earth, Water, Heart and Yam.
> Day, Night and both the Evenings,
> And Dharma knows the men's manner of thinking.
>
> This śloka should be written in the affidavit [*pratijñāpatra*]. And the affidavit should be drafted in two neatly [literally, evenly] written lines. Agahaṇa, Caitra, and Vaiśākha are universally appropriate for taking all oaths. Winter, spring, and rainy seasons are [appropriate] for [oath by] fire. Autumn and summer are [appropriate] for [oath by] water. That's it.[97]

Arguably the most remarkable issue that comes up for relatively extensive treatment in the fourth section is the issue of recording the sale/purchase of slaves. One of the documents provided a rather detailed description of the transaction, complete with the price of each member of the family being sold,[98] as well as the terms of the

[95] This is a literal translation after disaggregating the compound word, '*taptamārgākarṣaṇadivye*'. It is also possible that the phrase stands for a particular type of oath.

[96] It seems that the person taking the oath is merely invoking the verse to seal his claim that he has already paid rather than to actually spell out anything that he still owes to his (erstwhile) creditor.

[97] *Likhanāvalī*, document no. 82, pp. 59–60.

[98] The prices specified are as follows: six rūpya-ṭaṅkas for the forty-four-year-old male, four rūpya-ṭaṅkas for the thirty-year-old woman, three rūpya-ṭaṅkas for the sixteen-year-old boy, and one rūpya-ṭaṅka for the eight-year-old girl. See *Likhanāvalī*, document no. 55, pp. 42–3.

transaction. The sold slaves' obligations included almost everything under the sun, as they were to 'plough the land, clear the left-overs, fetch water, carry the palanquin, and perform all other chores'.[99] The terminology used to refer to those being sold too, is equally remarkable: the first reference to the family members is couched in the vocabulary of the varṇa (śūdra–śūdrī), while the word *dāsam* (slave) appears interchangeably the second time. Indeed, the entire text of *Likhanāvalī* provides records for a spectrum of conditions of 'various degrees of freedom and un-freedom'—from the subjection of women within the family on the one hand, to bonded labourers and slaves on the other. As Indrani Chatterjee pointed out recently, connected social histories of these practices are only beginning to be posed as a project by historians.[100] One such condition of relative un-freedom could also be located in the perpetual indebtedness in which a whole variety of people, from peasants and householders to fishermen and even traders, are 'framed' by the text. The largest number of documents, twelve out of a total of eighty-four, is devoted to debt deeds, again a contingency that we are more familiar with from the historiography of a century later.

* * *

The debate around Benedict Anderson's tracing of processes of the rise of nation-states notwithstanding, it is difficult to dispute that 'imagining' modern national communities into existence was made possible only with modern technologies of print, census, textbooks, mass media, and so forth. We may extend the logic back in time and ask: what were the social, technological, and educational prerequisites for the rise of the imperium that the nation-states eventually displaced? After all, state-building, whether local or trans-local, did not automatically follow from war-victories in any period, let alone the medieval or early modern. Once the battlefields quietened and

99 *Likhanāvalī*, document no. 55, pp. 42–3.

100 For an interesting discussion on the possibilities of such history, and a useful framing of the problematic, see Chatterjee, 'Renewed and Connected Histories'.

messy processes of institution-building for sustained governance/exploitation started, another kind of army was required, one that was equipped with a different kind of expertise: a ready knowledge of respected ideals of governance; the ability to conduct a massive 'public relations' exercise on behalf of the state and reassure the subjects that nothing much had changed; the skills to carry out this exercise through communications couched in widely respected terminologies of power and hence likely to evoke awe, authority, and acceptance; and finally to be well-versed in norms of social order and ethical conduct. If this skill-set promised careers more lucrative than soldiery in the off-season of the agricultural cycle, it was also more difficult to acquire, and probably accessible only to an exclusive group. In an immediate sense, our analysis above suggests, it was this politico-educational need that texts like *Likhanāvalī* responded to.

To pursue these questions, as I have tried above, is also to admit what should have been obvious but is rarely realized in the context of the fifteenth century: that the political processes that contribute to the making of states, including imperial states, could not and did not stop with the disintegration of the Delhi Sultanate. The processes of the cultivation of prized skills, the fructification of grand ideas, in short the disciplinary formations—ideational as much as coercive—continued to gather even as scholars and poets competed for patronage from smaller, often subordinate, states with humbler ambitions. It is only fair to assume that political imagination did not necessarily shrink with imperial fortunes.

The brief survey of the contents of *Likhanāvalī* hardly leaves any doubt that its documents dealt with an extraordinary range of issues/concerns, and did not merely reflect life in the small chieftaincy to which the author was himself beholden for patronage. If we try to reconstruct some vignettes of the imagined state by putting together the ideas articulated in *Likhanāvalī*, several salient imperatives of state building emerge: sovereignty of the ruler, loyalty of subordinates and subjects, forming and maintenance of alliances, agrarian taxation to the limit of the payee's tolerance and ability, maintenance of army including the continuous recruitment of commanders, rehabilitation of deserted and fallow lands, looking out for better varieties of seeds, farming out common property resources like river bodies, leasing out commercial rights for a negotiated price, and so on. One may add another item, in some senses central to all the rest: insistence on consigning every single administrative, economic, military, diplomatic, and judicial transaction to 'properly' written records, a process that may be seen as a precursor to what came to be known in modern times as 'archiving'. That archives make states as much as states make archives, is no longer a secret among historians writing about the colonial or modern period.[101] The relationship between state and archives in the days of pre-modern, pre-print, and pre-mass politics could hardly be any simpler.

On several occasions in the course of describing the contents of the text above, we noted the similarities of contexts and concerns that the documents raised, with the concerns of the Mughal state, more than a century later. However, the attempt here is not to suggest a linear teleology of causation between the archive and the state. It would be premature, if not outright problematic, to suggest that writing manuals like the one composed by Vidyapati 'produced' states like those of the Turko-Mongols. Yet, one cannot deny that an empire had to contend, often comply, with existing webs of ideas and ideals, and those with knowledge of such ideals played crucial roles in the imperial enterprise. If colonial archives could be seen, as Ann Stoler saw them in the modern context, as 'both transparencies on which power relations were inscribed and intricate technologies of rule in themselves', may we not cast our critical gaze at the documents of *Likhanāvalī* in a similar spirit?[102] That is why, to make sense of the model documents of *Likhanāvalī*, one also had to look beyond the territorial boundaries of Mithila. Equally, one had to connect the finer strands of Vidyapati's oeuvre beyond the chronological limits defined by Timur on the one side, and Babur on the other.

The English East India Company, after it assumed political control over some of the Indian territories in the late-eighteenth century, produced an edition and translation of the famous early-seventeenth-century Persian writing manual, *Insha-i Harkaran* of Harkaran Das, 'so that it could serve as a model text for its own early administrators

[101] For a discussion of the complex range of meanings associated with the term 'archive', see Chapter 2 in this volume.

[102] Stoler, 'Colonial Archives and the Arts of Governance', p. 87.

when they dealt with the knotty problems of inherited Mughal administrative practice and terminology'.[103] Clearly, cultivating the skill of framing grammatically correct sentences and coherent prose was not enough for aspiring scribes in the fifteenth, sixteenth, and seventeenth centuries. As the celebrated Lahore-born Persian scholar, Chandar Bhān Brāhmaṇa, head of the chancellery (Mir Munshi) under Shah Jahan, wrote in a letter to his son in the middle of the seventeenth century, aspiring munshīs needed, first and foremost, to get 'training in the system of norms [*akhlaq*]'.[104] Not surprisingly, an almost identical idea is found in the Puranic tradition of Sanskrit. *Matsyapurāṇa* noted that the qualities of the ideal lekhaka included not only the knowledge of different scripts and the ability to produce neat and legible writing, but competence in the *śāstras*.[105] It is hardly surprising then that the author of *Likhanāvalī* did not confine himself only to teaching the science of writing in his text on writing. He went beyond framing the 'writs/orders' of the state, and also provided templates for personal communication within 'ideal' families, affidavits that attested to 'acceptable' sexual conduct, and a whole range of communications that traversed through and stitched together various threads of social and political relationships. Indeed, it would appear that the crucial factor for political order, for Vidyapati in *Likhanāvalī*, was not so much the strength of an institution per se, whether that of the raja or the minister, but stability of the web of loyal and virtuous relationships within which the political order must sustain itself. Nor was state-building envisaged as a terminable enterprise. Rather it came across as a never-ending process where loyalties had to be continuously

[103] Alam and Subrahmanyam, 'The Making of a Munshi', p. 61. As Alam and Subrahmanyam note, 'Since such materials fell into a branch of knowledge that was regarded as secular, in the sense of being distinctly this-worldly and largely devoid of religious or theological connotations, we are not entirely surprised to find that many of their authors, including Harkaran himself, were Hindus, usually Khatris, Kāyasthas, or Brāhmaṇas.'

[104] Alam and Subrahmanyam, 'The Making of a Munshi', p. 62. For a recent bio-historical work on Chandar Bhān Brāhmaṇa, see Kinra, 'Secretary–Poets in Mughal India and the Ethos of Persian'.

[105] Ali, 'The Image of the Scribe', p. 168.

tested, adversaries befriended or crushed, new and deserted lands brought (back) under cultivation, search for new varieties of seeds had to go on, military contingents had to keep expanding, and so on. His recipe for state-building was carefully calibrated and anchored in specific codes of everyday conduct. It should not come to us as a surprise then that the same author also wrote a treatise on political ethics entitled *Puruṣaparīkṣā*, the text at the centre of the next chapter.

4 *Political Ethics or the Art of Being a Man*

This chapter focusses on the famous *Puruṣaparīkṣā*, a treatise on manliness, written 'under instructions from Raja Śivasiṃha'[1] of Tirhut. It is a compilation of stories narrated with a view to put forth examples of (re)commendable manly conduct. *Puruṣaparīkṣā* is an *udāharaṇakathā*, a genre that had been in relative disuse in Sanskrit since the time of *Pañcatantra* and *Hitopadeśa*, though *kathā* as a genre was much discussed and debated among Sanskrit literary theorists since Bhāmaha and Daṇḍin from the seventh century onwards.

The chapter seeks to uncover the ways in which the treatise articulated 'authoritative knowledge' about legitimate social and political power. How did Vidyapati, a learned Sanskrit scholar, construct that power in relation to gender, caste, politics, and dharma? This line of investigation helps to open up the whole question of the (as yet underexplored) world of medieval political thought

[1] Vidyapati, *Puruṣaparīkṣā*, p. 3.

in Sanskrit, especially in the North Indian context. Moreover, it allows for rethinking the issue of how 'secular' authority was constructed within Brāhmaṇic discourse at a time when Rajas, Sultans/Suratrāṇas, Rājapūtas and Maliks operated together as well as in rivalry with each other. With these objectives in mind, I take a close look at the framing, language, and genre of the text in a historical perspective as well as what it has to offer in terms of content and what it presumed but left unsaid.

The chapter is divided into seven sections. The first gives some details about the text. The second section explores the history of the kathā genre in North India—in Sanskrit literary theory as well as in compositions. The third, fourth, and fifth sections examine depictions of gender, caste, and politics, respectively, in *Puruṣaparīkṣa*. In the sixth section, I try to investigate the epistemological frame deployed by Vidyapati before offering some ideas by way of a conclusion in the last. Reference will also be made, wherever relevant, to two comparable Sanskrit texts on politics: Merutuṅga Ācārya's *Prabandhacintāmaṇi* and Caṇḍeśvara's *Rājanītiratnākara*.[2] The former was written in Western India, and focusses primarily on Gujarat, Malwa, and the western Deccan in general. The latter was composed in Mithila itself. The first one may broadly be categorized as a kathā in the *prabandha* (a continuous or connected narrative; also a generic term for any literary composition) form of history[3] while the latter was organized in the form of a general treatise on politics, rājanīti. Both belong roughly to the early-fourteenth century. Occasional reference to comparable ideas in certain Persian texts will also be made with a view to underline the as yet unexplored aspects of their dynamic (cross-linguistic/cross-confessional) character.

[2] See Caṇḍeśvara, *Rājanītiratnākara*; Merutuṅga, *Prabandhacintāmaṇi* or *Wishing-stone of Narratives*, trans. Tawney. Where necessary, I also refer to the original Sanskrit version published earlier: Merutuṅga, *Prabandhacintāmaṇiḥ*, 1888. Henceforth, Tawney's translated volume is cited as Merutuṅga, *Wishing-stone of Narratives*, and the Sanskrit original as Merutuṅga, *Prabandhacintāmaṇiḥ*.

[3] For an interesting discussion of prabandha literature in Sanskrit, with useful references to *Prabandhacintāmaṇi* itself, see Ali, 'Temporality, Narration and the Problem of History'.

In Chapter 2 in this volume, I took critical stock of the recent historiographic interest in the study of precolonial literary cultures in the subcontinent. In this chapter, my reading of *Puruṣaparīkṣā* (as of *Likhanāvalī* in the last chapter) explores possibilities of several meaningful departures from the ways in which pre-Mughal literary cultures in general and the fifteenth century in particular have hitherto been approached. Locating *Puruṣaparīkṣā* within larger histories of aesthetic and genre-related trends in Sanskrit literary cultures is an important part of this exercise. The identification of its more temporal co-ordinates in the spatial and chronological context is an equally important component. It is interesting, for example, that in this instance, Vidyapati picked up several dispersed literary techniques to cobble together a text that gestured substantively to the philosophical debates of four or more centuries earlier while simultaneously attempting to address a larger audience who would be drawn more towards stories than 'dry' texts on political or philosophical thought. As I try to demonstrate, most of the ideas about masculinity or political ethics offered by Vidyapati in *Puruṣaparīkṣā* were also offered in earlier compositions. The novelty of this collection of tales lay in its sharper focus, in weaving together stray and vague ideas into a neatly classified schema. Like the *ubhayavidya* (one with expertise both in folklore and Vedic lore) who he celebrated in one of his stories, Vidyapati used his erudition in classical lore along with his creative talents in retelling popular tales to package an abstruse set of nīti ideals in an accessible genre. From the point of view of literary history, it is difficult to imagine such a text in an earlier age.

In the last fifteen years or so, historians have increasingly turned to the study of literary aesthetics, vernacular and cosmopolitan cultures, and the formation of regions as phenomena largely linked to novel techniques of reading, writing, and performative practices.[4] More recently, interesting studies by Bronner, Shulman, Kapadia, and Ahmad have tried to delineate paradigms within which local/universal flavours of a text may be isolated and described.[5] Steadily this has released a whole gamut of new questions, not all of which, I would

[4] See Chapter 2 in this volume for a discussion of these aspects.

[5] Ahmad, 'The Long Thirteenth Century of the *Chachnāma*'; Bronner and Shulman, '"A Cloud Turned Goose"'; Kapadia, 'The Last *Cakravartin*?'

like to suggest, may be answered within the terms hitherto offered by these debates. The question of literary aesthetic is surely a question of choice between the regional and the cosmopolitan/universalistic (or the local and the imperial) just as it is also the problem of looking at cross-generic and cross-linguistic borrowings or 'inter-confessional' appropriations. While beginnings of 'literarization' and aesthetic choices made by litterateurs may have been implicated in the process of regionalization and vernacularization, the problem that remains obscure is how a new regime of literary aesthetics (with or without supporting 'local political regimes') reimagined and rearticulated ritually and socially discriminatory regimes of power in the pre-Mughal period. To put it narrowly and within the modest ambitions of this chapter: how are varṇa and gender regimes reaccommodated within these new knowledge practices? Such a study must necessarily combine an analysis of the style and aesthetics of a text with the more conventional attention to their 'contents', not to positivistically discover a society as it was, but to describe a particular literary dynamic whereby texts claimed authority and constituted ideals.

The Text

Historians are notorious for reducing books and documents composed in the distant past into sources that they selectively mine for pieces of information, with complete disregard for their textual integrity, and sometimes, even contextual specificity. Increasingly, however, scholars agree that the historicized reading of a text is impossible without critical attention paid to its structure.[6] Let us begin then, with a brief outline of the composition at the centre of focus in this chapter.

Puruṣaparīkṣā begins with salutations to Ādi Śakti, broadly identified with the goddess popularly known in present-day Mithila as Bhagavatī.[7] The author records that he is composing the text under

[6] For a recent restatement of the idea in the medieval context, see Spiegel, 'Genealogy: Form and Function in Medieval History Narrative', p. 46.

[7] Grierson, in his translation of *Puruṣaparīkṣā*, refers to the goddess as 'Durgâ' before qualifying her with a literal translation of Ādi Śakti as 'Primeval Potency Energy'; See Grierson, *The Test of a Man*, p. 1.

instructions from Raja Śivasiṃha, son of Raja Devasiṃha.[8] It is written in easy Sanskrit prose, and contains about forty-four stories. It is divided into four parts, one of which is rather distinct. The first three parts describe and illustrate each of the three chief traits of a man. The fourth part deals, again through stories, with the rewards (*phalaṃ*) of being a 'true man'.[9] Table 4.1 below lists the stories in the

Table 4.1 Tales about Different Kinds of Men in *Puruṣaparīkṣā*

Puruṣa Typologies		
Different Types of *Vīra* (Valorous) ↓	Different Types of *Sudhī* (Intelligent) ↓	Different Types of *Savidya* (Learned) ↓
Dānavīra (Generous)	*Sapratibhaḥ* (Quick-witted)	*Śastravidya* (Expert in Weapon Use)
Dayāvīra (Compassionate)	*Medhāvīḥ* (Alert)	*Śāstravidya* (Learned in Sciences)
Yuddhavīra (Battle-Adept)	*Subuddhi* (Judicious)	*Vedavidya* (Learned in Vedas)
Satyavīra (Truthful)	*Vañcaka** (Wily/Cunning)	*Lokavidya* (Learned in Folklore)
*Caura** (Thief)	*Piśuna** (Slanderous)	*Ubhayavidya* (Learned both in Vedas and Folklore)
*Bhīru** (Fearful)	*Janmabarbara** (Imbecile by Birth)	*Citravidya* (Expert in Painting)
*Kṛipaṇa** (Miser)	*Saṃsargabarbara** (Imbecile by Company)	*Gītavidya* (Expert in Singing)

(*Cont'd*)

[8] It is interesting to note that *Bhūparikramaṇa*, an earlier composition of Vidyapati (which was expanded into *Puruṣaparīkṣā*), was written under instructions from Śivasiṃha's father, Devasiṃha. See Vidyapati, *Bhūparikramaṇa*, p. 1.

[9] '*Puruṣasyalakṣaṇaṃ proktaṃ phalaṃ tasya nigadyate*' (Having described the attributes of a man, let me now write about its rewards). See Vidyapati, *Puruṣaparīkṣā* (henceforth, *Puruṣaparīkṣā*), p. 162.

Table 4.1 (*Cont'd*)

Puruṣa Typologies		
Different Types of *Vīra* (Valorous) ↓	Different Types of *Sudhī* (Intelligent) ↓	Different Types of *Savidya* (Learned) ↓
*Alasa** (Lazy)		*Nṛityavidya* (Expert in Dance)
		Indrajālavidya (Expert in Casting Spells)
		Pūjitavidya (Felicitated for Learning)
		*Avasannavidya** (Unappreciated in Learning)
		*Avidya** (Uneducated)
		*Khaṇḍitavidya** (Partially-educated)
		Hāsavidya (Expert in Comedy)

Source: *Puruṣaparīkṣā*.
Note: *signifies *pratyudāharaṇa kathā* or counterexample story.

first three sections. Table 4.2 lists the stories in the fourth section. A quick look at these tables conveys how meticulously the author framed and followed the scheme of classification. It is noteworthy that the stories in the fourth section are not divided into 'example stories' and 'counterexample stories'. Rather, they map a spectrum of possibilities on different levels of attainment accessible to men on the path of each of the four *puruṣārthas*, that is, *dharma* (righteousness), *artha* (material well-being), *kāma* (sensual pleasures), and *mokṣa* (salvation).

Manuscripts of *Puruṣaparīkṣā* have been found in different parts of Mithila, Nepal, and Bengal. Although a range of scholars established its historicity long ago, it may be noted that there is one story in *Puruṣaparīkṣā* that is almost certainly a later addition to the text. This is the story entitled *Niḥspṛihakathā*. It revolves around an ascetic called Vāmana, and another, Kṛiṣṇacaitanya. Caitanya

Table 4.2 Tales Illustrating Puruṣārtha or 'The Prescribed Goals of Men's Life'

Puruṣārtha Typologies			
Dharmakathāḥ (Tales about Righteousness)	*Arthakathāḥ* (Tales about Wealth) ↓	*Kāmakathāḥ* (Tales about Pleasure) ↓	*Mokṣakathāḥ* (Tales about Salvation) ↓
Tātvika (Knower of Truth)	*Maheccha* (Righteously Affluent)	*Anukūla* (Faithful)	*Nirbandhī* (Detached)
Tāmasa (Dynamic)	*Mūḍha* (Profligate)	*Dakṣiṇa* (Promiscuous but Faithful)	*Niḥspṛih* (One Untouched by Worldly Desires)
Anuśayī (Repentant)	*Bahvāśa* (Covetous)	*Vidagdha* (Accomplished [Lover])	*Labdhasiddhi* (One Who Attained Perfection)
	Sāvadhāna (Discreet)	*Dhūrta* (Deceitful)	
		Ghasmara (Henpecked)	

Source: Puruṣaparīkṣā.

or Kṛiṣṇacaitanya, the famous Vaiṣṇava saint from Bengal, was born in 1485, and hence there is no way that Vidyapati could have known him.[10]

In any case, when George Abraham Grierson (1851–1941) translated *Puruṣaparīkṣā*, early in the twentieth century, he noted that 'among the early books printed in Bengal was a translation into the Bengali language by Hara Prasâda Râya of the *Puruṣaparīkṣā*

[10] The story is fantastic in other ways too. Kṛiṣṇacaitanya is depicted in the story as a young man sitting in rapt contemplation in a Śiva temple in *daṇḍakāraṇya*, that is, in the general expanse of the Deccan plateau. In the epic tale of Rāmāyaṇa, it was supposed to be situated between the Vindhya and Saibala mountains. In an essay titled 'The Geography of Rama's Exile', Pargiter had argued that '*daṇḍakāraṇya*' comprised all the forests from Bundelkhand to River Krishna. See entry on *daṇḍakāraṇya* in Dey, *The Geographical Dictionary of Ancient and Mediaeval India*, p. 52.

probably in 1815'.[11] Incidentally, Grierson also noted that 'it became a textbook for government examinations and an edition by Sir G. Haughton appeared in London in 1826, and others in Calcutta in subsequent years'.[12] Another edition of the Sanskrit text appeared in 1888 with a translation by Chanda Jha.[13] An abridged version was published in 1911 for use in schools 'to replace the animal fables like *Pañcatantra* and *Hitopadeśa* and to provide young boys at school with an introduction to morals, but without the air of "unreality" that pervaded the fables. Accordingly, several study guides to the text were also published in subsequent years.'[14] It was soon included in the curriculum of the coveted Indian Civil Service examination.[15]

The best way to understand the organization of *Puruṣaparīkṣā* is to look at the way it actually begins, with a seed story after the peremptory salutations. Let me reproduce the story, which frames the forty-four stories that follow:

> In the city of Candrātapā, there once was a king by the name of Pārāvara, whose lotus feet were adorned by the pollen of the flowers in the garlands of thousands of kings from regions up to the oceans. He had a daughter by the name of Padmāvatī, who was beautiful in all aspects, and full of all the desirable virtues. As her childhood receded, the king was filled with anxiety about finding a suitable groom for her, appropriate to the family pedigree. For,
>
> > A man might be hardworking and earning riches by legitimate means,
> > Righteous, gentle, and free of anger and other vices,
> > Yet if he has a daughter, his heart will be filled with worries,
> > About finding a suitable groom and fear of being refused.

[11] Grierson, *Vidyapati's Puruṣaparīkṣā*, pp. xvii–xviii.

[12] Grierson, *Vidyapati's Puruṣaparīkṣā*, pp. xvii–xviii.

[13] Grierson, *Vidyapati's Puruṣaparīkṣā*. Grierson, for some reason spelt the scholar's name as Chandra Jha. See Grierson, *Vidyapati's Puruṣaparīkṣā*, pp. xi, xii, xvii, xviii.

[14] Ali, *Courtly Culture and Political Life*, p. 1. Also see Grierson, *Vidyapati's Puruṣaparīkṣā*, p. xviii.

[15] Mishra, 'Prakāśakīya', p. i.

What is to be done then, he asked Sage Subuddhi. Because,

> Never take a decision entirely on your own in important matters
> Even the wise are liable to commit mistakes and suffer from delusions.

The Raja said, 'O, Sage! I have a daughter by the name of Padmāvatī. Who should the groom for her be, kindly consider and give instructions.'

The Sage said, 'O, Rājan! Choose a man.'

'O, Sage! One who is not a man cannot be a groom in any case.'

The Sage said, 'There are many men on this earth who only have the physical shape of a man. What I mean is that you should give up on those who are men only in appearance, and choose a [real] man!' After all,

> Those looking like a man you can easily find, while real men are rare,
> It is difficult to find a man with qualities that I am about to declare.

Thus,

> The man who is valorous, intelligent, and learned is a real male,
> The rest are men merely by appearance, animals they are without a tail.[16]

The King said, 'How, then, does one identify the valorous one, and so on?'

[16] *Vīraḥ sudhīḥ savidyaśca puruṣaḥ puruṣārthavāntadanye puruṣākārāḥ, paśavaḥ puccha varjitāḥ*. My translation differs substantively from that by Grierson. He renders the couplet as follows: 'The hero, the intelligent, the skilled adept, and he who hath attained the four objects of life are each real men. Others are men-shapes only, mere brute beasts that have no tails'. See Grierson, *The Test of a Man*, p. 2. While puruṣārtha does refer to the four prescribed objects of life, *puruṣārthavān* occurs in the couplet as an adjective of the three kinds of men, that is, the valorous, the intelligent, and the learned, who according to Vidyapati were capable of attaining and enjoying the four ideal fruits of dharma, mokṣa, artha, and kāma. Hence, I have translated the word puruṣārthavān as a 'real male', that is, one possessing the requisite attributes of manhood that will earn him puruṣārtha.

The Sage replied:

Vīraḥ śaurya vivekābhyām utsāhena ca maṇḍitaḥ
Mātāpitror alaṅkṛitu kule kutrāpi jāyate
Śauryaṃ kārapaṇya rahitaṃ viveko dhīr hitāhite
Kriyā pravṛittirutsāho vīrastais tu bhavet tribhiḥ

(One adorned with bravery, discretion, and enthusiasm is a man of valour
Earning glories for parents, they might be born to whatever lineage
Lack of fear is bravery, discretion—the ability to discern the good from bad
Enthusiasm is the will to exert oneself, these three maketh a valorous man!)

There are four types of [valorous men]: *dānavīro dayāvīro yuddhavīraḥ satyavīraśca* (the generous one, the kind one, the warrior, and the truthful one).

Thus,

Hariścandra was the generous one, Raja Śivi the kind one,
Pārtha was the warrior type, the truthful one was Yuddhiṣṭhira.

'O, Sage!', the Raja quipped, 'These men belonged to another era. We cannot learn anything from their example in this era.' For,

Characters of the Kṛita-born cannot be a source of education in Kaliyuga,
Due to changes because of time, these examples cannot be followed!
Men no longer have that kind of intelligence, nor that strength,
For those born in the Kaliyuga, there is no such truth either!

Hence, please enlighten us about the character of the valorous through stories of men born in the times of Kali.

The Sage said, 'The learned have already told the stories of Satyuga, Dvāpari, and Tretā, I will tell you tales of the Kaliyuga.'[17]

A student of history will be quick to notice at least three interesting elements in this story: (*a*) that what appeared in the beginning merely as a problem about finding a suitable boy/groom swiftly opens up a wide didactic space for a full-fledged exploration of the constitution of a man, actually, a *real* man, possibly, a politically successful man; (*b*) that a man's

[17] *Puruṣaparīkṣā*, pp. 2–6.

valour does not depend on his birth, an assertion that is brought home with the phrase, '*kule kutrāpi jāyate*'; and (*c*) that the author consciously located the stories that are to follow in *this-worldly time*, and wanted his reader to note this detail. I will come back to these observations as I proceed, and will hopefully be able to see beneath and beyond them.

But what does one make of a text that details the true characteristics of a real man largely through stories? Of course, this is a treatise on the substance and fruits of being *puruṣārthavān*[18] or what we moderns might call the ideal way of being a man. Yet, it is surely much more than that. After all, the traits of valour, intelligence, and learning are not abstract qualities: *Puruṣaparīkṣā* constituted these qualities through ostensibly real-life stories, told in a manner that grounded the idea of the Real Man in the clumsy, tactile, and imitable world of lived experience. It is instructive to note that according to Vidyapati himself, one of the aims of the book was to make the young appreciate *naya*.[19] It is hardly surprising then, that from Grierson to more recent commentators, most scholars have variously referred to it as a manual on politics, as a treatise on political morality, or even ethics, and it is not an entirely inappropriate characterization. For, even apart from the author's own assertion, the content and tone of the stories in the book clearly establish the fact that it is meant as a didactic manual

[18] Strictly, in a literal sense, puruṣārtha, the four objects/fruits (dharma, artha, mokṣa, and kāma) of human life, are not gender specific. However, even apart from the fact that puruṣārtha is cognate with the very gender-specific *puruṣa*, it is rarely, if ever, used as a normative virtue for women.

[19] *Śiśūnām siddhayartha naya paricitenūñtanadhiyāṃ* (May the children/adolescents with fresh minds succeed in appreciating righteousness). See *Puruṣaparīkṣā*, p. 2. While 'naya' literally means 'righteous or virtuous conduct', it also connotes policy, political wisdom, statesmanship, civil administration, and even state policy; see Apte, *Sanskrit–English Dictionary*, p. 536. What is interesting is that naya comes close, both in a lexical sense as well as in historical usage, to nīti, on which there was a long history of scholarship in Sanskrit. Indeed, in the epilogue of the text, Vidyapati himself comments that he had just finished writing about the complex (*granthila*) subject of state policy (*daṇḍanīti*). As Apte has noted, *Mṛicchakaṭika* as well as *Raghuvaṃśa* used the word 'naya' in this sense. For a useful discussion of *Raghuvaṃśa* as a political document, see Singh, 'The Power of a Poet'.

for maintaining political order. The choice of the story mode could not have been incidental for an author as varied in the choice of his themes and genres as Vidyapati was.

Genre

Probably the first time we hear of anything resembling kathā as a genre in a classificatory scheme in Sanskrit is in the form of the *udāharaṇaṃ* (example) in Kautilya's *Arthaśastra*, which mentioned it as a branch of *itihāsa*: '*Purāṇam itivṛittaṃ ākhyāyikā udāharaṇaṃ dharmaśāstram arthaśāstraṃ ca itihāsaḥ*, i.e. *itihāsa* is ancient stories, recent history, traditional biographical narratives, stories as examples, law texts, and political narratives'.[20]

This is probably one of the earliest passages in Sanskrit seeking to set out a typology of compositions. How one interprets it depends critically on how one translates words like *itihāsa, purāṇa, ākhyāyikā, itivṛitta*, and so on. It is the translation by K.P. Jayaswal that I have cited above. It is noteworthy that he retained the word *itihāsa* (*iti.ha.āsa*, literally, 'so it has been') indicating that there is probably no close equivalent in English for this word. *Arthaśāstra's* account, of course, is not a classification of different genres of literature. Had there not been the unresolved issue of the precise time at which *Arthaśāstra* was composed, one might even have said that this was possibly an attempt in the 'pre-literary' era to list out different kinds of itihāsa, the closest equivalent to which in English is probably 'history'. Nor is there an agreement among scholars—and this includes medieval *alaṅkārika*s (language theorists) as well as modern historians—about the precise definition of terms like itivṛitta, udāharaṇaṃ, and ākhyāyikā. Udāharaṇa connotes 'examples' but it never evolved into a literary genre as such, unlike kathā and ākhyāyikā. Jayaswal translates itivṛitta as 'stories' though literally, itivṛtta would imply some sort of a 'finite account' of something. So far as ākhyāyikā is concerned, Jayaswal, like Warder, saw an element of history in it, probably because the term *ākhyā* carries a sense of 'reporting' and hence points to an 'actual' occurrence.

[20] Cited in Jayaswal, 'Introduction', *Rajanīti-ratnākara*, p. 27. The translation is by Jayaswal.

The first literary–theoretical treatise, *Nāṭyaśāstra* of Bharata, did not refer to kathā. For a text focussed on drama, that is hardly a surprise. However, some scholars have found the discussion of itivṛitta therein to be a discussion of kathā by another name.[21] It is true, as Sadhale has pointed out, that Abhinavagupta did read the term 'itivṛitta' as a reference to the *kathāvastu* of a drama. However, kathā could not be same as kathāvastu, literally, the 'plot' of a story or a drama, though the two words are cognate.[22]

Scholars of Sanskrit literary aesthetics, the alaṅkārikas, were fairly consistent with the ways in which they understood the basic contours of genres. Yet, this was not so with regard to kathā, let alone udāharaṇakathā, which is rarely mentioned. Bhāmaha, considered one of the foremost authorities on Sanskrit aesthetics (*alaṅkāraśāstra*), listed kathā as one of the five types of kāvya, which could be in prose or verse.[23] He went on to add that in a kathā, the protagonist does not himself describe his own qualities; rather, someone else praises him.[24] Daṇḍin (c. 700) however, denied any distinction between kathā and ākhyāyikā.[25] Not surprisingly, while the stories of several books of *Pañcatantra* are styled as kathās, one version is entitled *tantrākhyāyikā*, and in practice it was probably difficult to distinguish between them.[26] The abiding and increasing confusions between the seventh and the fifteenth centuries, both in theory and in actual

[21] See for example, Sadhale, *Kathā in Sanskrit Poetics*, p. 3.

[22] Sadhale, *Kathā in Sanskrit* Poetics, p. 3.

[23] *Sargabandhoabhineyārthaṃ tathaivākhyāyikākathe/Anibaddhañca kāvyādi tatpunaḥ pañcadhocyate* (It is said that kāvya may further be classified into five kinds: *mahākāvya*, which is divided into different thematic sections; *abhineya*, that which can be staged; *ākhyāyikā* [biography]; *kathā* [story]; and *anibaddha* [free/independent verses]). See Bhāmaha, *Kāvyālaṅkāra*, p. 10. Warder translates *sargabandha* as 'lyric', and identifies '*nāṭya*' (drama) instead of '*abhineya*' as one of the five types of kāvya that he attributes to Bhāmaha's classification; see Warder, *Indian Kāvya Literature*, vol. I, p. 122. See the section on 'genre' in Chapter 5 in this volume for a fuller treatment of this.

[24] Bhāmaha, *Kāvyālaṅkāra*, p. 15.

[25] Warder takes this to mean that Daṇḍin denied any distinction even between history and fiction. See Warder, *Indian Kāvya Literature*, vol. VI, p. ix.

[26] Keith, *A History of Sanskrit Literature*, p. 245.

practice, between kathā and ākhyāyikā, will be taken up for a somewhat detailed analysis in the next chapter.

Warder has argued that the twelfth century might be regarded as the period when story-telling (kathā) dominated kāvya, after which there are fewer such narratives though they did not disappear.[27] Sometimes, as Warder himself pointed out, short tales could be embedded within a *mahākāvya* (courtly epic) or other forms as an example or udāharaṇa. Stories within stories as well as stories as didactic tools of course, had as long a history in Indic traditions as kathā itself.[28] After the thirteenth century, in any case, the experiments in texts seem to have muddled, and multiplied beyond, the neat classifications of genres by alaṅkārikas like Bhāmaha and Daṇḍin, a fact that is reflected in the works of later theorists like Viśvanātha Kavirāja.[29] So, while 'kathā' as a genre may or may not have 'peaked' in the twelfth century only to 'decline' subsequently, stories continued to be told/composed in a variety of registers, languages, and mix of genres. These were stories about the past, both historical and semi-historical, but also 'fictive' stories of the mythological past. The prabandha texts from Western India that started appearing from the mid/late-thirteenth century, for example, were a motley of such story compositions. Many of them reflected several traits traditionally associated with kathā, and some associated with ākhyāyikā as well.[30] Indeed, as Ali has argued, prabandhas started off as biographical anthologies, though the style of their narration owed much to the kathā tradition.[31]

[27] Collections of Kṣemendra and Somadeva II also belonged to this century. Warder, *Indian Kāvya Literature*, vol. VI, p. vii.

[28] Warder, *Indian Kāvya Literature*, vol. VI, pp. 664–5.

[29] See the section on 'genre' in Chapter 5 in this volume, for details.

[30] For an interesting recent discussion of this 'genre' of literature, see Daud Ali, 'Temporality, Narration and the Problem of History'.

[31] It is doubtful if, either in theory or practice, Sanskrit (or any other Indic) literary culture had the tradition of composing a biographical anthology till this time. Persian, on the other hand, had a vibrant tradition of *tazkira*, a popular genre in the Sufic literary canon of North India by the time the prabandhas came into being. See Daud Ali, 'Temporality, Narration and the Problem of History', p. 253.

One of the most remarkable examples, if somewhat atypical, amongst these texts was *Prabandhacintāmaṇi* of Merutuṅga Ācārya. A brief comparison of this text with *Puruṣaparīkṣā* would help throw the uniqueness of the latter into sharper relief, and locate it within the history of the changing patterns of kathā and related genres in the fourteenth and fifteenth centuries.[32]

Merutuṅga of Vardhamanapura (or Vaḍhvān), completed his *Prabandhacintāmaṇi*, in the year 1361 of the era of Vikramāditya corresponding to 1305 in the Christian Era. Its manuscripts are reported to be in Jain Nāgarī, and it is part of the Jain corpus of Sanskrit literature.[33] The text starts with an invocation of Om, Ṣrī, and Lord Mahāvīra. It then calls upon 'Jina Ṛishabha, the divine son of Nābhi, the *Parameṣṭhin*, who makes an end of births' to 'protect the four gates of the glorious goddess of speech [Sarasvatī], which become her, in that she has four mouths'.[34]

As Hofrath Buhler noted, 'The objects with which the *Caritas* and *Prabandhas* were composed, were to edify the Jain community, to convince them of the glory and power of the Jain religion, or, in cases where the subject is a purely secular one, to provide them with an agreeable entertainment'.[35] To the modern observer, used to neat and exclusive formulations, however, the Jain moorings of the text might occasionally appear 'compromised' and even shallow. Brāhmaṇic mythological characters are frequently and approvingly referred to in several stories.[36] It is only in the retellings of the occasional clash with a Jain believer/*muni* that others are showed down.

[32] For a detailed discussion of the incidence and context of heightened experiments in genre and literary compositions in general in the fourteenth–fifteenth centuries, see Chapter 2 in this volume.

[33] Tawney, 'Preface', *Wishing-stone of Narratives*, p. xix.

[34] Merutuṅga, *Wishing-stone of Narratives*, p. 1.

[35] Cited by Tawney in his 'Preface' to Merutuṅga, *Wishing-stone of Narratives*, p. vi.

[36] See Merutuṅga, *Wishing-stone of Narratives*. Sarasvatī, the Brāhmaṇical/ Hindu goddess of learning/speech is invoked several times (pp. 35, 39, 46, passim); the Vedas and upaniṣads are referred to respectfully as repositories of knowledge (p. 156 for Upaniṣads; passim for Vedas); the author ends the text in the hope that his book might help the wise ones attain a stature like that of Viṣṇu himself (p. 204). This should not lead us to underestimate the

In any case, the author's stated intentions in *Prabandhacintāmaṇi* do indicate that the text was meant, like most other such compositions, to both entertain and educate. Thus, Merutuṅga stated at the beginning of the text that he was narrating the life-stories of men nearer in time to his own because the ancient stories had lost their entertainment value on account of having been narrated so often.[37] At the end of the book, however, he provided another reason for the composition of the book. Learning, he noted, was in decay and virtuous men were difficult to find. He, therefore, wove together stories of good men. Narrated 'in the service of future sages', these stories could make wise men wiser (like Viṣṇu).

The text is divided into five roughly even-sized chapters or prabandhas. The first four of the chapters are focussed on one or two rulers: the first one tells of the deeds of Vikramārka (Vikramāditya); the second, those of Bhoja and Bhīma; the third one is styled as a narrative about Siddharāja; and the fourth one about Kumārapāla. The fifth chapter, curiously, is styled as a 'miscellaneous chapter' in which 'those actions of the great men previously spoken of, which remain over and above their deeds already related, and others in addition to those' are described.[38]

It may be noted in passing that according to the alaṅkārikas, kathās were meant to be unbroken narratives, told either in a continuous and linear series, or in the form of stories within stories.[39] It is equally

---

intensity of Jain–Brāhmaṇism rivalry, but to underline the fact that culturally respected symbols and story-templates were used across sectarian boundaries in ways that may not make easy sense in modern times, when claims of exclusive sectarian domains are more common.

37 Merutuṅga, *Wishing-stone of Narratives*, p. 2. Let us recall the distinction that Vidyapati made between the truth of Kaliyuga and the 'more truthful' previous yugas. This distinction might also be seen, in modern parlance, as the distinction between the historical and that which is purely mythological.

38 Merutuṅga, *Wishing-stone of Narratives*, p. 169.

39 In contrast, ākhyāyikā was supposed to be divided into *ucchavāsas* (divisions in a literary text; singular, *ucchavāsa*; literally, a deep breath that one would take after a continuous session of reading/recitation)/*saṇdhis* (divisions in a literary text; singular, *sandhi*; literally, the joint between two

noteworthy that four of the five chapters in *Prabandhacintāmaṇi* are organized around historical personages (kings) and named as such, though the stories under these chapters are not entirely confined to the reigns of the ruler(s) named in the chapter title. Composed a century later, *Puruṣaparīkṣā* (also divided into chapters) made a sharp departure from this and other similar texts inasmuch as Vidyapati wove the whole text around specific traits of men, with stories as examples and counterexamples for each quality. In doing so, Vidyapati gave a far more direct and sharper didactic edge to his text than did Merutuṅga to his own. This is also evident in the explicit and unequivocal statement of the author at the end that his text was meant to edify the young in naya or political ethics.

A similar overlap *and* dissimilarity is evident in the manner in which the two authors handled time. Merutuṅga deployed two different registers of time. Frequently, he used the standard convention of 'once upon a time', popular among storytellers, to refer to an undifferentiated past. However, he also resorted, less frequently but significantly, to the epigraphic tradition of marking time, whereby the precise day, date, fortnight, month, and year were listed. On the other hand, Vidyapati invariably started his story in terms of 'once upon a time'. More interesting were the distinct reasons the two authors gave for choosing to tell the stories of *a* particular time. As noted above, Merutuṅga chose to relate 'stories nearer to his own time', *vṛittaistadāsannasatāṃ*, simply because the old stories, *kathāḥ purāṇāḥ*, had lost their charm due to frequent repetition.[40] Vidyapati gave more elaborate and very specific reasons for defining the temporal co-ordinates of his stories, as we have already seen in the very

different parts that make the whole)/*sargas* (divisions in a literary text; singular, *sarga*; literally, a natural flow or intrinsic trait). Bhamaha actually defined kathā as a composition that neither had *vaktra* (a particular metre in Sanskrit verse, wherein long and short vowels alternate as per a fixed scheme) or *apavaktra* (any kind of writing scheme that does not follow the fixed rule of alternating scheme of vowels as per the vaktra metre) metres, nor ucchavās. See Bhāmaha, *Kāvyālaṅkāra* (I. 28), p. 15. Also see Hemacandra, *Kāvyanuśāsana* (VIII: 7), p. 169.

[40] Merutuṅga, *Prabandhacintāmaṇiḥ*, p. 2.

first story of *Puruṣaparīkṣā* cited above. The truths of the earlier eras were no longer valid, he declared, and went on to narrate the tales of protagonists who people in his own age might hope to emulate with profit. Indeed, there could hardly be a more categorically stated case of consciously reconstructing what Daud Ali called 'useable pasts' in the context of prabandha compositions.[41]

A listener/reader of the two texts would not fail to notice another somewhat subtle, though equally consequential, difference in the style of their retelling. Vidyapati's stories always had a very well-defined plot, a clear beginning and end, a foregrounding of the quality that the story meant to illustrate, and a very clearly marked characterization. The stories of *Puruṣaparīkṣā* were shorn of all the details that did not fit into their didactic intent. Their heroes were always, without fail, an epitome of the virtue (or vice in the case of counterexample stories) they were supposed to exemplify. Merutuṅga's protagonists by comparison, even the celebrated characters such as Bhoja, were more realistic, prone to making mistakes and having to pay for it. Frequently, the stories of *Prabandhacintāmaṇi* seemed to meander through a variety of episodes, providing sundry details in ways that a modern historian might find useful. For a medieval 'consumer' of the kathās, however, *Puruṣaparīkṣā* served a more tightly controlled, neatly told, readymade corpus of modular stories, each geared towards delivering a very specific lesson.

There were other ways in which *Puruṣaparīkṣā* stood out in contrast with the prabandha compositions. The people who animated its stories were drawn from a vast range of places in North India and the Deccan. While sticking to the established convention of including the stories of Vikramāditya, Candragupta, and Bhoja, Vidyapati also introduced Turkish and Afghan sultans as well as three local heroes from Mithila as characters in his kathās. Very often he let his characters, both the heroes and anti-heroes, speak at length for themselves and hence set his ideas in a more dialogical context. What made *Puruṣaparīkṣā* truly unique, however, was

41 Ali, 'Temporality, Narration and the Problem of History', pp. 239, 242, and 246.

the fact that he formulated each one of his political ideals as the qualities of a 'model male' character.

Gender

That *Puruṣaparīkṣā* presumed the field of politics to be exclusively a male domain should not be hastily prejudged. Indeed, as far as medieval political theorists were concerned, only men were capable of, and hence expected to, cultivate the qualities of a good political subject: in the sense of those who had political power and initiative as well as in the sense of those who were 'subjected' to that power—the subjects of the state so to say.[42]

Reality though could sometimes shatter such idealism, as Vidyapati discovered soon. Within a decade of the composition of *Puruṣaparīkṣā*, the author of *The Test of a Man* ended up writing *Śaivasarvasvasāra* under instructions from a woman ruler of Tirhut, Viśvāsa Devī.[43] Yet, we should not forget that facts like these, whether we are talking about Viśvāsa Devī or Raziyya Sultan or several other queens that we come across, do not take away from the conceptually gendered terrain of politics. A more truthful reflection of the maleness of political power perhaps was the fact that even when a female ruler occupied the throne, the qualities she would be ideally attributed and praised for were masculine qualities.[44] Moreover, while it was still possible

[42] Most premodern treatises on political ethics illustrated their ideals through stories about the deeds of good men, whether in the Persian or in the pre-Persian Indic traditions. This would include, the above-mentioned *Prabandhacintāmaṇi* as also Nizam al-Mulk's *Siyasat Nama*, Ziya' al-Din Barani's *Fatawa-i Jahandari*, and other Persian texts in the tradition of the so-called 'mirrors for princes'.

[43] Padmasiṃha, the younger brother of Vidyapati's patron Raja Śivasiṃha, succeeded the latter to the throne of Tirhut. And Viśvāsadevī soon succeeded her husband Raja Padmasiṃha; see Vidyapati, *Śaivasarvasvasāra*, pp. 4–6. For the succession chart, see Chapter 1 of this volume.

[44] Juzjani, the author of the thirteenth-century chronicle *Tabaqat-i Nasiri*, for example, thought that Raziyya lacked the 'good fortune of being counted amongst men'; see Minhaj-i Siraj Juzjani, *Tabaqat-i Nasiri*, p. 457,

for a woman to become a Sultan or a Raja, it was near impossible for a woman to be appointed to any other important administrative position.[45] Indeed, the fourteenth-century political theorist Caṇḍeśvara explicitly prohibited 'rogues, women and children' from being appointed as ministers.[46]

Yet, women were not irrelevant to the construction of this exclusively male domain of politics. The author constructed the feminine, as much as the 'less than masculine', as a prop to throw the truly male into bolder relief. Narrating the characteristics of warrior men (*yuddhavīra*), the following śloka sets the tone of contrast between the yuddhavīra on the one hand, and children, fearful men, and women together on the other:

> Cowards, children, and women live the life of dependence,
> Lions and good men depend on their own prowess![47]

The possibilities for the 'less than male' were much wider than those for women. While women were repeatedly noted to be constrained by their ineffable nature, failings of men were due to

---

cited in Kumar, *Emergence of the Delhi Sultanate*, p. 260. Vidyapati too attributed traits to Viśvāsadevī in the beginning of *Śaivasarvasvasāra*, which he would associate with men in *Puruṣaparīkṣā*. See Vidyapati, *Śaivasarvasvasāra*, pp. 6–8. Note also, Talbot, 'Rudrama-devi, the Female King'.

45 It is a different matter altogether that historians of the Mughal state often celebrate the apparently cosmopolitan and universally inclusive character of its nobility without bothering to so much as mention that no woman could ever hope to be a *mansabdar* (literally, a rank holder. All high officials of the Mughal state were given ranks [*mansab*] that signified their position in the hierarchy. They were called mansabdar).

46 *Dhūrtaḥ strī vā śiśuryasya mantriṇaḥ syurmahīpateḥ/Anītipavanotkṣiptaḥ kāryābhau sa nimañjati* (A king who has a cunning man or a woman or a child for a minister, is blown away by the storm of the lack of righteousness and submerged into the ocean of work), says the author. See Caṇḍeśvara, *Rājanītiratnākara*, p. 25.

47 *Parāśrayeṇa jīvanti kātarāḥ śiśavaḥ striyaḥ/Siṃhāḥ satpuruṣascaiva nija darpopajīvinaḥ*. See *Puruṣaparīkṣā*, p. 20. Another śloka about women's destiny also expresses similar sentiments. *Puruṣaparīkṣā*, p. 56.

inclement circumstances. In the story about the 'brilliant one' (*sapratibha kathā*), a queen has this to say:

> A man's predicament might be condemnable, not he himself,
> Due to her son's virtues, a woman is called the bearer of gems![48]

Indeed, the best of men still needed to be cautious while dealing with women in their lives. For,

> Marked by turbulence and intensity, illusions and delusions,
> Women and rivers have identical characters.
> Always disposed to go down, even if you take them along a higher path,
> They will keep going lower and lower down without effort.[49]

Not surprisingly, a man was not masculine enough if he could be subdued by the charms of a woman. The śloka cited above actually occurs in the context of a *pratyudāharaṇakathā*, that is, 'counterexample story', about a ghasmara who is defined as 'a man who in spite of being valorous, intelligent, and learned, is fettered by feminine charms, and is under the control of a woman'.

While all the stories of *Puruṣaparīkṣā* seek to illustrate, through *udāharaṇakathā*, how to be a real man, and through *pratyudāharaṇakathā*, how not to be one, there are no dearth of descriptive and didactic observations about women. All the stereotypes (and more) associated with women can be found here. Thus, her sexual appetite is interminable and eight times that of men;[50] she would do anything to seduce a man once she was seized with desire;[51] she would laugh at cowardly men while she was always available to

[48] *Puruṣaparīkṣā*, p. 60.

[49] The śloka is recited, incidentally, by the Lord of the Yavanas, Sahāvadīno (almost certainly referring to Muhammad Shihab al-Din Ghuri), who, armed with this wisdom, proceeds to use his rival Jayachandra's wife and chief queen in order to defeat him. See '*Atha Ghasmara Kathā*', in *Puruṣaparīkṣā*, pp. 218–30.

[50] See *Puruṣaparīkṣā*, '*Atha dhūrta kathā* (the story of the cunning one)', p. 216.

[51] *Puruṣaparīkṣā*, '*Atha nispṛha kathā* (the story of the abstinent)', pp. 236–44.

a 'manly' man. In fact, women were represented almost as fruits of masculinity, trophies to be won.[52] It was the rare woman, the *sati*, one in a thousand, who remained chaste if she was unmarried, and who remained faithful if she was married.[53] Rare as these qualities may be, *Puruṣaparīkṣā* argued, unsurprisingly from an entirely masculine perspective, they marked the true power of a woman.

Although *Puruṣaparīkṣā* refrained from explicitly laying out the ostensibly positive details of the woman's burden in this gendered division of duties and traits, *Likhanāvalī* did briefly touch upon it. Thus, a model letter written by a travelling young man to his mother at home makes it a point to mention the nurturing role of a mother, and compares her with Ganga.[54] Another letter written by the mother of a young married woman advises her thus:

> [W]e have heard reports of your ill-repute on account of dissatisfaction with [your] sister-in-law[55] and quarrels with the co-wife. That distresses us. Though daughter–children are always a source of anxiety for parents, yet it is painful to hear so many stories so unbecoming of you, [one] who is [otherwise] so very virtuous, expert in household work, and devoted to your elders. Even if your sister-in-law is vicious, co-wife is jealous and ill disposed towards you; still you should give up garrulity and conduct yourself according to your own nature. Indeed, humility helps in both the worlds and brings good fortune. Be devoted to your lord [that is, husband] and follow his instructions every moment....[56]

It is hardly surprising that Vidyapati confined women to the household and focussed primarily on their supporting role to men within the family. And of course, neither *Puruṣaparīkṣā* nor *Likhanāvalī* recognized the clear tension in suggesting that women were incorrigible by nature, even as they prescribed a whole set of virtuous practices for them. More interesting for us, however, is the fact that the conduct of women was often framed in the context of a larger political and social order, and not individuated into awarding or denying character

[52] *Puruṣaparīkṣā*, pp. 51 and 77.
[53] *Puruṣaparīkṣā*, pp. 110–14.
[54] Vidyapati, *Likhanāvalī*, p. 5.
[55] *Nananda*, that is, husband's sister.
[56] *Likhanāvalī*, pp. 27–8.

certificates to specific women. Two very different stories vividly illustrate this point.

The first one is ostensibly about the infallible wisdom of a Brāhmaṇa learned in the Vedas, wherein a Raja of Avantī, consumed with sexual desire for a Vaṇij[57] woman, relentlessly pursues her. When all his machinations fail in the face of the resolutely *pativratā* (a woman who has taken a vow to serve her husband under all conditions) and *sati* (a woman who lives truthfully for her husband and is willing to die with him) woman, he tries to bring her into disrepute by accusing her of adultery. When a Vedavidya Brāhmaṇa publicly demonstrates the innocence of the woman, the Raja faces ignominy, and can save himself and his kingdom only after he falls at the feet of the Brāhmaṇa (not at the feet of the woman) and apologizes.[58] Even more instructive is Vidyapati's version of the story about how Jayachandra of Kānyakubja lost his kingdom to the Lord of the Yavanas, the ruler of Yoginīpura (that is, Delhi), Sahāvadīna (Shihabuddin). When Shihabuddin is faced with repeated defeats in battle with Jayachandra, he conspires to target the chief queen of Jayachandra. Even though Jayachandra was blessed with Vidyādhara, an extraordinarily loyal and learned minister, the latter could not save his master's kingdom since the queen herself had turned disloyal. With his larger objects accomplished, Shihabuddin also snubs the unfaithful queen and kills her. The story ends with a couplet:

> Women are a means for fun, love her and treat her like a beloved,
> Prohibited it is to be under their control, else your misery is assured![59]

What this śloka did not specify—even if it was asserted in the stories—was that a gendered conduct was a necessary condition for both, individual happiness and social and political stability. At stake in the story cited above is not the historical veracity of Vidyapati's retelling of the well-known incident; more insightful is the way our author moulded the story to suit his own didactic agenda. As we shall see later, many of these ideas were reminiscent of *smṛiti* texts as well as

57 A caste associated with trading.

58 *Puruṣaparīkṣā*, pp. 110–14.

59 *Puruṣaparīkṣā*, p. 230.

philosophical treatises, both of which had a long and deep history in Sanskrit literary tradition. The earlier articulations of these ideals were either presumptive (as in the Puranic and folk tales) or stark and bald (as in the *dharmaśāstras*). The novelty, one may argue, of *Puruṣaparīkṣā* lay more in its aestheticized representation of these ideals in the form of entertaining stories while still maintaining a sharp didactic edge. The tradition of telling stories to teach ethics was at least as old as *Pañcatantra*, one of the earliest didactic texts on political ethics that wilfully styled, indeed camouflaged, itself as a series of entertaining stories.[60]

A century before Vidyapati, in Mithila itself, another Brāhmaṇa scholar, Caṇḍeśvara, delineated the desirable qualities of a king, on the authority of Yājñyavalkya, in the following words: 'A king should be full of enthusiasm [*mahotsāhaḥ*], resolute in his goals [*sthūlalakṣaḥ*], grateful, disposed to serve the elderly, humble, valorous [*satvasampannaḥ*], noble by birth, truthful, pure, energetic [literally, not lazy, *adīrghasūtra*], of good memory, above pettiness, duty-bound [*dhārmika*], free of all bad habits, learned [*prājñyaḥ*], heroic and knower of the secrets'.[61]

Qualities that were identical, similar to, or comparable with the ones cited by Caṇḍeśvara here are easy to find in *Puruṣaparīkṣā*. As noted though, the two texts are very different in the manner in which they approach their readers/listeners. *Rājanītiratnākara* was a simple account of the important components of an ideal state. The author described functions and desirable traits of each of these institutional components, one after another, from the king and ministers to spies and tax collectors. A non-specialist might be forgiven for having no patience with such a bland and erudite essay.

[60] The seed story of *Pañcatantra* relates that the author, Pandit Viṣṇu Sharma, told the stories to his patron-king's three sons. The king wanted his sons' minds to be illuminated, *buddhiprakāśo*, as they were disinterested in the sciences (*śāstravimukho*) and lacked discretion (*vivekarahito*). Moreover, he warned Sharma that they were resistant (*paramadurbhedaso*) to learning. Sharma reassured his patron that his wish would be fulfilled within six months, and promised that 'he would impart knowledge with entertainment' (*sarasvatīvinodam kariṣyāmi*). See Pandit Viṣṇu Sharma, *Pañcatantra*, pp. 3–7.

[61] Caṇḍeśvara, *Rājanītiratnākara*, ed. Gairola and Jha, p. 5.

A more interesting correlation is the recurrence of comparable, if not similar, ideas—more than a century later and a thousand miles away from Mithila—in Delhi, in a number of Persian texts. If the Sanskrit tradition framed the political ideals in the fifteenth century in an explicitly gendered way, the Persian tradition too had an indispensable place for manliness in politics. While trying to explain the failure of Humayun in holding on to his inherited territories in Hindustan, 'chroniclers such as Bayazid Bayat and Jawhar ... consistently compared the emperor with his rivals, including his brother Kamran and his Afghan enemy Sher Shah, in such a way as to suggest that Humayun had fallen short specifically in fulfilling gender roles appropriate to a warrior king'.[62] *Jawanmardi* (manliness), for example, was a critical attribute of a successful political agent, whether a fighter in the battlefield or a ruler in his court. When Humayun praised Mast Ali Qurchi's valour, it was the latter's jawanmardi that was highlighted as crucial.[63] Jawanmardi in the Persianate political world (as puruṣa in the Sanskrit tradition) was not to be contrasted only with the feminine. As Anooshahr noted in the context of the Persian accounts of the sixteenth century,

> 'unmanly' need not imply effeminacy, because, unlike modern perceptions, the strict binary opposites of male/female do not occur exclusively in the texts of these periods.... Rather, the masculine attributes of soldiers would have included aggressiveness and bravery, some sense of mercy, and the ability to bear with pain and hardship. Against these we encounter in the 'unmanly' a kind of pathetic weakness (*zabūnī*) which may be manifested in the inability to exact revenge as well as a love for fineries and comfort.[64]

It is difficult to miss the fact that many of the masculine qualities that the Persian chronicler listed with approval, for example, mercy, aggression, and bravery, had parallels in terms of qualities like *dayā*, *parākram/adīrghasūtra*, and *śaurya* as they figure in *Puruṣaparīkṣā*. If *ayyashi* (the vice of indulging in unrighteous material and physical

[62] Anooshahr, 'The King Who Would Be Man', p. 328.
[63] Anooshahr, 'The King Who Would Be Man', p. 329.
[64] Anooshahr, 'The King Who Would Be Man', p. 329.

pleasures) was the undoing of a prince, so were the *vyasanas* (unethical addictions geared to provide material and physical pleasures). While jawanmardi was rooted in the Perso-Islamic ecumenical tradition, its contemporary commonsensical echoes (and political salience) might not have been very different from the idea of being *puruṣārthavān*. If the idea of the perfect puruṣa looked back to the earlier articulations of an ideal social order in the smṛiti tradition, the Perso-Islamic ideal of the 'true' man, *insan-i kamil,* had its genealogy in *hadith, tawarikh,* sufi lore, and eventually Ibn al-Arabi. Each tradition had its own deep and long history to look back to and work out of. The word jawanmardi, for example, had a variable trajectory of connotations in Perso-Arabic literature from the ninth century onwards, when it had a close association with mystical and 'deviant' Islam.[65]

Two centuries later, jawanmardi came to have a set of connotations that might easily be compared to those of puruṣārtha. Kaykavus (eleventh century) in his *Qabus-namah,* devoted a full section to the 'Institution of *Jawānmardī*' wherein he posited, to begin with, three components of jawanmardi: to always fulfil one's promise, to always speak the truth, and to always act with patience. Other virtues followed soon: to be brave (*delir*) and manly, to be pure in sexual life and thought, never cause loss to anyone for one's own gain, never oppress the weak or extort anything out of prisoners, be generous towards the needy, and have endurance in hardship. Gratitude, the 'condition of being abundantly armed', and always protecting the one who has surrendered to you (or has come to take refuge with you) are also mentioned a little later.[66] Though a large number of texts seem to have been written on the theme of jawanmardi (or *futuwwa* in Arabic) in the Middle Ages, most of them seem to be concerned more with jawanmardi brotherhoods 'as formal institutions with an initiation ceremony, a uniform, a hierarchy of authority and codes of conduct'.[67] What is more interesting, however, is that parallel stories

[65] Tor, *Violent Order*, pp. 229–31.

[66] See Kaykavus, *Kitab-i Nasihat Namah, Ma'ruf bah Qabus Namah*, pp. 179–81, cited in Tor, *Violent Order*, pp. 247–8.

[67] Flatt, 'Courtly Culture in the Indo–Persian States', p. 175. While the section titled 'Historical Development of *Jawanmardi*' in Flatt's thesis is rich in detail about different forms of jawanmardi in the Middle Ages, she does not

for each of the aspects of jawanmardi listed by *Qabus-namah* (except the injunction on 'never to extort anything from a prisoner') can be found in *Puruṣaparīkṣā* (see Tables 4.1 and 4.2).

The point, however, is not to match the Persian and Sanskritic tradition, idea for idea. In fact, some of the details of these concepts may not match at all across the two literary traditions. The significance of this parallel lies in the fact that both major literary traditions articulated their political ideals in ways that each would find familiar in the other.[68]

Caste/Varṇa

The ideal political domain for Vidyapati was exclusionary in other respects as well. His incredibly elaborate inventory of manly traits was not represented as accessible to any and every man. In fact, only men of certain social standing determined by birth might aspire to the qualities outlined in *Puruṣaparīkṣā*. Other men and all women were mere props for the privileged few who had the opportunity and the ritual sanction to cultivate the virtues valorized in these stories. Consider the fact that in each of the udāharaṇa kathās of the book, upper-caste men were usually the protagonists with illustrious characters—roughly half of them were Brāhmaṇas, a quarter were Rājapūtas, while the rest were either Vaiśyas or of unidentifiable ritual status. On the other hand, in the pratyudāharaṇa kathās (wherein a counterexample is given to demonstrate the opposite of prescribed conduct), the protagonists were more heterogenous and included characters from varied social backgrounds.

A story about the 'back-biting' kind, set during the reign of Candragupta Maurya, illustrates the author's essentialist perception about caste/varṇa and endogamy. A boy was born to a poor Brāhmaṇa

seem to be aware of Tor's book (cited above), which meticulously traced a more diachronic account of the Persianate–Arabic concept.

[68] Unfortunately no nuanced or detailed study of any of the major medieval Indian states' approach to or investment in jawanmardi/puruṣartha has yet been undertaken, though some interesting general accounts of the significance of manliness for service under the Mughals do exist. See for example, O'Hanlon, 'Manliness and Imperial Service in Mughal North India'.

couple. But his father died early and his mother was forced to abandon him. A *vaṇij* neighbour named Somadatta took pity on him and brought him up. He got his saṃsakāras (literally, to make perfect. Also refers to one of the twelve [sometimes sixteen or more] sacred/purificatory rites prescribed by *Dharmaśāstras*. It is in the latter sense that the word occurs here) done by a Brāhmaṇa, and arranged for a Kāyastha to teach him. However, a Buddhist monk (*kṣapaṇaka*) who saw the boy recited the following śloka:

> Born to mean Brāhmaṇa parentage, fed by a Vaṇij's bread
> Educated by a Kāyastha, he will be mean-minded![69]

When the Brāhmaṇa boy grew up and started receiving generous patronage from the court, instead of being grateful to the Vaṇij, he started extorting money from the latter by invoking his newfound power and position. While the Vaṇij was reduced to penury, the Brāhmaṇa boy became even more ambitious and tried to badmouth the famous minister (Rākṣasa) to the king and vice versa. However, the clever minister and the king discovered the boy's ploy to create mistrust between them. But the story does not end here. 'Going by his conduct', said Rākṣasa, 'he appears to be an illegitimate child [*jārajoayamiti*, literally, "born to someone else", that is, by someone other than his mother's duly wed husband]'. On further enquiry, the minister proved to be right, as the boy's mother admitted that he was born not of her Brāhmaṇa husband but a Cāṇḍāla who had once sneaked into her hut!

It is not difficult to see that this is a cleverly crafted story. The Buddhist monk was at least partially right so far as the boy's character was concerned. However, use of the phrase, 'mean Brāhmaṇa parentage (*hīna-dvija-kule*)' by the monk proved to be misplaced, as the author revealed in the end that Kṣudrabuddhi was actually born to a Cāṇḍāla father.[70] A more interesting irony in the story is the fact that it was

[69] '*Kṣudrabuddhi*' is the word. See *Puruṣaparīkṣā*, p. 84.

[70] It would appear that it was almost a formulaic ploy in stories to discover the lowly origins of a man after he was found to have conducted himself in an immoral manner. Nizam al-Din Awliya's *malfuz*, *Fawa'id al-Fu'ad* has a similar story about a Sayyid's son from a slave girl whose conduct was unbecoming

Candragupta Maurya, a ruler that Vidyapati did not hesitate to identify as 'low born',[71] who insisted on finding out the parentage of the boy.

Within these paradigms, the reference to the historical Candragupta could have been an embarrassment for Vidyapati: his social origins could not be simply reinvented; they had to be explained. Vidyapati's resolution was quite ingenious. He made no effort to hide the monarch's low social origins, and deliberately used the uncommon term *vṛiṣala* or outcaste to describe him. He could have used the more familiar terms Śudra or *antyaja* to communicate the low social origins of Candragupta, but used vṛiṣala since it was apparently used by Cāṇakya, the monarch's minister, to describe his master.[72] The link appears to be deliberate since Vidyapati went on to credit Candragupta's ascension to the throne of Kusumpur to the avenging Brāhmaṇa, Cāṇakya. In fact, in the story about the ubhayavidya (that is, one learned both in the Vedas and folk wisdom), Candragupta is rarely mentioned, and when he is, Vidyapati is careful to craft him as the incidental recipient of the Brāhmaṇa's grace.[73] Clearly, the historical Candragupta did not stretch Vidyapati's didactic disposition too much.

As we saw in the last chapter, the whole text of Vidyapati's writing manual might be read as a reflection on a series of relationships that are either political or perceived as crucial for political harmony. As far as caste/varṇa is concerned, the fault line that emerged there was just one: that between the Śudras on the one hand and the rest of the society on the other. Śudras, in fact, were insouciantly treated as a subhuman slave category, especially in the fourth section (that related

---

of his Sayyid provenance. It was later found that the slave girl had cohabited with another slave. See Sijzi, *Fawa'id al-Fu'ad*, p. 352.

71 *Puruṣaparīkṣā*, p. 124.

72 See Apte, *Sanskrit–English Dictionary*, p. 386. It is noteworthy that in the Middle Ages, the most likely source of information on Candragupta and Cāṇakya was probably the famous Sanskrit play *Mudrārākṣasam* by Viśākhādatta. In this play too, Candragupta is referred to by Cāṇakya as a *rājavṛiṣala* (royal Śūdra). That Vidyapati was familiar with the play is borne out by the fact that he narrated a story about Viśākhādatta in *Puruṣaparīkṣā* at the end of which it is duly noted that he was the author of *Mudrārākṣasam*. See the *sapratibha kathā* in *Puruṣaparīkṣā*, pp. 58–66.

73 See '*Atha ubhayavidya kathā*', *Puruṣaparīkṣā*, pp. 122–8.

to administrative and business transactions), but also occasionally in the first three. Here, for example, is a letter, written presumably by an upper-caste man to his elder brother:

> May it be well. To the most adorable elder brother, a tree-like resting place for affection and care,[74] comparable to father, Ṭhakkura Śrī so and so goes this letter from so and so village, by Śrī so and so, conveying a hundred salutations. By the boundless affection of the respectable brother's feet, all is well here. [I] wish all is well there [too]. The matter is that I cannot disobey the order you gave to free the fettered Śūdra even though he wishes harm [to me], and even though I had tied him up in great anger and with a purpose, hence he was freed the moment I saw your writing. So, therefore, [kindly] do not renounce the flow of affection towards my ever-obedient self.[75]

Indeed, as we saw in the last chapter, compared to *Puruṣaparīkṣā*, *Likhanāvalī* is an elusively simple text. It claims to do no more than teach how to write certain kinds of letters, and appears merely to describe what the author might have considered a 'normative reality'. The letters lack the melodramatic suspense exhibited by most of the stories in *Puruṣaparīkṣā*. Nor do these model missives have the palpably oral texture that gives the tales of *Puruṣaparīkṣā* the quality of being grounded in lived experience. Yet, a careful reading of the letters and documents of *Likhanāvalī* has its rewards. Here is a document from the fourth section, titled '*Vyavahāra Likhanāni*' or 'Conduct-related Writing', of *Likhanāvalī*:

> Siddhiḥ. In the year two hundred and ninety-nine of the erstwhile King Śrī Lakṣamaṇa Senadeva in the tradition of the most revered kings, on Friday the fourteenth day of the bright moon in the month of Bhādra, accordingly when written numerically in the sequence of month, fortnight, date, and day—Lakṣamaṇa Era 299, Bhādra, bright moon, on fourteenth, the Friday. Further, in the realm of the most revered, adorned with all due procedures, light of good deeds, King of all the three lords [namely] the lord of horses, the lord of elephants, and the lord of men, served by thousands of kings, recipient of the grace of

[74] *Sneha mānyatobhaya vyatikara viśrāma mahīruheṣu*. See *Likhanāvalī*, p. 6.

[75] *Likhanāvalī*, p. 6.

Khoda, lauded by panegyrics, Great Suratrāṇasāha's subordinate, Śrī so and so, with all due procedures, like Nārāyaṇa to the Kaṃsas who are his enemies, committed to the devotion of Śiva, a man of character and light of good deeds, in his kingdom of Tirhut, in the country of Ratnapura, subdivision of Mīgo and village Mīmbrā, Śrī so and so Datta puts in his money for buying male and female Śūdras.[76] The recipient of this money, needy Rāutta Śrī so and so sold his slave[77] of Kevaṭa caste, forty-four years old, dark complexioned, named so and so for six silver Taṅkas,[78] similarly his wife [that is, the slave's wife]—thirty years old and fair complexioned named so and so for four silver Taṅkas, similarly their son—sixteen years old and fair complexioned named so and so for three silver Taṅkas, and similarly their daughter, eight years old, dark complexioned named so and so,[79] to look after the cows and perform other duties[80] for the purchaser[81] for the duration of the moon and the sun [that is, forever]. Hereby sold male and female Śudras—four; sale amount—fourteen. For the performance of miscellaneous duties due from both parties—two each. At the residence of the purchaser, these Śudras will plough the land, clear the leftovers, fetch water, carry the palanquin, and perform all other chores. If ever they flee, they will be brought back to slavery with this deed as proof [of legitimate claim over them] even if they are hiding beneath the Royal throne. Witnesses for the purpose are Devadatta, Yajñadatta,

76 *Śudra śudrī krayaṇartha.*

77 The word I have translated as slave is '*dāsam*'.

78 '*Rūpya ṭaṅkasat*' is the phrase. In several documents, rupya (Sanskrit) and taṅka (Persian) are mentioned together. It is possible that the author wanted to create a template which could be used verbatim with minimum alterations in different exchange circles. It is equally likely that the term *rupya-taṅka* was meant to refer to a silver (rupya) *tankha*, a high-denomination currency during this period in north India. It is difficult, however, to trace a definite pattern in the way currencies/denominations are mentioned in *Likhanāvalī*. Several other currencies figure as media of exchange in other documents. These include purāṇas, *paṇas, kākinī, kapardaka*, and so on. Occasionally, a document simply uses the word *mudrā* (money) without specifying the currency.

79 No price for the eight-year-old daughter is mentioned. It is probably to be assumed that since the price for her father, mother, and brother adds up to thirteen ṭaṅkas, the price paid for her is one ṭaṅka!

80 The term is '*gotrāgotra nivārakaṃ*'.

81 '*Dhaniṣu*', literally, 'for the affluent one'.

> Viṣṇumitra, and so on, and it was written by the Kāyastha Śrī so and so with the permission of both parties. Payment due for writing, equally from both—Rupya 1 each. This is also the payment voucher for the sum of 14 silver taṅkas as sale amount. Money received after due verification [for which] the witnesses are the same as for this deed.[82]

This is only one of the several deeds that purport to record trade in humans. The manner of their trading is hardly different from the manner in which other 'commodities' were bought and sold.

In some senses, this document, probably the longest in *Likhanāvalī*, is also somewhat 'representative' of the text: in its longish and stylized characterization of rulers, in recording all the details of the transaction, and in marking the political hierarchy by first referring to the sultan and then to the subordinate raja. One cannot miss the remarkable fact that though the transaction is dated, it still referred to the reigning Sultan as well as the chieftain. This reference was not meant simply to mark time. Rather, it historicized the transaction, giving its executors 'history'. Equally, it also sought to fortify the terms of the transaction in a way that in some senses transcended even the state. The legitimacy of the transaction lay in the fact that it was 'duly documented'. Hence the clear assertion that if the sold Śudras tried to flee, 'they will be brought back to slavery with this *deed as proof even if they were hiding beneath the Royal throne*' (emphasis mine). In their format and texture as well as in their claim to being legal testimony, a majority of the documents in the fourth section of *Likhanāvalī* appear to have borrowed their style from the copper plate Sanskrit inscriptions of North India from the Gupta period onwards.[83] Indeed, the text of the copper plate inscription that recorded the grant of taxes of the village Bisapī by Raja Śivasiṃha to Vidyapati, also makes for interesting comparison with the documents of *Likhanāvalī* in this context.[84]

82 *Likhanāvalī*, pp. 42–3.

83 For the format and framing of 'typical' Sanskrit inscriptions from North India, see Salomon, *Indian Epigraphy*, especially the Appendix entitled 'Selection of Typical Inscriptions', pp. 262–309.

84 For the full text of the inscription, consisting of thirty-eight lines in Sanskrit, along with an English translation and comments on its disputed authenticity by Grierson, see *Indian Antiquary*, vol. XIV, 1885, pp. 191–2.

Clearly, from the high pedestal on which the author seated himself, the Śudras appeared merely as subhuman labouring machines, hardly the kind who could aspire to be real men, the long list of whose qualities were difficult enough to achieve even for those who had the required opportunity, ritual sanction, and material means. Once we understand this, it becomes easier for us to account for the evocative śloka in the opening story of *Puruṣaparīkṣā* that at first sight appears mouth-wateringly liberal and even anti-caste:

Vīraḥ śaurya vivekābhyām utsāhena ca maṇḍitaḥ
Mātā pitroralaṅkṛtu kule kutrāpi jāyate

(One adorned with bravery, discretion, and enthusiasm is a man of valour,
Earning glories for parents, they might be born into whatever lineage!)

It should still be noted that Vidyapati was careful to use the phrase '*kule kutrāpi jāyate*' only in the context of a *vīra puruṣa*, that is, the valorous one, valour being one of the three virtues that he expected in a real man. For the other two traits, namely, intelligence and learning, the field was probably not so wide open.

My point is not, however, to argue that a Brāhmaṇa courtier of the fifteenth century believed in the caste/varṇa hierarchy, or that he treated politics as a sport played among men, preferably *real* men. That would amount to belabouring the obvious. What is more interesting is the manner in which Vidyapati shaped and deployed gender and caste norms in the context of social harmony and political power. It would be helpful, then, to shift the focus from his construction of gender and caste, and consider the author's notion of the state and political power as it is formulated and expressed in *Puruṣaparīkṣā* and *Likhanāvalī*. We will take up a comparable exercise in the context of Vidyapati's *Kīrttilatā* in Chapter 5 in this volume.

Politics

It is extremely difficult for a modern readership to isolate the author's views on the state and politics from a bunch of homilies on a host of themes like sin (*pāpa*), meritorious conduct (*puṇya*), and kindness (*dayā*)—stories and model letters cannot be expected to present an exposition of any idea in a sustained manner. Yet, political power, even the state, is ubiquitous in both texts. Almost every single story in *Puruṣaparīkṣā* is framed either in the backdrop of a state or more directly in terms of how the conduct of a political agent (a king, prince, minister, or courtier) can help or harm the interest of the state. As already seen, this is also true of *Likhanāvalī*, in which a majority of letters are exchanged between political agents and often carry substantive ideas about prescribed and prohibited political conduct. The very first letter written by a king to a priest of the Vīreśvara temple in Varanasi 'whose inner being has been purified by the ultimate wisdom of the Vedic doctrines' lists the reasons for his own (that is, the king's) contentment in a way that might well be read as a checklist of conditions for the political stability of a state:

> With the grace of your feet and by the blessings sent [by you], we are all well and [there is] happiness in our family, good conduct prevails in the realm, the army is powerful, attendants are sinless [loyal?], [our] enemies' morale is low, and the treasure is flawless [full?], and so [I am in a position to] embrace happiness and peace.[85]

Elsewhere, the king is approvingly addressed as 'full of mercy, charity, moral propriety, discretion, and other qualities worthy of a ruler'.[86] In a comparable way, yet another letter counts the qualities of a chief advisor (*mahāmattaka*) as 'accomplished in the six skills of alliance, antagonism, invasion, firm opportunism, strategic ambivalence, and tactical retreat (or refuge)'.[87] He is also described in the same letter as one who 'overcomes the impact of wrong-doing [in the realm] through his aggressive pursuit of justice,[88] is careful in [cultivating] the three bases of mokṣa, deft at defending and adding to the royal treasure, bright and magnificent, soft in speech and tough in action,

85 *Likhanāvalī*, letter no. 3, p. 3.

86 *Likhanāvalī*, letter no. 10, p. 8.

87 *Sandhi vigraha yānāsana dvaidhāśraya*. See *Likhanāvalī*, letter no. 12, p. 10.

88 *Pracaṇḍa daṇḍanīti nirākṛta sakala durvvṛitta prabhāveṣu*. See *Likhanāvalī*, letter no. 12, pp. 10–11.

discerning in [giving] advice, informed about the secrets of the opponents, discreet in [performing] his duties', and so on.[89] *Puruṣaparīkṣā* occasionally refers to the king as a giver of sustenance,[90] an expression that *Likhanāvalī* also uses for the father. If the king did not perform his duties as per norms, all sorts of prohibited conduct could flourish. Loyalty to the king is counted as a virtue, but deserting,[91] even deposing,[92] the king (albeit only by ministers) is allowed in specific circumstances. Reclamation of deserted land for agriculture,[93] looking for good varieties of seeds,[94] mobilizing experienced and skilled soldiers of high ancestry,[95] punishing erring subordinates,[96] and so on, are all counted as normative initiatives that a state could take.

One could go on stitching together Vidyapati's views on statecraft with the help of these two texts. However, that would be a separate exercise in itself and outside the scope of this chapter. I am more interested here in looking at how these expressions could be inflected by the genre of the text. More importantly, I want to explore the way Vidyapati wove together notions of social and perhaps 'religious' propriety with political power. That can help us in understanding how 'religiously' sanctioned norms of caste and gender could constitute important building blocks for the apparently secular pursuit of power. It would also allow us to engage with contentious arguments among scholars about the status, if any, of secularism and religion in premodern India.

Predictably, *Likhanāvalī* often articulated ideas about political conduct in neat formulaic expressions that were probably abbreviated references to established ideas. *Puruṣaparīkṣā*, on the other hand, got itself into clumsier terrain, often putting its precepts in the laboratory of history under testing circumstances, and driving home some of the

[89] *Likhanāvalī*, letter no. 12, pp. 10–11.

[90] *Puruṣaparīkṣā*, p. 106.

[91] *Likhanāvalī*, letter nos. 26 and 53, pp. 21 and 39–40.

[92] See the story of the repentant one (*anuśayīka kathā*), *Puruṣaparīkṣā*, pp. 170–8.

[93] '*Ujjaṭa bhūmi vāsārtha*', *Likhanāvalī*, letter no. 10, p. 8.

[94] *Likhanāvalī*, letter nos. 34 and 52, pp. 26 and 39.

[95] *Likhanāvalī*, letter no. 15, p. 13.

[96] *Likhanāvalī*, letter nos. 19 and 20, pp. 17–18.

same points that find mention in *Likhanāvalī*. In the stories narrated in *Puruṣaparīkṣā*, political prescriptions could be challenged in a more dialogical context, where the author got an opportunity to elaborate on the details of—occasionally even the rationale behind—his beliefs.

The story about the repentant one provides an interesting perspective on the whole question of the sources and limits of political power.[97] King Ratnāṅgada of Kampilā, the story went, was disposed to be unjust (*anyāya pravṛitto babhūva*). Through a series of ślokas, the reader is warned about the ill consequences that such a disposition holds for the king and his subjects. I reproduce one of the ślokas here:

> When women turn immoral and kings turn away from dharma,
> What is not possible then? It is as if an elephant has gone mad!

All the king's ministers deliberated over the issue. Reluctant to commit the sin of sedition, they invited sages to preach the path of righteous conduct (*dharmopadeśaḥ*) to the king. When the sages tried to persuade the king to give up the path of sin and pursue religious merit (puṇya), the king asked, 'What is puṇya?' The sages said: 'Puṇya is the fruit of staying away from committing violence or coveting others' possessions, and so on, and being inclined to kindness, generosity, providing for subjects, conducting *yajñas*, *vratas*, and so on, and generally acting in accordance with the knowledge contained in the Vedas'.[98]

It was not clear how any of this could be 'puṇya' or religious merit. Certainly the king was perplexed and he asked, 'What comes out of that [that is, such conduct]?' The sages replied, 'that helps accomplish the triumvirate (*trivargaḥ sādhyate*)', referring presumably to '*artha, dharma,* and *kāma*', that is, profit, righteousness, and pleasure.

> The Raja retorted, 'Where is the proof [of that]?'
>
> The sages replied, '*vedāḥ pramāṇam, parmeśwaraḥ praṇetā* (Vedas are the proof. God is the promulgator)'.
>
> 'How can the Vedas be His creation, when God himself is non-existent? If He existed, He would have showed up (*upalabhyate*; literally, would have been available), I would have seen Him too. If He does not

97 *Anuśayika Kathā*, *Puruṣaparīkṣā*, pp. 170–8.

98 *Puruṣaparīkṣā*, p. 172.

show up, then He does not exist. You are all respected sages, why are you pestering me with such fallacies? If you say [these things] again, you will attract punishment.'

Thus snubbed, the sages went away. The story goes on to note that the 'ministers and soldiers' deposed the king and placed his younger brother on the throne, but the rest of the story is not significant for my argument. The cited debate is exceptionable in its concern about the authority of the Vedas, which hinges either on their divine provenance or their practical utility. In fact, one might easily place it in the larger history of the dispute between the Vedic, especially the nyāya sytem, and the Cāravāka system of philosophy. In a composition entitled *Sarva-darśana-saṅgraha* (literally, Compilation of All Philosophical Systems), written in the Vijayanagar kingdom around the time of Vidyapati's birth, the very first chapter was devoted to the Cāravāka system.[99] Interestingly, the text notes that the Cāravāka system 'admits of only that evidence which can be seen and does not allow speculation or any non-tangible source as a valid source of knowledge'.[100] Indeed the Cāravākas explicitly ridiculed the authority of the Vedas and claimed that the offerings made to the sacred fire, the three Vedas, the three staves of the ascetic, and the practice of smearing one's body with ashes are mere means of livelihood for those devoid of any intelligence or manliness.[101] In his summary condemnation of the Cāravākas, Vidyapati was echoing the sentiments expressed eloquently by the late-ninth-century commentator and exponent of the nyāya system, Jayanta Bhaṭṭa (ninth–tenth centuries), when the latter argued that 'the wretched Cāravākas, on the other hand, should

[99] The authorship of the text is disputed. Most scholars believe it to be a work by Mādhavācārya, while some attribute it to Cannī Bhaṭṭa. In any case, this was surely one of the better-known works on the philosophies of the subcontinent in the Sanskrit tradition. See Agrawal, 'Introduction', *Sarva-darśana-saṅgraha*, pp. ii–vii.

[100] *Pratyakṣaikapramāṇavāditayā anumānādeḥ anaṅgīkāreṇ pramāṇābhāvāt.* See Mādhavācārya, *Sarva-darśana-saṅgraha*, p. 4.

[101] *Agnihotraṃ trayo vedāstridaṇḍaṃ bhasmaguṇṭhanaṃ/ Buddhipauruṣahīnānāṃ jīviketi Bṛhaspatiḥ iti.* The author of *Sarva-darśana-saṅgraha* attributes these views to Bṛihaspati. See Mādhavācārya, *Sarva-darśana-saṅgraha*, p. 7.

only be neglected since their unworthy logic has no scope for being enumerated as one of the branches of learning'.[102]

Clearly, the story inhabits an episteme that is primarily philosophical and ontological. From a 'modern' perspective, we might add, it is simultaneously secular and religious. To us in the modern age, the conversation between the king and the sages may appear incongruous in the larger scheme of *Puruṣaparīkṣā* (since this text was supposed to instruct the young about naya or 'ethical/righteous conduct'). It is doubtful if that would have been the case for a reader of the text in the fifteenth, or for that matter, even in the seventeenth century.

However, this is not to say that no distinction could be made in the pre- or early-modern period between the explicitly 'religious' and the *laukika*. The very existence of terms like laukika (literally, this-worldly) and *alaukika* (other-worldly) indicates that such distinctions were made and respected. We will revisit the question a little later in the chapter. For Vidyapati, probably the important issue at stake was the valid source of 'authoritative' knowledge.

Epistemology

It would be interesting then to examine the question of authority that our author, Vidyapati, was trying to access to give legitimacy to his own ideas. That would take us to the layered epistemological basis that produced the knowledge on nīti, and on ways of being *puruṣārthavān*. On what grounds did Vidyapati make his claims about gender, caste, and politics? Where did the author himself derive his authority from?

Let us, for a moment, go back to the opening story of *Puruṣaparīkṣā* with which we started. For, that is the only story that the author tells us directly. He attributed the other stories to the character Subuddhi,

[102] *Cārvākāstu varākāḥ pratikṣeptavyā eveti kaḥ kṣudratarkasya tadīyasyeha gaṇanāvasaraḥ*. See Bhaṭṭa, *Nyāyamañjarī* Part I, trans. Bhattacharya, p. 4. The English version I have cited in the text is the translation by Bhattacharyya. See Bhaṭṭa, *Nyāyamañjarī*, vol. 1, trans. Bhattacharya, p. 5. V.N. Jha breaks up the sentence in translation but his rendition is more literal: 'the followers of *Cāravāka*-system are pitiable indeed and therefore, they are surely worthy of being discarded (from consideration). Thus, where is the scope to count here their bad logic?' See Bhaṭṭa, *Nyāyamañjarī* (Āhnika-I), trans. Jha, p. 6.

a muni or sage. Where did the sage's knowledge come from? We saw that Raja Pārāvara stopped him from drawing upon the truths of Kṛtayuga, Tretāyuga, or Dvāpariyuga. Was not the truth of Kaliyuga different from that of the earlier yugas: '*na vā satyaṃ*'? Nor did the sage claim to base his ideas in Śaiva, Vaiṣṇava, Buddhist, or any other sectarian philosophy. Just in case the reader/listener failed to notice the non-sectarian and 'historical' basis of the sage's pronouncements, the author reasserted the fact through a conversation between Sage Subuddhi and Raja Pārāvara at the beginning of the fourth section.[103]

Here, Sage Subuddhi, having finished his exposition on different types of valour, intelligence, and learning, prepared to elaborate on the fruits of puruṣārtha. The Raja expressed his doubts. There were, said the Raja, Buddhists, and there were the followers of the Vedas, and there were others too. All of them get into verbal disputations, and it was natural for them to try and disprove each other. What should a mere mortal do? Even the intelligent might find it difficult to steady their faith in any one of these traditions. Subuddhi's response was two-fold. First, he said that in whatever family and tradition the Almighty caused you to be born, you should follow that tradition. Was there not only one God? And if there was any discrepancy in your conduct even after that, then only God was responsible!

Second, in what might appear to be a volte-face, however, the sage was quick to add that in reality the most enlightened path was the one shown by the Vedas. How did he justify this? Is it possible to resolve the contradiction in his assertions? Was the sage simply following his own dharma by preaching the faith of his own ancestors?

The path of the Vedas, Subuddhi went on to explain, was the best because of three reasons: (*a*) intelligent and logically minded people had traversed this path (*yena gacchati dhīmantas tarkanisṇāta buddhayaḥ*); (*b*) there was evidence that the predictions of astrological, astronomical, and other such sciences were true; and (*c*) a close linguistic examination yielded visible results (*anvaya-vyatirekābhyāṃ sadyo dṛiṣṭa phalodayam*), and its meaning, message, and sentence

[103] This section claims to deal with the fruits of puruṣārtha since the characteristics of puruṣārtha were already described and illustrated in the first three sections.

(*artha-saṃvādi-vākyam*) all prove to be of practical value.[104] Thus, concluded Sage Subuddhi, 'the path proper (*dharma samīcīna*) ... [was the one] ... informed by the Vedas (*vedabodhita*)'.

No reference, one notes, was made (unlike in the story cited earlier about the repentant one) to the Vedas being the revealed word of God or any other claim from the realm of faith. Actual physical corroboration, practical aspects derived through linguistic analysis, and the example set by 'logically thinking men' were the three reasons cited for the supreme authority of the Vedas. Again, it would appear that our author was keenly aware of the raging debates about the authority of the Vedas among Indic philosophers in Sanskrit, a debate that seems to have peaked around the ninth–tenth centuries. Explicating the *sūtras* (literally, a thread; also refers to a formula/equation or a cryptic expression succinctly carrying an instruction or the key to an idea) of Gautama, for example, Jayanta Bhaṭṭa's *Nyāyamañjarī* emphasized precisely these aspects to validate Vedic knowledge in response to imagined objections, presumably from the Buddhists and Cārvākas. Even a cursory look at the section on the 'definition of *pramāṇa*' (*pramāṇalakṣaṇam*: literally the traits/symptoms of pramāṇa) is enough to demonstrate how central linguistic analysis was to the whole question of the authority of the Vedas.[105] Indeed this is true probably of almost all the 'schools' of philosophy under question with the possible exception of the Cāravākas. Equally ubiquitous were claims that Vedic lore could be empirically verified. The 'words (*śabdaḥ*) couched in logic (*tarka*)' too, appears to be a throwback to the *Nyāyikas* as the word 'nyāya' itself could be held (as it was held by Bhaṭṭa) to mean logic.

Coming back to the story, what about the differences amongst the followers of the Vedas themselves? Here, the sage was more cryptic as he merely pointed out that the difference is only in the name

104 *Puruṣaparīkṣā*, pp. 162–4. Alternatively, the phrase may be translated as follows: 'its utterances (*saṃvādi-vākyam*) accord with the goals (*artha*)'.

105 Bhaṭṭa, *Nyāyamañjarī*, Part I, ed. Shukla, pp. 12–14. To get a sense of how contentious these debates around pramāṇa (instrument of true knowledge) were, see Kataoka, 'The *Mīmāṃsā* Definition of *Pramāṇa*'; Kataoka, 'What Really Protects the Vedas?'; Hegde, 'The Nature and Number of *Pramāṇas*'; and Kastura, 'Dharmakīrti's Theory of Truth'.

(*nāmnaiva bhinna mahaḥ*). For, the sages had already determined by logic that there was only one God in this world (*nirṇīta munibhiḥ satarka matibhiśced viśvam ekeśvaraṃ*).[106]

Can we say, then, that our author anchored the authority of the sage in the Vedas and in logic, fully cognizant of the fact that the Vedas did not merely denote the four famous tomes, but were shorthand for a whole variety of literature of ancient times? Were the Vedas supreme only because their knowledge could yield tangible and desirable results? Let me briefly get into another story, probably the most complex story of *Puruṣaparīkṣā*:

> [Once upon a time] there lived Raja Vikramāditya in the city of Ujjayinī. One day, a certain Brāhmaṇa came to the gates [of his palace]. The Brāhmaṇa said:
>
>> Never should a Raja give up the holy task of providing for his subjects,
>> More so if the subject is a miserable Brāhmaṇa suffering from an ailment.
>
> Hence, 'His Highness must protect me, a miserable and ailing Brāhmaṇa.' The Raja's heart was filled with pity upon seeing the Brāhmaṇa in that condition. Curious as to what will happen to the Brāhmaṇa, the Raja said to Varāha, an expert in astrology, 'O, Varāha! Will the Brāhmaṇa survive?' Varāha said, 'He will be cured without having to take liquor (*madyapāna*). He will live for the duration of a man's age [that is, for a hundred years].' On hearing this, the Raja thought, 'Being learned in *śastras*, how could he say such a thing? How can he rule out something that has not even been mentioned? Where is the context for the Brāhmaṇa drinking liquor? Alright, let's see.'
>
> The Raja called for a vaidya [doctor] by the name of Hariścandra and asked, 'What is his ailment and what is the cure for it?' The vaidya said, 'It is the *brahmakīṭa*[107] and there is no antidote for it.' The Raja said,

[106] Another composition of Vidyapati entitled *Vibhāgasāra* also has an interesting conversation, at the very beginning of the text, between Śiva and Viṣṇu over the possession of Ganga. The message of that short conversation is also similar to the one put in the mouth of Subuddhi in *Puruṣaparīkṣā*. See Vidyapati, *Vibhāgasāra*, p. 39.

[107] This is a compound word, *brahma+kīṭa*. *Kīṭa* simply referred to an insect or a worm. *Brahma*, when used as a prefix before a noun, carried the

'The Almighty would not provide medicine for a disease? That is just not possible.' The vaidya said, 'The *brahmakīṭa* gnaws at the flesh in his head and that is why he is going crazy with pain. The *brahmakīṭa* does not burn in fire; iron cannot cut it; water cannot dissolve it; it is killed only by alcohol. Hence, alcohol is the medicine for it!' The Raja touched his ears and said, 'Fie! Do not utter another word—such a sin. You will offer alcohol to a Brāhmaṇa?'

'Without that he will not survive', said the vaidya, 'that is certain.'

The Raja was most committed to *dharma* and keen to alleviate others' pain: he called for Ācārya Śabarasvāmī,[108] learned in the *dharmaśāstras*, and asked, 'What is permitted [under the circumstances]?' The ācārya said, 'If the disease cannot be cured by any other means [and] if the vaidya is absolutely sure about it, then the Brāhmaṇa will not fall from grace upon drinking alcohol.' The vaidya said, 'If he is cured by any means other than taking alcohol, then the sin will be mine!' Having understood that both were convinced about their own knowledge of their śāstras, the Raja instructed the brāhmaṇa to drink alcohol. As alcohol was brought in, a voice from the sky proclaimed, 'O, Śabara! Don't you dare!' Śabarasvāmī insisted, 'O, Brāhmaṇa! Go ahead and take the drink. The god of the speech is expert merely in the sum of letters, phrases, and sentences. Where is His understanding of dharma's rulings?' Later on, flowers were showered on Śabarasvāmī's head.

Overwhelmed, the Raja and the courtiers put their trust in Śabarasvāmī and gave alcohol to the Brāhmaṇa. All his life, the Brāhmaṇa had never tasted alcohol. As a result, the *brahmakīṭa* fell to the ground by the sheer smell of the substance (the Brāhmaṇa did not have to even take a sip). To test the veracity of the vaidya's assertion, the Raja threw the *brahmakīṭa* into fire. Yet, the worm did not burn in fire, nor did it dissolve in water, nor could it be cut with iron. But it dissolved in a drop of alcohol. Seeing this, everyone was amazed.[109]

---

sense of being divinely blessed to be immortal, indestructible, accurate, perfect, or infallible. Thus, a *brahmakīṭa* would probably denote a worm that was indestructible/immortal/incurable.

108 The context suggests that this is the same Śabarasvāmī who famously wrote a commentary on *Pūrvamīmaṃsāsūtra*, entitled *Mīmāṃsā-śabara-bhāṣya*. See Kataoka, 'The *Mīmāṃsā* Definition of Pramāṇa', pp. 90–1. Also see Pollock, 'The Languages of Science in Early Modern India', p. 36 and endnote no. 52.

109 '*Śastra vidya kathā*', *Puruṣaparīkṣā*, pp. 104–8.

It is pertinent to note that this story is an illustration of the Śastravidya (that is, one learned in the śastras) and not of the *Vedavidya* (that is, one learned in the Vedas), for which there is a separate story. Yet, as we saw earlier, the author cited the tangible truths of astronomy, astrology, and so on, as proof of the veracity of the Vedas. Nor should we miss the momentary clash between the gods in the skies and the apparently logical and practical wisdom of the learned man, Śabarasvamī, which was resolved in favour of the latter. The truth of the śāstras and the Vedas, in the epistemological world of Vidyapati had to be demonstrated empirically, if need be, even in the face of the gods. Both logic as well as empirical veracity, then, are deployed by the author to prove the truth of his homilies. To be sure, he also invoked the authority of the Vedas, but only after reassuring the readers/listeners that the *Vedavākya* was in line with the thoughts of logically thinking men as well as empirical evidence.

Yet there was another source of authority tapped by Sage Subuddhi and the author Vidyapati Ṭhakkura to buttress their arguments. This was the authority of 'history' or more appropriately, *itihāsa*. The choice of the genre of '*udāharaṇa kathā*' could not have been incidental. As noted above, *udāharaṇa* (literally, example/instance) was known in Sanskrit literature since ancient times.

That Sage Subuddhi claimed to have learnt his lessons from an examination of the past went well with the genre of *udāharaṇa kathā* in which he was himself a character. We have already seen that the lessons in nīti/naya were illustrated through and authorized by 'stories' taken from 'this-worldly' time. This recourse to history by Vidyapati should not be lost on us. In one of his uncharacteristically nebulous formulations, for example, Pollock made the following claim back in 1989: 'History, one might thus conclude, is not simply absent from or unknown to Sanskritic India; rather it is denied in favor of a model of "truth" that accorded history no epistemological value or social significance'.[110]

As noted earlier in the chapter, many of the precepts of *Puruṣaparīkṣā* reflected directly upon the debates between the *nyāya*,

110 Pollock, 'Mīmāṃsā and the Problem of History in Traditional India', p. 610.

mīmāṃsā, and *sāṅkhya* schools of Vedic philosophy on the one hand, and the Buddhists and Cāravākas on the other. These long-debated and respected ideals, now woven into a discourse on nīti, carried with them some of their own 'authority'. After all, as Jayanta Bhaṭṭa pointed out, narratives of bygone times (*itihāsapurāṇas*) should be one way of supporting the Vedic lore.[111]

A literary device that helped Vidyapati accomplish this was the tradition of '*subhāṣita*' in Sanskrit literature. In fact, the whole text of *Puruṣaparīkṣā*, and occasionally even *Likhanāvalī*, is liberally sprinkled with independent couplets of (un)identifiable origin. These were drawn from the free-floating reserve of an ever-growing śloka tradition, called subhāṣita, literally, 'well said', a 'witty saying', or an aphorism. As such subhāṣita belonged both to the folk as well as to the classical tradition, and very often, to a classical rendering of folk traditions. As Daud Ali pointed out, '[g]iven the close imbrication of the written and oral dimensions of the *subhāṣita* world, we may plausibly suggest that the anthology [of *subhāṣita*] functioned as an instrument of fixity which actually helped sustain rather than ossify the continued renewal, transmission, and circulation of this open-ended knowledge'.[112] They represented no particular ideology as such, and somewhat like Hindi film songs, one could find just about any idea expressed in them. Indeed, one could even compose a customized couplet oneself and simply represent it as part of subhāṣita.

As such subhāṣita represented not a defined set of ideas, but an open ended, ever growing literary genre: any beautifully crafted Sanskrit couplet was a subhāṣita. Ali's understanding of subhāṣita as an 'artefact of ethical life', however, is a little different from mine. Subhāṣitas, according to him, 'formed a communicative idiom rather than simply a legitimatory discourse', thus underlining 'a deeply dialogical aspect of ethical practice'.[113] Yet the very fact, one may argue, that characters in a tale often sought refuge in subhāṣitas for

[111] *Itihāsapurāṇābhyāṃ vedaṃ samupabṛhṃyet.* See Bhaṭṭa, *Nyāyamañjarī*, Part I, ed. Shukla p. 3.

[112] Ali, 'The *Subhāṣita* as an Artefact of Ethical Life', p. 32. I am indebted to Whitney Cox for this reference.

[113] Ali, 'The *Subhāṣita* as an Artefact of Ethical Life', p. 34.

justifying their actions meant that these were *also* intended as floating touchstones for contingent truthlets. That such truth claims could be countered with other subhāṣitas did not mean that they had no legitimatory role; rather, it meant that their authority was not absolute and they could be challenged in what Ali calls 'a deeply dialogical' context.

* * *

The conversational and dialogical framing of *Puruṣaparīkṣā* (bolstered by clever deployment of subhāṣitas) gave this text on nīti a wider reach and accessibility. This was very much in keeping with a general tendency towards a more dynamic and expansive literary culture in the fifteenth century. Paradoxically, it was also accompanied in *Puruṣaparīkṣā*, as the discussion above suggested, by parallel strategies of exclusion where women and 'lower' castes were concerned. Five important points emerged through the chapter. First of all, in order to develop a historical–critical understanding of Vidyapati, we need to rescue him from the tyranny of labels—Śaiva, Vaiṣṇava, or Śākta—as well as from the confines of 'regional' history that has so 'naturally' embraced the fifteenth century. The varied literary traditions of Sanskrit, among other things, helped Vidyapati set aside his own Śaiva/Śakta predilections and claim that his ideas about puruṣa and nīti were not anchored in any sectarian ideology. In matters of 'secular' law and public morality, there was a higher truth beyond the sectarian quibbles of Śaivism, Vaiṣṇavism, Buddhism, and so on.[114] His protagonists could receive their share of divine grace from Śiva, Narāyaṇa, Buddha, or Khoda—these details did not matter so long as the secular power was duly constituted through all established procedures, and was committed to protecting the subjects (*prajāḥparipālayan*) as well as (Vidyapati's notion of) the normative social order. In any case, the learned courtier was writing in the 'secular' tradition of the nīti texts as against the other, equally vibrant, tradition of *dharmaśāstras*, but I will come back to that a little later.

[114] If Buddhism continued to be a point of reference (long after its decline) in the early-fifteenth century, it suggests that Vidyapati was probably participating in a long tradition of dialogues between various philosophical/sectarian systems.

The futility of tags such as 'local/sub-regional' for a courtier–scholar writing in Sanskrit in the middle of the 'vernacular millennium', however, may not be immediately obvious. Yigal Bronner and David Shulman in their study make a clear distinction between 'regional Sanskrit poetry' and 'erudite and theoretical Sanskrit compositions' of the second millennium. They identify a regional composition as one that (*a*) aims at a local audience, (*b*) shows evidence of local linguistic materials, and (*c*) is primarily concerned with issues or themes rooted in the culture, society, and history of specific places.[115] Put to this litmus test, where would the two texts examined above figure? *Puruṣaparīkṣā* is neither poetry nor erudite and theoretical. There are too few intra-textual signs to suggest that it was aimed at a local audience, either in terms of the thematic or the manner of articulation. It is true that occasionally, the author did use certain local vernacular words, but these did not interfere with the overwhelmingly non-local Sanskrit flavour of his compositions.

Notwithstanding his attachment to the subordinate local principality of Tirhut, Vidyapati invoked ideas that looked beyond his immediate geographical confines. In fact, all of Vidyapati's Sanskrit compositions, and probably even the Apabhraṃśa texts as we shall see in the next chapter, speak from, and speak to, a larger trans-local sphere defined by the boundaries of a cosmopolitan Sanskrit literary heritage. It is pertinent to recall here that *Puruṣaparīkṣā* itself was an expanded and slightly reworked version of the much shorter text that the author had evocatively titled *Bhūparikramaṇa*. A list of the places where the stories of *Puruṣaparīkṣā* were set makes for impressive reading, and testifies to the (literally) expansive horizon of the scholar.[116] As a character in one of his stories remarked, seeing different places (*deśānagatvā*) was crucial for cultivating a tender (*komaladhiyā*), and probably higher sensibility.[117]

[115] Bronner and Shulman, '"A Cloud Turned Goose"'.

[116] These include, apart from Mithila/Tirhut, Candrātapā, Ujjayinī, Yoginīpura, Raṇastambha, Kānyakubja, Kāśī, Kamboja, Dvārakā, Gauda, Devagirī, Viśālā, Yuthikāpura, Kauśambī, Dhārā, Avantī, Vijayapura (Vijayanagar?), and so on.

[117] *Puruṣaparīkṣā*, p. 76.

Second, if we look beyond the binary of a universalistic or a local Sanskrit, a more interesting aspect emerges that concerns the presence of Persian—the 'other' equally vibrant literary culture of the period. Occasionally Vidyapati would very imaginatively deploy Perso-Arabic words such as *kāphara*[118] in *Puruṣaparīkṣā* to refer to political rivals. As discussed in the last chapter, as well as earlier in this chapter, in the imagined norm of Vidyapati's writing manual, both the Nārāyaṇa-like Raja as well as the recipient of Khoda's grace, Suratrāṇasāha, could be invoked to mark the purchase of slaves. The very fact that he chose to write on the art of writing, might in fact be a valuable piece of 'evidence'. As we have already seen in Chapter 3 in this volume, it is very likely that in composing *Likhanāvalī*, Vidyapati was actually drawing upon the Persian genre of insha texts.[119]

Third, as we saw, Vidyapati articulated his political ideals through a discourse on puruṣa or rather how to be (or identify) one. He drew legitimacy for his ideas rather eclectically from the established tradition of the wisdom of a sage, the authority of the Vedas verified with the power of logic, even the perspicacity of a wandering Buddhist monk. Above all, he yoked his teachings to an examination of a past that was, at least conceptually, not very distant from his present. Recreating a world populated by competing kingdoms, sultans, and rajas, he grounded his stories in contemporary flavour, and appealed to his readers' historical common sense more than anything else.

Clearly, much more was happening in the fifteenth century than what a narrow focus on regional history, or for that matter, a unitary Sanskrit cosmopolis—dead or living—would allow the historians to account for.

However, gestures towards Persian, history, and common sense, I would argue, should not obscure the fact that there were serious limits to the apparent universalism of Vidyapati's ideas. And this brings me to the fourth point. *Puruṣaparīkṣā* was an atypical text on nīti in the form of an udāharaṇa kathā. One may point out that because it laid down its nīti through 'real life stories', it also exposed the extent

118 Persian: kafir or non-Muslim. It was against a host of such kafir rajas that the exemplary protagonist of the *satyavīra kathā* fought. See *Puruṣaparīkṣā*, pp. 28–32.

119 For a detailed discussion of this aspect, see Chapter 3 in this volume.

to which nīti was undergirded by dharma precepts in the lived world, as against the neater division of textual traditions. Interestingly, even Caṇḍeśvara's *Rājanītiratnākara*, a fourteenth-century digest on politics from the same region, referred thirty-six times to Manu and eleven times to Nārada, while only once citing from *Arthaśastra* and twice from *Kāmaṇḍaka*, the latter two being among the few conventional nīti texts cited.[120] Let us recall that unlike typical texts on nīti such as those from medieval South India or ancient India, *Puruṣaparīkṣā* did deal in some detail, not just with artha and kāma but also with the other two fruits of puruṣārtha, namely, dharma and mokṣa. Once we understand this, it becomes possible for us to account for the fact that our author managed to explicitly lay out *dharmaśāstric* precepts about distinct (and discriminatory) gender and caste roles, and weave them together with his ideas about politics and statecraft. If we posit political power in the broader (both modern and postmodern) sense, then it is easy to see how dharma-sanctioned gender and varṇa categories themselves become a source of authority.

Since the overarching epistemological structure of both *Puruṣaparīkṣā* and *Likhanāvalī* is marked by primarily this-worldly/laukika concerns, and since it took many of its 'social' precepts for granted, Vidyapati could treat gender, varṇa, and state as part of a continuum, a singular domain of socio-political order. The fact that a ritual hierarchy presumed to be axiomatic underpinned the discourse on puruṣa and nīti indicates that in the lived world of the fifteenth century, the discriminatory regimes of gender, varṇa, and politics could be expressed and probably experienced as commonsensical knowledge derived from an examination of a this-worldly past.

At the historiographical edge of this discussion, let me offer brief comments on two interesting issues. In a well-argued piece in 2009, Velcheru Narayana Rao and Sanjay Subrahmanyam tried to dispel doubts about the existence in India of works on political theory (other than those in the ancient 'classical' period) in the precolonial era, by noting the existence of a varied body of Telugu materials between the fourteenth and the late-eighteenth centuries.[121] To begin with,

[120] See Jayaswal, 'Introduction', *Rājanīti-ratnākara*, p. 37.

[121] See Rao and Subrahmanyam, 'Notes on Political Thought'.

I would like to add at least two more works from North India to the Rao–Subrahmanyam list: Vidyapati's *Puruṣaparīkṣā* and Caṇḍeśvara's *Rājanītiratnākara*, from the fifteenth and the fourteenth centuries, respectively. However, my reading of Vidyapati also inflects the argument of Rao and Subrahmanyam when they point to a clear conceptual separation of nīti and dharma in the minds of the Telugu writers as they theorized on politics during the fourteenth through the seventeenth century. To be sure, Vidyapati also operates with the 'conceptual' distinction between nīti and dharma. Yet, as I have tried to show, such textual distinctions notwithstanding, the ideals of politics in medieval Tirhut were heavily underwritten by ideas that one might usually associate with *dharmic* traditions, not just in the sense of 'ethical duty' and legal injunctions but also in the more contemporary and anachronistic sense of the 'religious'. That is why, in spite of all measures of discrimination, Vidyapati's text on nīti could claim to be universalistic in its reach through a complex discourse in which it was possible 'legitimately' to chant '*kule kutrāpi jāyate*', and still stick to a strict ritual regime.

More substantively, my explorations complicate the contrast that Pollock raised between this-worldly and other-worldly knowledge in the context of 'the languages of science in India'. Pollock observed: '[T]he vehicle of organized, systematic *laukika*, or this-worldly, knowledge before colonialism was Sanskrit, while the regional languages, at least in their incarnation as literary idioms, were in the first instance the voice of *alaukika*, or other-worldly wisdom (a situation closely paralleled by Latin and the European vernaculars).'[122]

On the face of it, there is little to contest in this formulation. The words laukika and alaukika are integral to Sanskrit literary traditions, and have not been invented by Pollock. These words also help escape the anachronistic parallel of religious–secular, though a modern reader is likely to understand laukika as 'secular' and alaukika as 'religious' unless the differences are clearly laid out by the author. It would be even more problematic, both historically as well as politically, to curtail this discussion without remarking on the almost organic interdependence of the two. And let me strike another note

[122] Pollock, 'The Languages of Science in Early Modern India', p. 25.

of caution about falling back on the worn-out construct of 'legitimation of secular power by religious authorities'.[123] As I have tried to demonstrate in this chapter, at least in the context of Vidyapati and the world of fifteenth-century Sanskrit knowledge he articulated, the two apparently distinct categories of laukika and alaukika were formulated within a singular epistemology in which artha and kāma were posited together alongside dharma and mokṣa within the ritually hierarchized and gendered notion of puruṣārtha.

Finally, as argued in Chapter 2 in this volume, if knowledge formations constituted the wider field within which the ideas of what passed for legitimate authority were cultivated, it is crucial to map the grids of these dynamic formations. Texts on philosophy and dharmaśāstras might have formed a pool of prescriptives, but it was popular genres like stories that mediated these prescriptives in accessible and durable, if somewhat open-ended, ways to people at large. It is to be noted that stories circulated continuously through the middle ages within and across languages. It is no coincidence that most collections of stories after the ninth–tenth centuries often tended to recycle already known stories, many of which were compiled in earlier collections like *Pañcatantra*, *Hitopadeśa*, and *Bṛihatkathā*. Some of the stories in *Puruṣaparīkṣā* too, might be traced to certain other collections of stories.[124] Unlike abstruse treatises or law books, stories had a vibrant life in oral cultures. If the former set out the do's and don't's in neat and conceptualized ways, the latter preached in the

123 For my take on the problems in the way the issue of 'legitimation of authority' is typically dealt with in modern historiography of pre-modern times, see Chapter 2 in this volume.

124 Apart from the obvious examples of the Cāṇakya and Viśākhadatta stories of *Puruṣaparīkṣā*, some of the Vikramāditya and Bhoja stories too, were recycled from earlier compilations. Thus, for example, the story about Raja Vikramāditya throwing himself into fire every night to ensure that one of his rival kings' treasuries are full, can be found in an earlier and more elaborate version in Bilahaṇa's *Vikramāṅkadevacaritam*. See *Puruṣaparīkṣā*, pp. 6–14; Bilahaṇa, *Vikramāṅkadevacaritam*, pp. 177–84. What is significant, however, is that in the Maithil Brāhmaṇa's text, the story serves not so much to glorify its protagonist as to illustrate the best example of generosity as a trait of the ideal man.

name of entertainment. The authors of kathās and prabandhas, it cannot be a mere coincidence, always claimed to entertain. The objective of propagating a set of ideals went hand in hand with entertainment as we saw in the case of both *Prabandhacintāmaṇi* and *Puruṣaparīkṣā*. It was precisely for this reason that these must have been more effective as a means to orient political imagination in specific ways.

Earlier in the chapter, it was noted how it would have been difficult to imagine a text like *Puruṣaparīkṣā* being composed in an earlier era. One may add that in its political salience, the *Test of a Man* could transcend its immediate environs and age. We know that it continued to be useful even to the British in the nineteenth century in a very different context. So, we may well ask: wouldn't texts like these have played some role, in terms of preparing the 'subjects', a *prajā*, for state builders in the fifteenth and sixteenth centuries too?

An interesting point that came out of the brief comparison of *Prabandhacintāmaṇi* and *Puruṣaparīkṣā* was that the latter too took up popular 'legendarized' historical protagonists like Bhoja and Vikramaditya, alongside more recent characters, to weave in its tales. Yet, compared to his early-fourteenth-century counterpart, Vidyapati, more than a hundred years later, was far more focussed on divesting his stories of all excrescences that did not fit into his didactic scheme. Indeed, the overarching narrative structure used by Vidyapati was always about delineating the ideal man in sharp relief. A few years before he wrote *Puruṣaparīkṣā*, however, he also composed another text that told the story of an ideal man. This text did not have the same theoretical rigour in defining the characteristics of the ideal male protagonist, but it engaged far more directly with the contemporary world of realpolitik, and revolved around only one protagonist (may be two, depending on how one looks at it). The text was *Kīrttilatā*, and the protagonist was the poet's then patron Kīrttisiṃha. It is this text that I take up for extended consideration in the next chapter.

5 *Entangled Vines of Glory*

Kīrttilatā *and Its Many Worlds*

The unification of vernacular language not only partakes of the logic of the unification of a new type of political space but is historically co-present with it.

—Sheldon Pollock[1]

I am familiar with the occupational hazard of historians, namely that a historian preparing herself to write, say, about the eighteenth century ends up writing mostly about the seventeenth century because it comes to seem so fundamental to the question at issue.

—James C. Scott[2]

1 Pollock, 'India in the Vernacular Millennium', p. 58.
2 Scott, 'Preface', in *The Art of Not Being Governed*, pp. xi–xii.

This chapter focusses primarily on Vidyapati's only major extant Apabhraṃśa/Avahaṭṭha work, namely, *Kīrttilatā*, and seeks to map out its many worlds.[3] It is divided into seven sections. The first three sections are focussed on the organization of the text, its language, and its genre. These sections attempt to locate the language and the genre of *Kīrttilatā* within a long history of Apabhraṃśa vis-à-vis Sanskrit, Persian, and other 'literary languages'. All of these traditions were dynamic and complex, thus making it imperative to place their fluid histories within their specific place–time–character co-ordinates. In the process, these sections help to complicate the story of 'vernacularization' in the second millennium. A focus on the historical development of ākhyāyikā as a separate genre, in Sanskrit and in other languages on the other hand, helps to throw the uniqueness of *Kīrttilatā* in bolder relief.

The next three sections are more engaged with the 'contents' of the text. Each of these three sections analyse the three different 'worlds' illuminated by the text: that of the local domain of Mithila; that of the city as a cosmopolitan space where conventional boundaries of propriety appear to break down; and that of the 'imperial' court (and might) of the Sharqi state that ostensibly patronized an ethical ('dhārmic') order. In the light of the literary and historical analysis of the preceding sections, the last section, 'Literature and Politics', tries to work out a more nuanced understanding of the fifteenth century literary-political and knowledge formations in Mithila.

In the entire oeuvre of Vidyapati, *Kīrttilatā* is probably one of the better circulated, and definitely the best preserved text. Not surprisingly, scholars of the medieval Hindi language, and of Hindi literature in general, have written extensively about it, publishing several critical editions, translating it into Hindi and Maithili, investigating its language and subject matter, and generally remarking

[3] Vidyapati also reportedly wrote another text in Avahaṭṭha, namely, *Kīrttipatākā*. However, the extant manuscripts of this text are severely damaged, and questions have also been raised about whether it was composed by Vidyapati himself or is wrongly attributed to him. It may be pertinent to note here that one of the two plays by the author, namely, *Gorakṣavijaya*, is a bilingual text with a large part of it in Avahaṭṭha and Maithili. See Vidyapati, *Gorakṣavijaya*.

on its 'greatness'. It was Haraprasad Sastri who first 'discovered' a manuscript of the work in the Durbar Library of Kathmandu in Nepal in 1898. Several manuscripts have since been found. As the 'Foreword' in one of the critical editions reports, they are preserved in the British Museum, London; Nagari Pracharini Sabha, Kashi; Jayaswal Research Institute, Patna; Patna College Library, Patna; Sanskrit Vishvavidyalay, Darbhanga; Ganganath Jha Research Institute, Prayag; Bhaudaji Collection of the Asiatic Society, Mumbai; and Anup Sanskrit Library, Bikaner.[4] Some of these manuscripts are exact replicas of each other and appear to have been copied at unspecified dates from another one in this group. Find-spots of some of these are known, while for others, they might be guessed with a fair amount of certitude. The one in the Durbar Library of Kathmandu, belongs to the same cultural zone as that inhabited by Vidyapati, and it might be safe to assume that this copy was prepared in the same region. The one in the possession of the Nagari Pracharani Sabha was found in the village of Asanī, Fatehpur district, in the undivided state of Uttar Pradesh. The copy that is preserved in the Anup Library, Bikaner, also has a Sanskrit *chāyā* (translation in Sanskrit), and mentions that it was prepared for Sūra Bhaṭṭa, younger brother of Gopāla Bhaṭṭa. This is also the oldest of the dated manuscripts with the year 1672 of Vikram Saṃvat (1615 CE) given, not in figures but in coded words, following an established Sanskrit convention.[5] This manuscript is also the most complete one. The script of all the manuscripts is Devanāgarī. Of all the critical editions published so far, the one annotated by Virendra Shrivastav and published by the Bihar Rāṣṭra Bhāṣā Pariṣad appears to be the most carefully edited with variable readings in the different manuscripts noted in the footnotes. This is the one that I have followed and all citations of *Kīrttilatā* in this chapter refer to this edition.

Kīrttilatā also happens to be the only text of Vidyapati that occasionally caught at least the fleeting attention of some of the major scholars writing in English, from Jagdeesh Narayan Sarkar

[4] Varma, 'Prākkathana', in Vidyapati, *Kīrttilatā*, ed. Shrivastav (henceforth *Kīrttilatā*), p. *ga*.

[5] Shrivastav, 'Prastāvanā', in *Kīrttilatā*, p. 3.

to R.S. McGregor, David Lorenzen, and Francesca Orsini. There are three different sets of plausible reasons for this: (*a*) it is one of the few 'vernacular' medieval texts that explicitly reflects on the choice of its language; (*b*) it provides one of the most detailed and specific descriptions of a cityscape, its residential quarters, and market place, as well as its palace complex; and (*c*) those researching the emergence of religious/ethnic/sectarian identities and/or conflict in premodern times find in it one of the earliest examples of a Brāhmaṇic/Hindu author apparently drawing a neat contrast between the 'Hindu' self and the Turk (read Muslim) other.

Yet there is more to *Kīrttilatā* than these issues. In the course of my discussion, I will engage with these and other themes. However, for a textually grounded understanding of the relevant historical issues, it would be useful to start by exploring the structural, linguistic, and generic traits as well as constraints that may have bound *Kīrttilatā* as a text.

The Text

Following a long-established tradition, the first few verses of salutation and dedication in the text are in Sanskrit even though the rest of it is almost entirely in Apabhraṃśa. These early verses beautifully set the tone of the text and the expectations of the listener/reader. The opening verse of salutation is somewhat unusual as it draws a sketch of a conversation between the child Gaṇeśa and Lord Śiva, his father:

> 'O Father, give me that stem of the lotus in the Ganga on your head.'
> 'O Son, this is not the stem of a lotus, it is the lord of the snakes.'
> Upon this, [toddler] Gaṇeśa is crying and Śambhū smiles.
> May Gauri's amusement on seeing this protect all.
> Moon, Sun, and Agni are [His] three sparkling eyes.
> I pray at the lotus-feet of Śambhū who destroys the darkness of ignorance.[6]

[6] *Kīrttilatā*, ed. Shrivastav, p. 47. All translations are mine, unless otherwise indicated.

This is followed by a śloka dedicated to Sarasvatī, the goddess of learning, who is hailed as 'a means to all aspirations, the dancer in the theatre of the tongue, the flame that lights up the elements, the flowing joy-stream of *sṛingāra*, and so on, and the companion of glory till the end of time'.[7] The next two verses refer to the author's patron, Kīrttisiṃha, and remark how, in Kaliyuga, literature is found in every home, its listeners (*śrotā*) in every place, connoisseurs (*rasajñātā*) in every country, yet patrons are difficult to find in the world. What follows is a series of couplets in Apabhraṃśa, nine to be precise, which reflect on the character, purpose, and language of, as also expectation from, the text at hand. It would be best to let the author speak for himself:

> How will the vine of glory spread in the farmland of the three worlds?
> If a high perch is not secured on top of the syllable-post?
> That is why, somehow, with effort, I put together this composition[8]
> The rogues, being rogues, will disparage it [but] good men will appreciate [it]
> The rogues revile and the good men appreciate, it is only fair
> A poisonous snake must spit venom, good men spread amṛita only
> Good people secretly wish to befriend every single person
> Antagonism even by mistake [should be avoided], may the rogues never be enemies
> Rogues' scorn does not affect either the toddler moon[9] or Vidyapati's language[10]
> One adorns God's forehead, the other charms the aesthetes[11]
> How do I raise awareness? Who must I apprise?
> How to arouse interest among the dull?
> If my language is appealing
> Those who follow would consider it appreciatively
> A black bee relishes the juice of flowers, an aesthete grasps the spirit of literature
> Good men do good unto others while the rogues are full of spite

7 *Kīrttilatā*, p. 47.

8 *Kabba*—Sanskrit, *kāvya*.

9 *Bālacanda*—Sanskrit, bālacandra.

10 *Bhāsā*—Sanskrit, *bhāṣā*.

11 *Nā-ara*—Sanskrit, *nāgara* (literally, city-bred).

Sanskrit speech is dear to the intellect-driven[12]
No one grasps the essence in Prakrit
Desi speech[13] is sweet to everyone
Hence I accordingly compose in Avahaṭṭha[14]

Going by the standard conventions followed by Indic authors around this time, this is an unusually long explanation/apologia for the text and its language by the author, indeed, for Vidyapati himself; he was far less expansive in his other compositions. It testifies to the author's keen awareness of having embarked on a somewhat unusual project, definitely with regard to its language, and possibly having to do with its subject matter as well. We would have occasion below to remark upon the anxiety expressed in these lines by a Sanskrit scholar keen to reach out to 'simple folks' in a language more accessible to them. We will come back to the matter of the language in question, Avahaṭṭha, a little later. Let us first take a brief look at the way *Kīrttilatā* is organized through a skeletal outline of the narrative.

[12] *Buha-aṇa*—Sanskrit, *buddhajana.*

[13] *Desila ba-anā*—Sanskrit, *deśīvāṇī.*

[14] My translation of these famous lines is close to the Maithili translation by Govind Jha. See Vidyapati, *Kīrttilatā*, ed. and trans. Jha, p. 5. But it differs somewhat from that by McGregor who renders the couplet as follows:

> 'Sanskrit appeals to the learned but who does not grasp and relish natural speech,
> To everyone the speech of his region is sweet and so one should speak in Avahaṭṭha'.

See McGregor, *Hindi Literature*, p. 30. The Hindi translations of these two lines also vary confusingly. Shivprasad Singh's translation in Hindi, translated again into English, is closer to mine:

> Sanskrit speech is dear only to the learned
> Prākṛit lacks the essence of aesthetic flavours
> Desi language is relished by everyone
> That's why I speak in the same Avahaṭṭha.

See Singh, *Kīrttilatā aur Avahaṭṭha Bhāṣā*, pp. 229–30.

The work is divided into four sections (*pallavas*) of verses. The narrative boundaries in each of the pallavas seem to be carefully marked. The first pallava, after the usual salutations and the unusual prefatory comments mentioned above, introduces a conversation between a female and a male black bee (*bhṛiṅgī*), with the former asking the latter what is the 'essence of the world'?[15] The rest of the story unfolds as a part of this conversation, and the male bee prepares the ground for introducing the 'great' Kīrttisiṃha by declaring that the essence of the world lay in being born a hero (*vīra*) and living a life of honour (*māna*). The author's patron, Kīrttisiṃha is then mentioned as the man who was born a vīra, and who was living a life of māna. The rest of the first pallava provides the ancestry of Kīrttisiṃha and a summary praise of his achievements. The 'action' part of the story starts with the second pallava as the male bee recounts how a certain Arsalan killed Kīrttisiṃha's father when the prince was a child, and how after attaining youth, he set out on an arduous journey to seek the reigning Sharqi Sultan's help in avenging his father's murder and recovering the lost throne of Tirhut. This is the section with the famous passages describing the city of Jaunpur as seen by Kīrttisiṃha and his companions, including Vidyapati himself. The end of this pallava sees Kīrttisiṃha and his companions at the doorsteps of the grand Sharqi palace in Jaunpur.[16]

The third pallava starts with Kīrttisiṃha meeting Sultan Ibrahim Shah and asking for help. The sultan appears sympathetic, but news of disturbance in certain places comes, and the Sharqi army

[15] The phrase '*saṃsārahi sār*' might alternatively be rendered as the 'essence of the cycle of life and death'.

[16] Vidyapati refers to it as Joṇāpura, but there can be little doubt that this is a reference to the capital city of Jaunpur. However, at least one scholar, Indrakant Jha, has argued that the term Joṇāpura in *Kīrttilatā* is actually a reference to Delhi. See Jha, *Vidyapatikālīn Mithilā*, pp. 14–17. Jha pointed out, rightly, that Delhi often figured in medieval Sanskrit parlance as Yoginīpura. However, his inference that Joṇāpura is an Apabhraṃśa spin-off of Yoginīpura is not borne out by other pieces of evidence. The most important of these is the direct reference in *Kīrttilatā* itself to the ruler Ibrahim Shah of Jaunpur. The sultan at Delhi around this time was of course, Nasiruddin Mohammad Tughluq.

sets out on a mission towards the west rather than the east. At the end of the third pallava, the Sharqi army comes back victorious, and the Tirhut prince makes another representation to Ibrahim Shah. At the beginning of the fourth pallava, the Sharqi army moves eastward into Tirhut to challenge the 'usurper' Malik Arsalan. The battle scenes are described in some detail with the prowess of the protagonist Kīrttisiṃha being foregrounded. In the end, the Tirhut prince defeats Arsalan in a one-to-one combat, and the latter flees the battlefront. The Sharqi sultan performs the *rājatilaka* ceremony for Kīrttisiṃha 'with his own hands', and everyone, presumably, lives happily ever after.

Language

'*Kīrttilatā* is an object of extreme significance from the perspective of language', wrote Shivprasad Singh in a study of the text. 'None of the compositions from the medieval period', he noted, 'managed to preserve the elements of such an old and fast-developing language [Avahaṭṭha] in such diverse forms'.[17] It is not easy, however, to identify and locate the language of the narrative within the historians' now (in)famous world of premodern vernacular and cosmopolitan languages. Vidyapati called it Avahaṭṭha. But we have little scholarly work, let alone an authoritative account, that can help us place this language in the dauntingly large number of non-Sanskrit, non-Persian dialects and languages that mark the literary world of the middle and early-modern ages in North India: Rajasthani, Śaurasenī, Apabhraṃśa, Awadhī, Braja, Hindavi/Hindui, Maithili, Bangla, and a number of others in which literary works were either rare or not composed as yet. In fact, a whole range of similar sounding words were in currency to refer to languages that might or might not have been a mere substitute word for Apabhraṃśa. This included, apart from Avahaṭṭha, confusingly close terms like Avavbhaṃsa, Avahaṃsa, Avahattha, Avavbaṃsa, and so on. It is not within the scope of this chapter to dwell on the separate histories of each of these terms and the languages they denoted, if at all.

[17] See 'Preface to the First Edition', in Singh, *Kīrttilatā aur Avahaṭṭha Bhāṣā*, p. 5 (my translation from the Hindi text).

It would be pertinent, however, to briefly dwell upon references to 'Avahaṭṭha', the language in which Vidyapati claimed to have composed *Kīrttilatā*. That Avahaṭṭha is etymologically related to Apabhraṃśa cannot be denied. However, the precise nature of Avahaṭṭha and its relationship with Apabhraṃśa has hardly attracted any sustained attention. Scholarly opinion on Avahaṭṭha, though varied, is mostly presumptive and not researched. Ronald Stuart McGregor, in his authoritative work on the history of Hindi literature, acknowledged the existence of 'different Apabhraṃśa traditions', both in terms of its literary corpus as well as its lexical and grammatical variations.[18] Specifically on Vidyapati, he noted that a 'significant feature of the language of *Kīrttilatā* is Vidyapati's use of Sanskrit loanwords in a way not usual in earlier Prakrit–Apabhraṃśa poetry, but now established in passages of literary style'.[19] Yet, he had little to say about Avahaṭṭha in particular, and used the word interchangeably with Apabhraṃśa. The more recent intensification of interest in vernacular literary traditions, or vernacularization for that matter, has not occasioned an analysis of Avahaṭṭha either. Sheldon Pollock does not specifically say much about its identity, or differences, with Apabhraṃśa.

The scholars' lack of patience with the nuances of difference between Apabhraṃśa and Avahaṭṭha is not incidental. One reason for it is the fact that marking boundaries within a world of extremely fluid, unstable, and overlapping lexical and grammatical practices may not always be analytically fruitful. Even nearly two centuries after Vidyapati, writing about a relatively more stable language, namely, Brajabhāṣā, Bhikhāridās noted that the reason why Brajabhāṣā might be called interesting was that its vocabulary consisted of words taken from at least six different languages: Sanskrit, Braj, Māgadhī, Nāgabhāṣā, spontaneous Persian, and Yavan[20] (languages with much older histories of written grammar and composition, for example, Sanskrit or Persian, were of course easier to identify and name).

[18] McGregor, *Hindi Literature*, p. 11.

[19] McGregor, *Hindi Literature*, p. 30.

[20] Singh, *Kīrttilatā aur Avahaṭṭha Bhāṣā*, p. 20.

For our purposes, it is still useful to see what language practice came to be known as Avahaṭṭha because it would help us understand the literary–political significance of the choice of this language for composing *Kīrttilatā*. One way to go about it is to map the chronological and spatial co-ordinates of the usage of this word by composers themselves. So far, I have been able to trace only three such instances among extant texts including *Kīrttilatā*. At least one instance also comes from a Sanskrit commentary by Vaṃśīdhar, *Prākṛit Paiṅgalam*.

The first instance comes from *Sandeśarāsaka*, whose author, Addahamāṇa (Abdul Rahman), identified himself as a 'lotus of the lineage in Prākṛit poetry, *kulakamalo pāiyakavvesu*'.[21] Evidently modelled on Kalidas's famous *Meghadūta*, *Saṅdeśarāsaka* is a message-poem, a sub-genre in Sanskrit. Its language is Avahaṭṭha, which is listed by Addahamāṇa as one of the four languages (besides Sanskrit, Prakrit, and Paiśācī) that 'great poets adorned with ornaments of grammar and metre'.[22] An extremely interesting and astonishingly under-researched text, the date and place of its composition are not certain. The author claims to belong to a family from a 'famous Mleccha country in the west' but it is not possible to identify the country. His plentiful references to gods like Rama and Brahmā, mythic figures like Udayana and Airāvata, and indeed the texts, languages, and genres of Indic traditions, are sufficient, however, to establish him as an inhabitant of the subcontinent, irrespective of where his ancestors came from. One of the two chief characters in the text is described as a resident of Vijayanagar, *Vijayanayarahu*, while the other, a resident of Sāmora, is shown to be travelling from Mulatthān (Multan) to Khambhāta (Cambay). The fact that the language shows close affinity to western Rajasthani dialect, along with the above information may suggest the location of the text broadly to be in the western and southwestern parts of thc subcontinent.

One of the commentaries on the *Saṅdeśarāsaka* by Lakṣmīcandra is dated 1409 CE. It would appear, as the editor of the text has

[21] Rahman, *Sandeśarāsaka*, p. 2.

[22] *Avahaṭṭayasakkayapāiyaṃmipesāiyaṃmibhāsāe/Lakkhaṇachaṃdāharaṇe sukaittaṃ bhūsiyaṃ jehiṃ*. See Rahman, *Sandeśarāsaka*.

shown, that the text itself might have been composed sometime between the mid-thirteenth and the mid-fourteenth centuries.[23] This is curious, of course, in the light of the fact that the life of Apabhraṃśa as a language for literary composition is said to have been coming to an end by the fifteenth century.

Another reference to Avahaṭṭha comes from Jyotirīśvara's *Varṇaratnākara*, arguably the first extant composition in Maithili/ Old Maithili, written sometime around the mid-thirteenth century. Haraprasad Sastri, who is credited with the modern 'discovery' of this text at the end of the nineteenth century, reported that '[t]he subject-matter of the book is very curious. It gives the poetic conventions. For instance, if a king is to be described, what are to be his qualities; if a capital is to be described, what are to be the details; and so on.... This book seems to have guided the genius of Vidyāpati'.[24]

The reference to 'Avahaṭha' occurs in the context where the text provides the standard expressions and conventions for describing the *bhāṭas* (panegyrists; loosely, poets). Again, the expression comes as the third in a list of six languages: *Sanskrit, Parākṛit, Avahaṭha, Paisācī, Saurasenī, Māgadhī.*[25] (It may be noted that counting to six, so far as the number of languages is concerned, was probably a convention, though the lists sometimes varied.) Most of the lists, however, mentioned Apabhraṃśa and at least one of these—that by the ninth-century scholar Rudraṭa in fact matched the list provided by Jyotirīśvara, except that where Rudraṭa mentioned Apabhraṃśa, Jyotirīśvara put in Avahaṭṭha. The time of composition in the case of *Varṇaratnākara* is the thirteenth century. That Jyotirīśvara lived and composed the text in the Mithila region is not disputed.

It is perhaps no coincidence that Vaṃśīdhar's commentary, *Prākṛit Paiṅgalam* is also dated around the same time in the heyday of the Delhi Sultanate, though it is difficult to trace the place co-ordinates for him.

It would be useful in this context to consider another work titled *Uktivyaktiprakaraṇa* on the Apabhraṃśa languages by Dāmodara

23 Mayrhofer, 'Introduction', *Sandeśarāsaka*, p. xii.

24 Sastri, 'Report on the Search of Sanskrit Manuscripts', p. 23.

25 Jyotirīśvara Kaviśekhara, *Varṇaratnākara*, ed. Chatterji, p. 44.

Paṇḍita.[26] Paṇḍita reflected on 'how the popularly used Apabhraṃśa language, current in one's time and place might be related to the grammar-system of Sanskrit, and how one may note the presence of a rough structure of Sanskrit grammar in the people's usages of bhāṣā words and expressions, etc'.[27] What is of significance for us is the fact that the language that the text analysed appears to have strong affinity with the kind of Apabhraṃśa that Vidyapati and Addahamāṇa called Avahaṭṭha. It may be noted that this extraordinary treatise cannot be placed before the thirteenth century.

Considering that Vidyapati also lived in the early-fifteenth century, the temporal context becomes very clear; all the commentators and poets who used the word 'Avahaṭṭha' (instead of Apabhraṃśa), or composed in, or commented on that language lived between the twelfth and the early-fifteenth century, that is, in the last three centuries or so of the career of Apabhraṃśa. In his detailed analysis of the language of *Kīrttilatā*, Shivprasad Singh noted that Apabhraṃśa was genealogically related to Avahaṭṭha as the former's later avatar. T. Nara, another scholar who had considered the question in some detail, also concluded that Avahaṭṭha was a 'late literary form of Apabhraṃśa'.[28] What distinguished Avahaṭṭha from Apabhraṃśa, it would appear, among other things, was an increasing number of *tatsam* words—loanwords from Sanskrit. Equally striking was the inclusion of a large number of Persian words.

The question Pollock asked in this regard more than fifteen years ago, is relevant here: '[W]hat else in the social and political world is being chosen when a language-for-literature is chosen?'.[29] An answer to this question is possible only once the historical character of Avahaṭṭha is ascertained. Neither Apabhraṃśa, nor Avahaṭṭha, may easily be placed in the binary formula of the cosmopolitan and the vernacular languages. As Pollock himself

[26] Dāmodara, *Uktivyaktiprakaraṇa*. This text was also known as *Uktivyaktiśāstra* and *Prayogaprakāśa*.

[27] Dāmodara, *Uktivyaktiprakaraṇa*, p. 7.

[28] See Nara, *Avahaṭṭha and Comparative Vocabulary of New Indo-Āryan Languages*, cited in Mayrhofer, 'Introduction', p. xiii, footnote no. 1.

[29] Pollock, 'The Cosmopolitan Vernacular', p. 7.

admitted, 'to define vernacular over against cosmopolitan appears to submerge a number of relativities'.[30] While no one can dispute the fact that Apabhraṃśa or Avahaṭṭha never travelled as far as Sanskrit or Persian, it is noteworthy that almost all the major commentators on the science of poetic aesthetics (*alaṅkāraśāstra*) included Apabhraṃśa together with Sanskrit and Prakrit in the list of three literary languages with possibly a trans-regional reach.[31] However, if Braja 'was rendered rootlessly cosmopolitan by the elimination ... of local dialectal difference in the fifteenth to sixteenth centuries',[32] Apabhraṃśa in the literary history of the subcontinent was always perceived as such. Pollock also admitted that 'Prakrit and Apabhraṃśa [were] two languages that under the influence of Sanskrit had been turned into cosmopolitan idioms, and which therefore could be and were used for literary composition anywhere in the Sanskrit cosmopolis'.[33] On the other hand, the mutative Avahaṭṭha further built on this status of Apabhraṃśa by adopting Persian as well as Sanskrit words with abundant infidelity.

It should therefore come as no surprise that the spatial co-ordinates of the authors and texts in/on Avahaṭṭha discussed earlier in this chapter do not seem to fall into a pattern. If Addahamāṇa's Avahaṭṭha in *Saṅdeśarāsaka* may be traced to Western India, Jyotirīśvara and Vidyapati are placed firmly in the eastern quarters of the subcontinent. Indeed, despite all its dynamism and expansive propensities, Apabhraṃśa could never match Sanskrit/

[30] Pollock, 'The Cosmopolitan Vernacular', p. 7.

[31] The first of the great authors on the science of poetics in Sanskrit, Bhāmaha (I.16), noted the following while trying to define kāvya:

Śabdārthau sahitau kāvyaṃ gadyaṃ padyaṃ ca tad-dvidhā
Saṃskṛtaṃ prākṛtaṃ cānyadapabhraṃśa iti tridhā

(Kāvya is the combination of words and meanings. It is of two types: prose and verse. Sanskrit, Prakrit, or else Apabhraṃśa: these are the three kinds.)

See Bhāmaha, *Kāvyālaṅkāra*, p. 9.

[32] Pollock, 'The Cosmopolitan Vernacular', p. 7.

[33] Pollock, 'The Cosmopolitan Vernacular', p. 11.

Persian in its horizontal spread. A qualitative difference between them has to be located more substantively elsewhere. Let us go back to Vidyapati's own explanation on why he chose to compose *Kīrttilatā* in the language that he did.

The fact that *Kīrttilatā* used the term 'indigenous dialect' (*desila ba-anā*) for Avahaṭṭha that was 'sweet to all' (*saba jana miṭṭhā*) surely indicates that common men appreciated the language more than they appreciated Sanskrit or Persian. Interestingly, in the thirteenth century, Hemacandra had noted in his *Kāvyānuśāsana*, that Apabhraṃśa itself could be divided into *śiṣṭabhāṣā* and *grāmya* Apabhraṃśa, the former a literary language and the latter a popular spoken dialect.[34] The former had a wider currency and consistency whereas the latter would be more vulnerable to 'corruption' through local influences in different regions. Around the same time, Śāradā Tanay in his *Bhav-prakāśa* noted in a somewhat similar vein that Apabhraṃśa was of three kinds: *nagarak*, grāmya, and *upanagarak*. While nagarak carried the sense of urbanity and sophistication present in śiṣṭabhāṣā, *upanagarak* posited another register of the language that was partly urbane and presumably also somewhat quotidian.[35] Earlier, the literary theorist Rudraṭa had probably referred to the variations inbuilt within the notion of *grāmyabhāṣā*, when he noted that the form of Apabhraṃśa also depended on the localities (*deśavideśādapabhraṃśaḥ*).[36]

We may presume a high level of intelligibility between the universalized literary register (*śiṣṭa*) and the local register (grāmya) of Apabhraṃśa. Keeping Sheldon Pollock's rhetorical formulation in mind, a composition in the former language thus had a potential reach at least all over North India, without forsaking the possibility of a deeper and popular local penetration. For a fifteenth-century author to use a language like this is particularly interesting. It remains to be seen whether this open-ended eclecticism of language was also reflective of a similar 'pragmatic' move towards a more expansive political culture in the text of *Kīrttilatā*. A more 'conventional' reading of the

[34] Hemacandra, *Kāvyanuśāsana*.

[35] Pandey, *Hindī Sāhitya kā Prāraṃbhik Yug*, p. 24.

[36] Pandey, *Hindī Sāhitya kā Prāraṃbhik Yug*.

text for its 'historical content' would allow for the exploration of such a possibility. However, an examination of *Kīrttilatā*'s genre antecedents is more valuable in opening up the question in closer proximity with the author's choice of literary techniques.

Genre

As noted earlier, *Kīrttilatā* is a biographical account in verse with the occasional use of prose. The title 'Vine(s) of Glory' plays on the fact that the word 'Kīrtti' (name of the protagonist) itself means 'glory'. While it seeks to tell the story of the glorious life and achievements of Kīrttisiṃha, it is clearly not meant as a mere *praśasti* (praise-text). The biographical literary tradition was known and practiced both in the Sanskrit as well as in the Persian tradition in the subcontinent. While a set of literary conventions came to be associated with the 'biography', both Persian as well as Sanskrit traditions left a lot of scope for an author to innovate, in theory as much as in practice. In the case of Sanskrit, nothing proves this better than the 'confusion' in the attempt to define ākhyāyikā, the category usually translated as 'biography'.

The first of the classical scholars on poetics in Sanskrit, Bhāmaha (I.18), noted early in the seventh century that literature (kāvya) may be classified into five kinds:

i. *sargabandha* (*mahākāvya* or 'epic poem')
ii. *abhineya* (that which can be performed, literally, 'acted')
iii. *ākhyāyikā* (biography)
iv. *kathā* (story/tale/novel)
v. *anibaddha* (free or independent verses)[37]

Even though *Kīrttilatā* was also a story of sorts, if we go by the above classification, it would surely fall in the category of ākhyāyikā and not kathā. Bhāmaha added (I.25) that the ākhyāyikā was written in prose with words pleasing to the ear and in tune with the content; that it consisted of vaktra and *apavaktra* metres; that

37 *Sargabandhoabhineyārthaṃ tathaivākhyāyikākathe/Aanibaddhañca kāvyādi tatpunaḥ pañcadhocyate*. See Bhāmaha, *Kāvyālaṅkāra*, p. 10.

it must have an exalted purpose/meaning (*udāttārtha*) with the use of poetic imagination; that important themes in it included abduction of a girl (*kanyā-haraṇa*), a battle (*saṅgrāma*), separation (*vipralambha*), and the eventual triumph (*udaya*) of the hero; that the hero himself narrated the story;[38] and that it is divided into several parts (*ucchavāsa*).

Yet, Daṇḍin (I.23), writing in the late-seventh or early-eighth century, famously ruled out any validity in the distinction between ākhyāyikā and kathā. As Warder noted, '[Daṇḍin] also points out that some of the description [of biography] given by Bhāmaha had been infringed in practice'.[39] Modern scholars who sought to understand these genres with reference to only Bhāmaha and Daṇḍin, had to predictably quote disappointment. One such scholar, Susan Tripp has very aptly and usefully described the confusion:

> Some of the confusion apparent in Bhāmaha's and Daṇḍin's definitions of the prose genres arises, I suspect, from the fact that they are attempting to include under *kāvya* various kinds of works which do not properly belong there. Epic and other kinds of poetry, and drama, are highly coded on all levels; Sanskrit prose literature, on the other hand, is much less highly coded and much of it creates the impression of being distinctly more 'popular' than verse genres. Including works of this kind within the class of *kāvya* has the effect of redefining *kāvya* as the class of all pleasure texts. But Bhāmaha and Daṇḍin try to make prose into *kāvya* by assigning to it a set of formal options, parallel to those governing other *kāvya* texts. One cannot help suspecting that Bhāmaha posited two kinds of prose works merely to equal the epic/drama pair, and to fill out his scheme with the required five elements for the fifth level: a scheme which Daṇḍin rejected as artificial. Daṇḍin first presents specific rules for the prose genres, then declares

[38] Some scholars, for example, T.S. Nandi, the editor and translator of *Kāvyānuśāsana*, interpreted this provision as a reference to autobiography. See Hemacandra, *Kāvyanuśāsana*, p. 595. However, the context and the complete absence of any autobiography before, during, or immediately after this period, suggest a composition in which a protagonist (real or fictional) is made to tell a story in the first person. Hence, it should not be confused with autobiography.

[39] Warder, *Indian Kavya Literature*, vol. I, p. 183.

> that these are not mandatory; first lists two genres, then decides that there is really only one; and finally concludes that what really counts is whether the writer succeeded in accomplishing what he intended. One would not be able to form any accurate conception of the actual forms of Sanskrit prose literature from Bhāmaha's and Daṇḍin's descriptions; nor can one infer much from what is not said. They simply seem to flounder when they attempt to handle prose. What the attempts show, I think, is the difficulty of trying to construct a universal theory of genre on the basis of the kind of restricted, hierarchical code that the early *alamkāra* theorists sought to develop.[40]

Clearly, it is not possible to fit *Kīrttilatā* neatly into any of the existing categories of Sanskrit genre. Scholars like Hazari Prasad Dvivedi took the easier way out and simply declared that *Kīrttilatā* was 'written as per the convention of *kathā* or *ākhyāyikā* in Sanskrit Literature'![41] It is true, as Ali has pointed out, that 'A.K. Warder's distinction between the kathā as "fiction" or "novel" based upon the poet's imagination, on the one hand, and the ākhyāyikā as a "little history" or "biography" based on real events, on the other, is strongly borne out in neither poetic theory nor literary practice'.[42] What Ali does not point out, however, is the fact that neither 'poetic theory' nor 'literary practice' was unchanging. Nor, as I try to demonstrate below, is it the case that 'the *ākhyāyikā* remains a relatively stable and singular category in *alaṅkāraśāstra*'.[43] Indeed, it is possible to trace the interesting ways in which the two genres get mixed up, both in theory as well as in practice, along a certain time line.

Most of the later theoreticians after Bhāmaha and Daṇḍin, however, appear to have simplified the distinction between the two genres.[44]

[40] Tripp, 'The Genres of Classical Sanskrit Literature', pp. 226–7.

[41] Dvivedi, 'Foreword', *Kīrttilatā aur Avahaṭṭha Bhāṣā*, p. 10.

[42] Ali, 'Temporality, Narration and the Problem of History', p. 243.

[43] Ali, 'Temporality, Narration and the Problem of History', p. 243.

[44] Hemacandra (thirteenth century) appears to be one exception though. He divided literature into that which is 'seen' (*prekṣyaṃ*) and that which is 'heard' (*śravyaṃ*), and classified the latter category of literature (*kāvya*) into 'epic poem, biography, story, mixed type, and stray verses', *Śravyaṃ mahākāvyamākhyāyikā kathā campūranibaddhaṃ ca*. His descriptions also clearly seem to have borrowed from Bhāmaha. See Hemacandra, *Kāvyanuśāsana*, p. 167.

By the time of Rudraṭa (ninth century), who based his theory on the model of Bāṇa's two works, *Harṣa-carita* and *Kādambarī*, a clearer distinction emerged between ākhyāyikā and kathā.[45] This is how De summarized the characteristic features of ākhyāyikā as it obtained in the world of Sanskrit literary theory by the tenth century or thereabouts: (*a*) The subject matter gives facts of actual experience; (*b*) The narrator need not be the hero himself; (*c*) It is divided into chapters called *ucchvāsas*, which should (excepting the first) open with two stanzas, preferably in *āryā*, indicating the tenor of the chapter in question; and (*d*) It possesses a metrical introduction of a literary character.[46]

In the eleventh century, however, Abhinavagupta, possibly the most sophisticated of theoreticians in the classical mould, tried to reduce it to a mere distinction of form when he commented that ākhyāyikā 'consisted of *ucchavāsa* and *vaktra–aparavaktra* verses, and the *kathā* was entirely devoid of these'.[47]

One of the characteristics of ākhyāyikā that emerged by the tenth century was that it could be written in both prose and poetry. In the case of *Kīrttilatā*, while prose often appears in between to explain a point or two, the flavour and the operative part of the narrative is primarily captured in verse. This would have made it possible for listeners to enjoy its recitation and retelling in a primarily oral culture. It would also facilitate retention among listeners and easier dissemination. If we try to apply whatever broad contours of the genres of ākhyāyikā, kathā, and *campū*[48] emerge, *Kīrttilatā* clearly comes closest to ākhyāyikā. It is interesting that *Kīrttilatā* fails the test if we apply the criteria put forth for ākhyāyikā by Bhāmaha in the seventh century. The changing character of the genre, at least in theory, in the following centuries, however, comes closer to the way our text is organized. Viśvanātha Kavirāja, writing in the late-fourteenth century in Orissa, invoked Daṇḍin to point out rather cryptically that so much was common (*antarbhāva*) between

[45] De, 'The *Akhyayika* and the *Katha* in Classical Sanskrit', p. 517.

[46] De, 'The *Akhyayika* and the *Katha* in Classical Sanskrit', p. 517.

[47] De, 'The *Akhyayika* and the *Katha* in Classical Sanskrit', p. 516.

[48] This is explained as a composition in prose and verse, mentioned by earlier commentators as well. See Viśvanātha Kavirāja, *Sāhityadarpaṇaḥ*, p. 728.

ākhyāyikā and kathā, that the two cannot be seen as separate categories.[49] After very briefly mentioning campū, and two new genres, namely, *viruda*[50] and *karambhaka*,[51] he found it necessary to remark that 'there were other varieties [of compositions] but because they were merely famous and different only in name and did not transgress the boundaries [of genres already defined, hence they were] not seen as separate'.[52] This last comment may be read as pointing towards an intensified experimentation with, and changes in, established genres—both in Sanskrit and in other literary traditions—by the time of Viśvanātha Kavirāja.

To keep the significance of my intervention in mind, it might be worthwhile to reformulate Pollock's rhetorical question regarding language and ask: '[W]hat else in the social and political world is being chosen when a language-for-literature *and a genre-for-literature* is chosen?' A vital aspect that we need to keep in mind as we reflect on this question concerns plausible precursors. While biographical compositions could theoretically be written in any of the three languages (Sanskrit/Apabhraṃśa/Prakrit) mentioned by Bhāmaha, in actual practice, Vidyapati could look to very few precedents for a political biography in Apabhraṃśa or Prakrit in the fifteenth century.

Two conventions within medieval North Indian 'vernacular' literature that might profitably be mentioned in this context are the *rāso* and the *carita* traditions. The most famous of the rāso texts is of course, *Pṛithvīrājarāso*, attributed to Cand Bardāi. This was composed in the Pingal language, 'a form of Braj Bhasa inflected by Rajasthani'.[53] Regarded for a long time as a contemporary work composed in the twelfth century itself, questions have been raised about the dating of this remarkable text. As early as 1886, Kaviraj Syamaldas, a scholar and poet attached to the Mewar court, argued in a rigorously

49 Viśvanātha Kavirāja, *Sāhityadarpaṇaḥ*, p. 727.

50 This is defined as a 'royal praise [*rājastuti*]' in a mix of prose and verse. See Viśvanātha Kavirāja, *Sāhityadarpaṇaḥ*, p. 727.

51 This is defined as a 'multilingual composition [*bhāṣābhirvividhābhirvinirmitam*]'. Viśvanātha Kavirāja, *Sāhityadarpaṇaḥ*, p. 727.

52 Viśvanātha Kavirāja, *Sāhityadarpaṇaḥ*, p. 729.

53 Talbot, 'Contesting Knowledges in Colonial India', p. 172.

researched piece that the great 'epic' was probably written between 1583 and 1613 of the Christian Era.[54] Though Syamaldas's arguments did not go unchallenged, historians in their scholarly opinions on *Pṛithvīrājarāso* have largely accepted the contention that it could not have been composed before the fifteenth, if not the sixteenth, century. Even within the Hindi literary scholarship, this view has been put forth strongly.[55]

Rāso, along with *vaṃśāvalī*, were 'Rajasthani narrative traditions of the late medieval period, [where] heroism was defined and celebrated as a continuing tradition, as an essence transmitted by hereditary lineage'.[56] Rāso as a genre, however, had a strong component of romance in it that was woven around the central male protagonist. It is interesting that it appears to have evolved rather late, and certainly not before the late-fourteenth century, even as they continued to be composed into the nineteenth century, mostly under patronage from the princely states of the colonial era.[57] As Sreenivasan has noted, a large number of rāso compositions, if not all, were written in tiny 'regional' kingdoms under the aegis of Rājapūta princes of diverse lineages. It is pertinent that *Pṛithvīrājarāso* was a political biography in verse, presented as an eyewitness account, much like Vidyapati's *Kīrttilatā*. It tells the story of the life and glories of the twelfth-century ruler, Prithvīrāj Cauhāna. Unlike *Kīrttilatā*, however, Cand Bardāī's account was not so much about how his protagonist ascended to power and glory. Rather it was more focussed on the heroic fall of the protagonist in the battlefield against his Ghurid adversary Shihab al-Din Muhammad.

Carita (or *cariu*) in Apabhraṃśa/Braj/Avadhī, on the other hand, may be traced more directly, at least where etymology is concerned, to the carita tradition of Sanskrit literature, a genre that became the

[54] Syamaldas, 'The Antiquity, Authenticity and Genuineness of the Epic Called the Prithvi Raj Rasa'. For a detailed discussion of the research method followed by Syamaldas, its remarkable success, and its epistemological context as well as contestations, see Talbot, 'Contesting Knowledges in Colonial India'.

[55] See for example, Singh, *Pṛithvīrāja Rāso kī Bhāṣā*.

[56] Sreenivasan, 'Alauddin Khalji Remembered', pp. 286–7.

[57] Svami, *Rāso Sāhitya aur Pṛthvirāj Rāso*.

benchmark for scholars of poetics during the 'classical' period to define the ākhyāyikā. As Knutson noted in a different context,

> in the early medieval period generally, from the seventh through the thirteenth centuries, historical personages emerged strongly as heroes of Sanskrit kavyas, in place of the mythical figures who earlier stood in for them, whether Harsa in Bana's *Harsacarita* (seventh century), Ramapala in Sandhyakara Nandin's *Ramacarita* (eleventh century), Vikramaditya VI (eleventh century) in Bilahaṇa's *Vikramāṅkadevacaritam*, or, at the Sena court, Laksmaṇasena in Dhoyi's *Pavanadūta* (twelfth and thirteenth centuries).[58]

Very much like the rāso texts, the vernacular caritas also seem to have flourished rather late, and mostly under the patronage of small sub-imperial courts. Thus, Vishnudas, a contemporary of Vidyapati at the Gwalior court, composed the famous *Pāṇḍavacarita* in what may be called a mix of Apabhraṃśa and Avadhī.[59] In fact most of the carita texts in Apabhraṃśa seem to have been composed in the late-fourteenth and fifteenth centuries, many of them at Gwalior, where one of the most prolific Apabhraṃśa authors, Raidhu, also lived. However, almost all of these caritas or carius were retellings of epic tales of Rāmāyaṇa or Mahābhārata, mostly in their Jain versions. Eva De Clercq noted recently that the cariu texts often consisted of the 'biography of a mythological or worldly hero'; her own account mentions very few works containing biographies of non-mythological/historical characters. As she points out in the context of one such work, *Sammattaguṇaṇihāṇakavva*, by Raidhu, 'the world which their protagonists inhabit often appears quite similar to the Jain Puranic setting inhabited by superhuman beings'.[60] To that extent, empirically at least, the carita genre of Apabhraṃśa and other (Avadhī/Braja) languages might actually be traced to the tradition of Kalidas's *Raghuvaṃśa* and other Purāṇic and epic-based works rather than the Sanskrit carita texts, which as noted by Knutson,

[58] Knutson, 'History Beyond the Reality Principle', p. 634.

[59] Vishnudas, *Mahābhārat: Pāṇḍav-carit*. For a brief note and interesting discussion of the work, see Bangha, 'Early Hindi Epic Poetry in Gwalior'.

[60] De Clercq, 'Apabhramsha as a Literary Medium', pp. 341, 349.

had historical personages as their protagonists. However, Vidyapati's *Kīrttilatā* might actually be placed in the longer history of Sanskrit caritas, revolving around historical characters, rather than the epic tales of Apabhraṃśa nearer his time.

Unlike the Sanskrit typologies of textual traditions, these 'vernacular' genres were rarely, if ever, theorized into strictly defined components. In fact, no theoretical treatises were composed in vernacular and Apabhraṃśa languages in general.[61] Accordingly, the non-Sanskrit genres evolved over a period of time, and left considerable agency with individual authors to experiment. This is one of the most important reasons why it is so difficult to definitively pin the generic antecedents of vernacular compositions.

In any case, it is doubtful if any language in the middle ages developed as sophisticated a tradition of literary theory as Sanskrit did, although some could match Sanskrit in terms of creative output and genre variations. Biographical traditions, on the other hand, developed early within the early Perso-Arabic tradition. By the tenth century or so, individual biographies and biographical anthologies also seem to have borrowed from existing techniques of history writing.[62]

[61] One limited 'exception' to the rule was the mid-fourteenth-century Maithili text, *Varṇaratnākara* by Jyotirīśvara Kaviśekhara, from the Mithila region itself, referred to above (see Jyotirīśvara Kaviśekhara, *Varṇaratnākara*, ed. Chatterji). As noted, it was a rather unusual composition that put together a collection of words/phrases and expressions that a writer could use in a given context or while describing a particular object/theme. Occasionally, it also defined certain terms. In a passage devoted to the description of the 'bhāṭas' (vernacular poets/singers), Jyotirīśvara mentioned six languages, seven 'sub-languages' (*upabhāṣā*), eight grammarians including Pānini and Dāmodara, a few learned in literary devices (*alaṇkāravijña*), some poets, and a few literary compositions which include *Kādambarī, Cakravāla, Vāyasu, Gadyamālā, Harṣacarita, Campū, Vāsavadattā, Śālabhañjī*, and *Karpūramañjarī*. It is intriguing that campū which was mentioned as a mixed (prose and verse) genre by several literary theorists, was included in this list of individual compositions. See Jyotirīśvara Kaviśekhara, *Varṇaratnākara*, ed. Mishra and Jha, p. 62.

[62] For the close relationship between biographical literature and history within the 'classical' Islamic tradition, see Khalidi, *Arabic Historical Thought*, pp. 204–10.

The best example of a political biography of a historical character within the North Indian Persianate tradition is probably Amir Khusrau's *Tughlaq Namah*, a text that might fruitfully be compared to the tenor and subject matter of *Kīrttilatā*. In fact, there seems to be some similarity of character and skills between the two authors themselves. Both were extremely prolific and of a pietistic disposition. Both were polyglots, and composed in several languages. They revelled in experimenting with genres, and took pride in their writing skills. If Vidyapati was reputed to be a scholar who could cite classical Sanskrit writers and narrate contemporary stories with equal ease, so could Khusrau vis-à-vis the Perso-Islamicate traditions. If his contemporaries saw Khusrau primarily as a poet and lyricist, Vidyapati's popularity too rested chiefly on his Maithili songs, both devotional and secular. It is no coincidence that neither was amenable to easy classification, leading one modern scholar to club them together as standalone figures under the heading '*phuṭakal racanāyeñ*', as we have already seen in Chapter 1 in this volume. It might be a coincidence though that both lived long and wrote for several patrons.

As in the case of *Tughlaq Namah*, *Kīrttilatā* is primarily about the author's patron–protagonist acquiring the throne with great personal heroism. Each story starts with the treacherous murder of a legitimate king (Gaṇesara in the case of *Kīrttilatā* and Mubarak Shah Khalaji in the case of *Tughlaq Namah*) by a debauched character (Arsalan/Khusrau Khan). The protagonists in both compositions start their campaign swearing vengeance against such conduct. They ostensibly do so, not on account of personal ambitions but in the cause of 'social order' based on faith, *din*[63] in one case, and Brāhmaṇical righteousness, *dhamma*[64] in the other. The route both protagonists

63 In captivity, when Khusrau Khan asked for forgiveness, Tughluq said, 'Since my enmity to you is for the sake of faith (din) I must punish you as you deserve.' See 'Appendix: The Tughlaq Namah', in Mirza, *The Life and Works of Amir Khusrau*, p. 252.

64 When the murderer Arsalan thought of (how he had transgressed) *dhamma*, he offered the throne back to Kīrttisiṃha. However, punishment for the wrong-doer is equally important in *Kīrttilatā* too, as we witness the protagonist take the longer route through the battlefield to claim the throne. See *Kīrttilatā*, pp. 64–6.

took through the battlefield was to restore the throne to its rightful claimant.[65] There are stylistic similarities too between the two texts. Unlike Apabhraṃśa, which did not have a fully established convention of political biographies, Persian heritage provided rich possibilities for Khusrau. However, Vidyapati innovated in his own unique way, composing a panegyric biography in verse, and broadly following the *mathnawi* style. More importantly, if Vidyapati seems to have followed Mammaṭa's advice that biographies should be composed in the 'raw and aggressive' style,[66] at least one modern author complained that the language deployed in *Tughlaq Namah* becomes 'at places ... positively gruesome'.[67] It is important at this point to guard against any lazy conclusion that such similarities in any way prove a direct 'influence' of Sanskrit poets on Khusrau or that of Khusrau on Vidyapati. Rather, it indicates how similar literary trends evolved simultaneously in the apparently parallel worlds of Sanskrit, Persian, and Apabhraṃśa/vernacular languages. That Khusrau generously employed a large number of Hindavi terms[68]—on occasion even Sanskrit—in his Persian text might not seem so unique if we recall the diverse lexical sources used in the composition of *Kīrttilatā*. These 'stray' practices gesture towards a shared common sense prevailing within the North Indian politico–literary domains across linguistic–territorial boundaries, a phenomenon also discussed earlier in the context of *Likhanāvalī*.

[65] In the case of Tughluq, however, this could not be done since all five sons of Mubarak Shāh had already been killed by Khusrau Khan. Thus, he 'accepted the crown after much hesitation and on repeated requests from the Maliks'! See Mirza, 'Appendix: The Tughlaq Namah', *The Life and Works of Amir Khusrau*, p. 252.

[66] Mammaṭa recommended different styles for *kathā* and *ākhyāyikā*, noting that the former should be written in a gentle (*sukumāra*) style, while a more aggressive (*vikaṭa*, literally, formidable/horrendous) style is suitable for the latter. See Mammaṭa, *Kāvyaprakāśa*, cited in Warder, *Indian Kavya Literature*, vol. I, p. 183.

[67] Mirza, 'Appendix: The Tughlaq Namah', *The Life and Works of Amir Khusrau*, p. 253.

[68] Mirza, 'Appendix: The Tughlaq Namah', *The Life and Works of Amir Khusrau*, p. 253.

The similarities between Amir Khusrau's and Vidyapati's biographical works, however, cannot be stretched too far. If Khusrau was one of the most influential poets in the court of probably the most powerful medieval state of North India before the Mughals, Vidyapati was attached to petty chieftains in a region that was only a minor territory for the major powers of the time. No less striking is the fact that in several episodes of the Apabhraṃśa biography, the protagonist Kīrttisiṃha was portrayed as a diminutive character, dependant on sympathizers, and a helpless supplicant before a superior Sharqi Sultan. In contrast, the Persian text in question always foregrounded Tughluq as the hero, towering above other characters in every single episode. Khusrau's linear account of Tughluq's ascent to power with the monochromatic world of court intrigues and battle scenes in the backdrop is in sharp contrast with *Kīrttilatā*'s narrative that invoked a whole range of emotions and described diverse political and cultural landscapes. It is in the light of this narrative complexity of the text that the rest of the chapter seeks to unpack its historical contents in all its varied colours and nuances.

The Local in *Kīrttilatā*

The first pallava of the text traces the ostensibly illustrious ancestry of Kīrttisiṃha. The Oiṇī dynasty (*baṃsa*) to which he belonged is described as one that had formidable command of logic (*takkakakkasa*), studied the Vedas, crushed penury with donations, understood the exalted meanings of the Supreme Soul (*parama bambha*), earned glories with wealth (*bitta*), and engaged with enemies in the battlefield for truth (*satta*). In an apparent reference to the somewhat unusual fact that this was a Brāhmaṇa dynasty, the poet added that one does not find (the qualities of) the god of the earth (*bhūdeva*) and the lord of the earth (*bhūbai*) in the same person. He then traced the lineage back to Kāmesara, the founder of the dynasty and his son Bhogīsa. It is appreciatively noted that Sultan Firuzshah (Piarojsāha Suratāṇa) honoured the latter by addressing him as 'dear friend' (*pia sakhā*).[69]

[69] *Kīrttilatā*, pp. 54–6.

Other rulers down to Kīrttisiṃha are then mentioned along with their individual accomplishments.

It is possible to argue that, like the contemporary Rājapūta narratives of Rajasthan and Gwalior, Vidyapati's biographical tale too, was geared towards 'legitimizing' the authority of its patron.[70] If our poet did not trace Kīrttisiṃha's ancestry back into the mythological past of the Surya-, Candra-, or Agni-vaṃśa, he made up for it by commending him as the 'ideal man' (a favourite trope of the author, as we have already seen in the previous chapter), and explicitly counting him as such alongside such illustrious mythological characters as Raja Bali, *Raghurāya* (Raja Ram), Bhagīratha, and Paraśurāma in a six-line verse in the *chapada* metre.

Purisa hua-u Balirāya jāsu kara kaṇṇa pasāri-a
Purisa hua-u Raghurāya jenne raṇa Rāvaṇa māri-a
Purisa Bhagīratha hua-u jenne ni-akula uddhari-u
Parasurāma puni purisa jenne khatti-a kha-a karia-u
Aur purisa pasaṃsa-oñ rā-aguru Kittisiṃha Ga-aṇesa su-a
Je sattu samara sammaddi kahuñ bappabaira uddhari-a dhu-a[71]

(Raja Bali was the man before whom [even] Kriṣṇa was a supplicant
Raja Ram was the man who killed Ravaṇa in the battlefield
Bhag Ram was the man who rescued his ancestors
Paraśurāma was the man who annihilated the Kṣatriyas
And I praise another man, the exalted among the kings, Kīrttisiṃha, son of Gaṇesa
Who crushed the enemy in the battlefield to avenge paternal animosity.)

Interestingly, however, all this is managed within the first pallava in the limited space left after the brief mandatory salutations, and not-so-brief reflections on language choice. The remaining three pallavas trace the travels and travails of Kīrttisiṃha through a whole variety of landscapes—geographical, cultural, and political, but also local, cosmopolitan, and universal.

70 Sreenivasan, 'Alauddin Khalji Remembered'. Also see Sreenivasan, 'The "Marriage" of "Hindu" and "Turak": Medieval Rajput Histories', pp. 87–109.

71 *Kīrttilatā*, p. 53.

Geo-culturally and politically, the local emerges through the first half of the second pallava, as the poet describes how Arsalan treacherously killed Kīrttisiṃha's father, Raja Gaeṇesar.[72] The time of this incident is referred to (the 252nd year of Lakkhaṇasen Ṇareśa, that is, Lakṣmaṇa Samvat, corresponding to 1371 CE), but the place is not mentioned. Even the physical setting of the occurrence, whether it is a court/palace/fort/seat of power is not specified. In the conversation between Kīrttisiṃha on the one side and his advisors and family members on the other that followed (presumably, about two decades later), the young prince is shown to overrule any possibility of rapproachment/compromise with Arsalan, who apparently offered the throne back to him. The conversation is reported to have taken place informally within the extended family without any description of the setting or reference to any place. While this might be ascribed to the fact that the family was out of power at this time, it is striking that at no point in the text has the poet described any fortress or palace/court, let alone a citadel, that we might associate with even a locally important ruler: not while describing Kīrttisiṃha's ancestors, nor while recounting the murder of his father, and not even at the culmination, when the aspiring ruler finally lays his hands on the 'throne' of Tirhut.

Unlike the Karṇāṭa dynasty that had a sprawling citadel at Simarāoñgarh/Simarāoñpura,[73] the Oiṇīvāra dynasty established by Kāmesar (Sanskrit: Kāmeśvara) in all likelihood operated out of a much humbler abode in the village of Sugauna in the Madhubani district of present-day Bihar.[74] As we have seen in Chapter 1, in contrast with the Karṇāṭa dynasty that often actively sought to throw off the yoke of the Delhi Sultanate, Raja Gaṇesara or his descendants rarely, if ever, claimed sovereignty. More crucial for our purposes is the fact that Vidyapati never applied the trope of hyperbole, a common device in a composition like this (and used generously in the subsequent sections), to present Kīrttisiṃha's political stature as anything more than that of a humble chieftain.

[72] The name of Raja Ganeśvara (Sanskrit spelling) is variously spelt in the Avahaṭṭha text as either Ga-eṇesar or Ga-enes.

[73] See Chapter 1 in this volume.

[74] Ansari, 'End of the Karṇāṭa Kingdom', pp. 161 and 171.

Interestingly, the poet did not show such restraint while describing the anarchy that ostensibly gripped the region in the aftermath of the killing of Raja Gaṇesara by Arsalan. Here is a glimpse:

Ṭhākura ṭhaka bha-e gela cora sappari ghara sajji-a
Dāse gosā-uni gahi-a dhamma ga-e dhaṅdha nimajji-a
Khale sajjana paribhavi-a koi nahi hoi vicāraka
Jāti ajāti vivāha adhama uttama kāñ pāraka
Akkhararasa bujjhinihāra nahi kavikula bhami bhikkhari bha-uñ
Tirhutti tirohi sabe guṇe Rā Gaṇeśa jabe sagga ga-uñ[75]

(Lords became thugs, thieves attacked and occupied houses
Slaves seized the ladies of the house, dharma disappeared, business drowned
Rogues prevailed over men of virtue, no one bothered
Rampant inter-caste marriages, no one to discern between inferior and superior
No connoisseurs of the written syllable, [while] poets became wandering beggars
All virtues disappeared from Tirhut when Gaṇesa departed for heaven.)

That the comprehensive breakdown of dharma needed to be reversed at any cost is thus established at the outset of the second pallava. Even though the aggressor Arsalan is shown to have repented and offered the kingdom back to Kīrttisiṃha, the latter would take the longer and harder route rather than compromise with the enemy or enjoy a kingdom at his foe's mercy. Thus, he decided to go against the counsel of his mother and ministers, as he declared:

Mātā bhaṇai mamattaya-i mantī rajjah nīti
Majjhu pi-āro ekka pa-i vīra purisa ka-i rīti[76]

(Mother speaks out of affection, ministers preach politics
But I prefer only the precedence set by the men of courage.)

His elder brother, Vīrasiṃha, almost always shown through the text as a quiet and loyal companion of Kīrttisiṃha, agreed and added

[75] *Kīrttilatā*, p. 61.
[76] *Kīrttilatā*, p. 65.

that it was 'better to embrace death than to allow one's inferior power (*nī-a sakti*) to be exposed before everyone'.[77] The two brothers, thus, set out *on foot* to meet the Sharqi overlord (*Pātisāha*). Interestingly, they are likened first to Balabhadra and Kṛiśṇa and then to Rama and Lakṣamaṇa. The Rāmāyaṇa parallel acquires particular salience in the way their journey is described. Unlike the godly brothers of the epic who were obliged by Kaikeyī's vow to move to the forest without any material support, there was no such bar for the 'sons of Raja Gaṇesara'. Yet, they chose to leave behind not just family and friends but also good quality horses (*vara turaṅga*) and lots of wealth (*dhana bahutta*). On the way, they faced terrible hardships but also received enthusiastic support from the common people. As the poet says rhetorically, 'someone gave clothes, someone gave horses, someone offered provisions, someone paid their debts, and someone helped them cross the river; someone carried their luggage and someone cleared the paths for them.'[78] It is clear that Vidyapati was making a deliberate attempt to make this journey appear as close a replica of the epic journey undertaken by Rama and Lakṣamaṇa as possible, probably to emphasize that the cause of dharma was central to both ventures.

Purely from the perspective of narrative strategies, the manner in which *Kīrttilatā* starts bears striking similarity with Valmiki's *Rāmāyaṇa*. As we saw above, the Avahaṭṭha text starts with a conversation between a male and a female bee wherein the true meaning of life and the world is seen as being born a man of valour and having lived a life of honour. This is followed by a long list of qualities that an ideal man must have but rarely possesses. The protagonist (Kīrttisiṃha) is then introduced as the man who boasts of all these qualities. Valmiki's *Rāmāyaṇa* starts with a conversation between the author and Sage Nārada wherein the latter asserts, in response to the former's query, that it is Rama who possessed all the qualities that were difficult to find in one man.[79]

Divested of this epic–literary context, the arduous expedition of Kīrttisiṃha and Vīrasiṃha might simply appear to be a badly planned journey! The parallel, of course, cannot be taken further than this

[77] *Kīrttilatā*, p. 66.

[78] *Kīrttilatā*, pp. 68–70.

[79] Valmiki, *Rāmāyaṇa*, pp. 1–2.

unless we stretch our imagination so far as to imagine the Sharqi Sultan as standing in for Śakti, the ferocious goddess, whom Rama had to placate and draw power from before he could kill Rāvaṇa! We will come back to the question of the local–political and the not-so-local literary in the intermediate[80] language of Apabhraṃśa at the end of the chapter. For the moment, lets move on with the two brothers into the hustle and bustle of the city of Jaunpur, outside of which they stood after a long and tiring journey.

The Cosmopolitan City

The description of Jaunpur marks a clear contrast with the familiar/familial and 'local' world of Tirhut that the two brothers left behind. The readers/listeners of the kāvya are alerted to the grand picture that awaits them in the very way the city is introduced:

> *Taṃ khaṇe pekhkhi-a na-ar so Joṇāpura tasu nāma*
> *Lo-ana kerā vallahā Lacchī ko visarāma*[81]
>
> (At that instant they beheld the city, Jaunpur was whose name
> Pleasing to the eyes, resting place for Lakṣmī.)

Immediately, the poet changes gear and breaks into *geetikā chhanda*, a metre that lends itself to vigorous celebratory recitation, with a crackling staccato:

> *Pekhkhia-u paṭṭana cāru mekhara jauṇ nīra pakhāriā*
> *Pāsāṇa kuṭṭima bhīti bhītara cūra uppara ḍhāri-ā*
> *Pallavi-a kusumi-a phali-a upavana cū-a caṃpaka sohi-ā*
> *Ma-araṅda pāṇa vimuddha mahu-ara saddeñ māṇasa mohi-ā*[82]
>
> ([They] saw the beautiful city surrounded by moats, rinsed by water
> Inside the walls were stone floors, outside—it was splashed with lime

[80] I use the word 'intermediate' for Avahaṭṭha to underline its uncertain status vis-à-vis the categories of local/vernacular *vs.* trans-local/cosmopolitan, as seen in an earlier section of this chapter.

[81] *Kīrttilatā*, p. 70.

[82] *Kīrttilatā*, p. 70.

Leafy, flowery, full of fruits, it is an orchard adorned with mango and campaka trees
Enchanting was the humming of the black bees, intoxicated on the sap of flowers.)

A detailed description of the cityscape follows—its ponds and dams, wide roads, and magnificent buildings (*nīka nīka niketanā*); broad staircases and large decorated windows too, find an appreciative mention. Paeans to the dazzling enormity of the place continue in the same vigorous metre, with a touch of hyperbole (*atiśayokti alaṅkāra*), as the poet tells us about 'hundreds and thousands of flagged milky-white houses (*dhavala gṛiha*), each decorated with a gold jar on top'.[83] The grandiose proportions of the physical setting were duly matched by a thriving city life: People spent their time in exclusive pursuits such as 'charity, honour, marriage,[84] festivities, songs, plays, literature, hospitality, supplication, and discrete recreational activities; anywhere you looked, you found them roaming around, playing, laughing and generally enjoying themselves'.[85]

If the city impressed with its sheer size and bustling life, it was even more striking for its affluence, evident as much in the vastness of its market and sheer magnitude of business as in the majestic buildings and entertainment avenues. As one entered the first gate of the market (*hāṭa*), one would notice the 'clinking of eight-metal (*aṣṭadhātu*) vessels being hammered into shape; the tinkering sound of brass utensils spread outside the metalsmiths'; a large number of villagers and towns-folk at the financiers'; separate markets of paddy, gold, betel leaves, delicacies, fish, and so on. If one tells this story truthfully, it would start sounding like a lie!' The rush was at its maximum in the afternoon 'when goods from all over the world [*sakalapṛithvī cakra*] came to the realm to be sold', and when all sorts of traders came and 'sold all their wares and bought everything in an instant, *khaṇa eke sabe vikkaṇathisabbe kichu kiṇa-ite pāvathi*'.[86]

83 *Kīrttilatā*, p. 71.

84 It is not clear why the author included 'marriage' in the list of activities that usually occupied people in the city.

85 *Kīrttilatā*, p. 72.

86 *Kīrttilatā*, pp. 74–5.

As 'the two princes went into the market, there were thousands of elephants and hundreds of thousands of horses, *tado ve kumaro pa-iṭṭhe bajāro jahī lakhkha ghorā ma-aṅgā hajāro*'. Further, there were 'low-born maid-servants, *ceṭi mandā* and slave women and men, *vādi vandā*'.[87] For Vidyapati, however, the most colourful manifestation of the city's opulence was its women in hundreds and thousands: There were trader-women—pretty, young, and virtuous sitting in the streets; but there were also a large number of courtesans and sex workers: women of easy virtue available for a price, living in such majestic houses that seemed to have been built by Viśvakarmā, the divine patron of metals and architecture, himself! A large number of verses are devoted to describing their make-up, hairstyles, perfumes, attire, and sheer bodily charms. It would be no exaggeration to say that the male-poet in Vidyapati, possibly aided by his 'rural' sensibility, was obsessed with the women of Jaunpur. A familiar Sanskrit trope, gendered but time-tested, to mark happy times is also invoked: 'hordes of beautiful women, with eyes as large as the leaves of land-lotus plants, *thalakamala patta pamāna netrahi* and with a gait like that of an elephant, *kuñjaragāminī*, roam around the roads and squares, turning back every now and then to check'.[88]

What confirms the status of *Kīrttilatā*'s Jaunpur as a truly cosmopolitan city, however, is its stunning ethno-cultural diversity, beautifully captured by the poet. Hordes of Brāhmaṇas, Kāyasthas, Rājapūtas, and many castes (*jātis*) 'lived together, *mili basa-i cappari*'.[89] Then there were a large number of *ghulams* (slaves) to be

[87] *Kīrttilatā*, p. 81.

[88] At another place, the poet claims, the young women met everyone's eyes with their sidelong glance, '*sabba-u kerā rijunayan taruṇī herai baṅk*' (*Kīrttilatā*, p. 77). The remark probably also alerted the reader/listener to the urban(e) sensibility the poet is addressing here. Govardhana, a poet in the court of Lakṣamaṇasena (late twelfth-century Bengal) and a contemporary of the more famous Jayadeva, remarked on the differences between rural and urban sensibilities with a verse about how the sidelong glance of a woman trying to seduce a man could, in rural areas, be interpreted as her being a witch. See Knutson, *Into the Twilight of Sanskrit Court Poetry*, p. 7.

[89] *Kīrttilatā*, p. 77.

bought, and there were also numerous Mīrs, Maliks, Salārs, Khojās, and an infinite number of Turks (*turakas/turuṣka/tullukas/tulukas*). Here is Vidyapati's somewhat exoticized and colourful description of the cultural mix:

Hindū Tuluka milala vāsa
Ekaka dhamme a-okāka hāsa
Katahu bāṅga katahu veda
Katahu bisamila katahu cheda
Katahu Ojhā katahu Khojā
Katahu nakata katahu rojā
Katahu tambārū katahu kūjā
Katahu nīmāja katahu pūjā
Katahu Tulukā bala kara
vāṭa jāyate begāra dhara

(Hindus and Turks live together
One's religion funny to the other
Bānga[90] here, Vedas there
Bismillah here, sacrifices there
Ojha[91] here, Khoja[92] there
Nakata[93] here, Roza[94] there
Copper vessel here, a kūzā[95] there
Namāj here, pūjā there
Sometimes the Turks use coercion
[forcing] passers-by into unpaid labour.)

[90] Persian: *banga* meaning 'the call to prayer from the minaret of a mosque'. See Steingass, *Comprehensive Persian–English Dictionary*, p. 152.

[91] A North Indian exorcist.

[92] An eunuch.

[93] From Sanskrit: *nakta*, meaning a type of 'religious vow or penance' whereby one eats only at night. See Apte, *Sanskrit–English Dictionary*, pp. 532–3.

[94] Persian: *roza*, a fasting day, especially during the month of Ramazan, when it is not permitted to eat till the evening. See Steingass, *Comprehensive Persian–English Dictionary*, p. 594.

[95] Persian: *kuza*, an earthen bottle with a long narrow neck, commonly used to minimize wastage of water in the water-starved Persian-speaking world during the middle ages. See Steingass, *Comprehensive Persian–English Dictionary*, p. 1061.

Almost everything in Jaunpur, it would appear, was awe-inspiring for Vidyapati. Yet, he probably found much there that was exotic, even alienating, for his rural–Brāhmaṇa self. There were two aspects in particular that he singled out for separate and extended treatment. The women of the city fascinated him. He kept coming back to the theme again and again through the second pallava, and glimpses of these literary vignettes we have already discussed above. Equally intriguing to him, it seems, were the Turks, who he described separately and at length in a metre (*bhujanṅgaprayāta chhanda*) that goes well with the authorial intent to surprise and amuse:

Kharīde pahūco bahutto gulāmo
Turuṣke Turuṣke aneko salāmo
....
Abe-be bhanantā sarābā pi-antā
Kalīmā kahantā kalāme jiantā
Kasīdā kāḍhantā masīdā bhamantā
Kitebā paṭhanta tulukkā anantā
Ati gah sumaru Khodā-e, khā-e le bhānga ka gunḍā
Binu kāraṇahi kohā-e va-an tātala tamakunḍā
Turuk tuṣārahi calala hāṭa bhami herā cāha-i
Āḍī ḍīṭhi nihāri davali dāḍhī thuka vāha-i[96]

(Countless slaves to be bought
Turks keep exchanging *salam* after salam
....
They spit out 'abe-be', drink alcohol
They recite *kalama*, live on poetry
Carve *kashidas* and visit mosques
Countless Turks recite *khutba*[97]
They heartily remember Khoda and swallow a mouthful of bhāṅga[98]
Get angry without reason, and then their faces resemble a hot copper pot
Riding snow-white horses in the market, they inspect animals[99]
When they cast a sidelong glance, spit spreads all over their beard.)

[96] *Kīrttilatā*, pp. 83–4.

[97] The congregational Friday prayer for Muslims. However, the word *kiteba* might alternatively refer to the book (Persian: *kitab*) meaning the Quran.

[98] A plant-based intoxicant found in the Indian subcontinent.

[99] Alternatively, this could be translated as 'he collects taxes on animals'.

Historians of medieval India would be familiar with the image of Turks as illiterate, uncouth, and lacking in good manners. Such stereotypes, it would appear, circulated in certain urban circuits of North India, as Persian accounts would also attest.[100] In fact, Turks were not the only ones among the migrant Muslims who were vulnerable to typecasting or ridicule. In the fifteenth century, this is what a Persian-speaking Mulla reportedly said when the Afghan ruler Sultan, Bahlul Lodi, came into his presence: 'Praise be to God: Strange people [Afghans] have appeared. I do not know whether they are the predecessors of Antichrist or possess the nature of Antichrist themselves. They call the mother, *Mur*; the brother, *rur*; the house, *gur*; the village, *shur*; and the man, *nūr*'.[101]

It is equally tempting to recall and tune into the now decades-long debate about the multiple, and historically contingent literary representations of the 'other' in Indic languages in the medieval period.[102] It is more pertinent, however, in the light of the larger textual dynamics of *Kīrttilatā*, as well as the concerns of this chapter, to take this 'othering' of Turks as part of our poet's wider project of presenting the cultural mosaic that the city of Jaunpur, appeared to be.

As the reference above to the use of force (*bala kara*) indicated, the poet was also cognizant of the potential discord that the tremendous density and diversity of the populace could engender. Indeed, it could, at least on occasion, even lead to chaos and breakdown of the social order. Some of it could be benign: It was easy for people to lose their way in the veritable 'ocean of humanity, *nara samudda-o*'.[103]

[100] Nizam al-Din Awliya in the fourteenth century, for example, approvingly narrated a story in which a pious Muslim described a Turk in similar terms. See Sijzi, *Fawa'id al Fu'ad*, cited in Kumar, *The Emergence of the Delhi Sultanate*, pp. 200–1.

[101] This is Siddiqui's translation of the relevant passage in Mushtaqui, *Waqi'at-i-Mushtaqui*, p. 9.

[102] For fascinating discussions of the contentious historiographic issues, see Chattopadhyaya, *Representing the Other?*; Pollock, 'Rāmāyaṇa and Political Imagination'; Talbot, 'Inscribing the Other'; Thapar, 'Imagined Religious Communities?'.

[103] *Kīrttilatā*, p. 75.

In the melee on the streets, one's body brushed against that of others so much so that the *tilak* on one's forehead might rub off on another's! But even these incidental transgressions were not always so benign: ladies' bangles could be crushed against male dancers disguised as women or, worse still, a Brāhmaṇa's sacred thread might fall on a cāṇḍāla's body. Again, the worst and most wilful excesses are attributed to the Turk:

> he catches hold of the Brāhmaṇa boy and rubs cow-fat [*gā-ika caruā*] on his forehead; licks up [the boy's] *tilak*, rips off his sacred thread, and seeks to crush him under his horse, *ūpara carāva-e cāha ghora*; he prepares alcohol with rice, demolishes the temple and builds a mosque; the whole earth is saturated with graves and domes and there is hardly any place to put one's foot on; he drives out people calling them Hindus, even the tiniest/youngest of Turks keeps threatening everyone, *choṭaho tuluko bhabhakī mār*.[104]

At one level, instances such as the one cited above, might be comparable to, if not worse than the scenes of anarchy that ostensibly gripped Tirhut in the aftermath of the killing of Raja Gaṇesara by Arsalan. It is doubtful, however, if Vidyapati himself thought so. Earlier in the section it was noted how he seemed to be in appreciative awe of the wonders of the city. Did his account of the excesses of the Turks and other instances of 'disorder' cited above militate against that spirit? At one stage, while describing the chaotic atmosphere of the city, the poet notes that 'the king [Rā-e] kept an eye over the city'.[105] At another point, in his narrative of the Turks running amok in Jaunpur, he is careful to point out how a government official, '*muqaddam* with an arrow [and a bow] keeps watch over him [the Turk] and forces him to sit still',[106] gesturing towards the presence of law-enforcing agencies in the city. He came back to the theme of law enforcement at the end of his account of the Turks, just in case the reader might have misunderstood him, and declared, 'May the Sultan under whose

104 *Kīrttilatā*, p. 88.
105 *Kīrttilatā*, p. 77.
106 *Kīrttilatā*, p. 84.

authority, even Turks such as these are in check, live long!'[107] That is why, notwithstanding the unruly conduct of certain rogue elements in the city, he was able to hold on to the view, expressed earlier in the section, that it was like 'a second incarnation of heaven [*amarāvatī*]'.[108] He reassured his readers/listeners repeatedly that 'everyone was good and all were wealthy, *save su-ana save sadhana*',[109] and added that

Sabba-u ṇāri viakhkhaṇī sabba-u susthita loka
Siri Ibarāhimasāhi guṇe ṇahi cintā ṇahi soka[110]

(All the women were sagacious and everyone was well-placed
By virtue of Śrī Ibrahim Shah, there are no worries and no troubles.)

To put it in the more familiar, modern historiographic vocabulary: Is it not possible to say that the dharma of the Sanskrit literary tradition was underwritten here, in Vidyapati's Apabhraṃśa rendering, by a state that was primarily invested in the Persian literary tradition? How did the poet perceive and represent the state under the Sharqi Sultan, Ibrahim Shah?

The 'Imperial' State of the Sharqis

The entire third pallava and a little of the fourth of *Kīrttilatā* focussed on Kīrttisiṃha's liaising with or, more accurately, his supplication before Sultan Ibrahim Shah. Vidyapati used the opportunity, however, to give a detailed account of the Sharqi kingdom: Its physical setting, majestic court, elaborate bureaucracy, its patronage to a large number of subordinate princes speaking a variety of languages, its infallible machinery of justice, and its large and apparently invincible army (consisting of foot soldiers, horses, and elephants) come in for embellished and evidently exaggerated treatment. After having told us in the sombre metre of a couplet (*dohā*) that the two brothers, in

107 *Kīrttilatā*, p. 89.
108 *Kīrttilatā*, p. 73.
109 *Kīrttilatā*, p. 77.
110 *Kīrttilatā*, p. 81.

curiosity and for work, entered the Sharqi court, the poet breaks into *padmāvatī chhanda*, another metre suited to celebrate heroism and invoke the vīra rasa:

> *Lo-aha sammadde bahuviha vadde aṃbara manḍala pūrī-ā*
> *Āvatte Turukkā Khāṇa Malikkā pa-a bhare patthar cūrī-ā*
> *Dūra hetti āvā baḍada-u rāvā dravali duārahi bārī-ā*
> *Cāhate chāhara āva-i bāhara gālima gaṇa-e na pārī-ā*[111]
>
> (The throng of people and [sound of] musical instruments filled the skies
> The feet of incoming Turks, Khans, and Maliks crushed the floor-stones
> Great kings from distant places too were stopped right away at the gate
> Favoured boys come out, ghulams cannot be counted.)

'People travel in all directions, from islands to mountains and seas, to meet the Rāṇas and Rauts but', added the poet, 'you would find all of them together here at the door [of the Sharqi court]'. Rājapūtas from '*Telaṅga, Vaṅgā, Cola and Kaliṅga* were all there. They, Rājapūtas and Brāhmaṇas [*paṇḍia*] alike, shivered with fear, gathered courage, and made submissions in their own languages, *ni-a bhāsā* [before the Sultan's court].'[112] The court, the poet noted more than once, was special and above the whole universe;[113] its king, *Pātisāha* was supreme, and only God, *Karatāra*, was above him. Persian names of each of the umpteen doors of the court are given, before wondering rhetorically if Viśvakarmā, the god of metals and architecture, had himself been at work there![114] Expectedly, the lord of such an exalted court was not easily accessible. On their first visit, the two brothers and their companions looked around, discovered its secrets (*rahasa*), and probably found out its procedures. They also

111 *Kīrttilatā*, p. 89.

112 *Kīrttilatā*, pp. 90–1.

113 *Ehu khāsa darabāra sa-ela mahīmaṇḍala uppari*. This is one of the many examples in the text of the juxtaposition of two very distinct linguistic traditions in one sentence/stanza: the [Persian] *darbar*, court denoted as the supreme arbiter over the (Sanskrit) *mahīmaṇḍala*, whole earth.

114 *Kīrttilatā*, p. 92.

got their identities verified with a well-behaved officer, *siṭṭha padika parica-a pamāni-a*.[115] On the next visit, they called upon the prime minister, *ujjīra*, told him about their work, and probably requested an audience with the Sultan. For, on the next visit, presumably after a(n) (unspecified) time lag, they met the Sultan at an auspicious moment, *subha muhutta*.

To their relief, Ibrahim Shah was sufficiently moved by their submissions and ordered the Khans and *umra* (singular: *amir*; refers to military commanders) to prepare with arms and provisions to move towards Tirhut. However, reports Vidyapati, news of some disturbance elsewhere arrived and the army embarked on a campaign towards the west rather than the east. This seems to have left Kīrttisiṃha crestfallen. His elder brother Vīrasiṃha recommended patience and persistence, before describing the equation between him and the Sultan with remarkable candour for a poetic composition like *Kīrttilatā*:

U viakhkhaṇa tummeṃ guṇamanta
U sadhamma tohe suddha oho sadaya tohe raja khanḍi-a
O jigīṣu tohe sūra uha rā-a tohe rā-a paṇḍi-a
Puhavīpati suratāna u tummeṃ rā-akumāra
Ekke citte ja-i sevia-i dhu-a hosa-i parakāra[116]

(He is sagacious, you are virtuous
He is with dharma and you are pure, he kind and you dethroned
He seeks victory and you are brave, he is king, you are a raj-paṇḍita
He is Lord of the earth, you a prince
If you persist in waiting on [him], surely some way out would appear.)

Kīrttisiṃha decided to accompany, though perhaps not participate in, the Sharqi campaign. The text noted terrible hardships for him during the journey, even as the march of the victorious army is described and celebrated in some detail. Particularly noteworthy in this description is the fact that Vidyapati likened Ibrahim Shah's expedition to a *digvijaya*, wherein the enemies were killed or chased away, and the territorial frontiers were extended up to the oceans.

[115] *Kīrttilatā*, p. 95.
[116] *Kīrttilatā*, p. 106.

There was not a single king who could stop his march: The only way to save one's life was to submit to him and become a tax-paying subject, *rai-ati*![117]

A second aspect that came in for renewed emphasis in the third pallava was the system of justice under the Sharqi dispensation: Once one became a subject, one was absolutely safe from all excesses.[118] One had to pay heavily even for the smallest of crimes. Earlier in the text, it was noted that even the poorest of the poor, *raṅka*, could prevail upon the court with their truthful solicitation for justice.[119] It comes as no surprise of course, that the dharmic order (*dhamma*) was re-established in Tirhut towards the end of the text, after a bloody battle that Kīrttisiṃha waged against the 'usurper' Arsalan with the help of the apparently invincible Sharqi military machine.

What the two princes from the 'local' chieftaincy of Tirhut witnessed in the Jaunpur court was truly remarkable: hordes of poets (*bhāṭṭā ghaṭṭā*) singing praises of the Sultan in the palace[120] and perhaps outside; scores of tributary princes from far-off places speaking diverse languages, but beholden in equal measure to the Sharqi sultan; a formalized system of justice, dispensing grace and punishment to all; a Turkish ruler with the Persian title of Badshah (Pātisāha), wedded to dharma (*sadhamma*), and engaged in a military campaign for the Sanskritic ideal of digvijaya; and finally, a territorial expanse that ostensibly reached up to the 'natural' frontier of the oceans. This, in any case, was how Vidyapati would have liked the 'audience' of the Apabhraṃśa composition to perceive the Sharqi state. It is remarkable that the Brāhmaṇa poet celebrated, in the process of eulogizing his patron of humble means and local aspirations, the ostensibly 'imperial' Sharqi state, that among other things, engaged in digvijaya, extended the frontiers of its domain endlessly to the limits of the oceans, and subdued princes from distant lands speaking a variety of languages.

117 *Kīrttilatā*, pp. 109–10.

118 Literally, 'nothing—not even weeds and leaves, *khara pā-ia* could touch you'; see *Kīrttilatā*, p. 111.

119 *Kīrttilatā*, p. 92.

120 *Kīrttilatā*, p. 90.

Literature and Politics

Reflecting back on the three 'entangled worlds' that *Kīrttilatā* constructed for its readers/listeners, it is not difficult to see that none of these worlds were simple or one-dimensional. The local political sphere of the Tirhut chieftaincy, for example, was firmly grounded literarily in the epic (or an Apabhraṃśa version of the epic Rāmāyaṇa) traditions, and ethically in the Sanskrit ecumenical as the refrain to dharma suggests. The territorial domain and aspirations of the Oiṇīvāra dynasty might have been localized and humble, but their protagonists were expected to match the high ethical standards (embedded in dharma) set by Puraṇic heroes. As we have seen in the last chapter, Vidyapati elaborated these ethics with reference to their more historical, as against mythic, exemplars later in his career in *Puruṣaparīkṣā*.

We know that even though the Sharqis did intermittently try to expand their territorial boundaries and ruled over a limited number of diverse linguistic–cultural zones, their domains never reached up to the oceans.[121] We also know that a number of other rival states co-existed with them in North India, and that they never held a position of decisive ascendancy relative to their rivals. One might point out that Vidyapati's depictions of the Sharqi state and its accomplishments are obviously inaccurate, even 'unreliable'. Nor is it my intention to argue otherwise. Rather, my interest lies in the poetic imagination that used *Kīrttilatā* as a vehicle for a set of very specific political ideals (that those ideals did not match the existing realities of the time is a different matter, though not completely irrelevant). At the core of these ideals was the aspiration for an imperial formation with universal claims, majestic courts, and supreme authority. Is this merely a continued and conservative/nostalgic adherence to the age-old Sanskritic ideal of *rājyam* that Pollock thought had disappeared during this time?[122] Perhaps not.

We have seen already, how the Sanskrit ākhyāyikā text was supposed to be written in the vikaṭa style, and celebrate the achievements

[121] See Nizami, 'The Sharqi Kingdom of Jaunpur'.

[122] Pollock, 'India in the Vernacular Millennium: Literary Culture and Polity: 1000–1500', p. 56.

of its protagonist. We have also seen that the carita/cariu genre in Apabhraṃśa and Prakrit was often wedded to the Puranic mode of mythologizing that could at best revolve around semi-historical characters. If Vidyapati still appeared, on occasion, to candidly provide some details not particularly favourable towards the eponymous hero of his composition (his helplessness while on the westward expedition of Ibrahim Shah or his tiny stature compared to Ibrahim Shah), it might be attributed to the indirect 'influence' of the history-inspired tradition of biography in Persian. However, we must not forget that unlike the Persian biographies that were invariably written in prose, this Avahaṭṭha composition was a versified work by a poet fully cognizant of its 'recital' possibilities (after all, Vidyapati was known in his lifetime, as well as later, mostly for his song compositions in the Maithili 'vernacular').

One way to approach the question is to revisit the unique character of Apabhraṃśa, or rather Avahaṭṭha, in which *Kīrttilatā* was composed.[123] It would be too simplistic to see Apabhraṃśa merely as something between the vernacular dialects and the cosmopolitan languages on a linear scale of 'how far the language travelled'. On the one hand, it was a medium appreciated by all, *sab jan miṭṭhā*, as against the language of the gods that only the 'chosen of the gods', namely, the intellectuals, *buajana* (mostly Brāhmaṇas), followed; on the other, it could carry the message much beyond its immediate locale, unlike the more rooted 'vernaculars'. The fact that manuscripts of *Kīrttilatā* were found as far as Fatehpur in Uttar Pradesh, and possibly in Rajasthan, only confirms the inter-intelligibility between various registers/versions of the language popular in different parts of North India. This double character of Apabhraṃśa gives the aspirational realism of Kīrttisiṃha's biography a very resonant and specific quality. It is crucial here to resist the temptation to look at *Kīrttilatā* or for that matter, Apabhraṃśa as mere exceptions to the otherwise binary world of vernacular sub-regional literary mediums

[123] One might safely put aside Sheldon Pollock's sweeping remark in this context that 'neither Prakrit after the fourth century nor Apabhramsha at any time was permitted a role in articulating political discourse of any stripe.' See Pollock, *The Language of the Gods*, p. 104.

on the one side, and the cosmopolitan Sanskrit on the other. Sheldon Pollock himself noted how,

> In prediscursive life there existed not languages but only language-continua, and along such a continuum, what in later discourse came to be named, say, Kannada imperceptibly merged into what was later called Telugu. In such a world, Kannada and Telugu should not even be regarded as pregiven points on a spectrum; the eventual segmentation of that continuum was an effect of, among other things, literary vernacularization itself.[124]

While there possibly cannot be any disagreement with the assertion about language continua, it is important to realize that at least in North India, 'vernacularization' did not necessarily and immediately lead to an irreversible segmentation of the language continuum. To put it differently, carving a vernacular out of the language continuum was not a zero-sum game. When Bengali was carved out through 'textualization' from this continuum, for example, it did not immediately lead to a situation wherein Maithili–Bengali- and Persian-tinged Apabhraṃśa works (such as those of Vidyapati and Jyotirīśvara before him) would stop being composed, or intelligible to the people, in what we now know as the region of Bengal. The same would hold true, evidently, for the numerous rāso texts from the Rajasthan region or the carita/cariu compositions from the Gwalior area during the fourteenth through the sixteenth centuries, composed in variegated lexical–syntactical shades of what we are used to imprecisely identifying as western Rajasthani, Śaurasenī, early Avadhī, and various shades of Apabhraṃśa, discussed in the first section of this chapter. The find-spots for most of these texts would suggest a pan-North Indian circulation and intelligibility. The fact that *Puruṣaparīkṣā* referred to certain minor princes (Cācikadeva in *satyavīra kathā*, for example)[125] from Rajasthan and Gujarat even though no Sanskrit work referred to them, also indicates the circulation of political lore in North India independent of Sanskrit.

To come back to *Kīrttilatā*, the universalist ideal that the text articulated would most likely be circulated much beyond the Mithila

[124] Pollock, *The Language of the Gods*, p. 415.

[125] See *Puruṣaparīkṣā*, pp. 28–32.

region. More critical for my analysis is the fact that the articulation of this political aspiration was not merely about thinly extending one's domain to distant lands without unsettling the sub-regional geopolitical realities.[126] Nor was this imperium mutually exclusive with regional or local aspirations. Rather it celebrated the local state formations reaching down to the lowest denominator among the taxpayers, even as it rode on these small and not-so-small domains and sought to integrate a variety of them within its fold. Late Apabhraṃśa, and even some of the 'vernaculars' (Avadhī, for example), intelligible outside of their immediate zones, were ideally suited vehicles for such an enterprise, for their simultaneous vertical and horizontal reach.

An interesting aspect of these linguistic registers was the abundant infidelity with which they cohabited lexically with Persian, the new cosmopolitan entity on the block, in language, as well as in the new set of ideational resources that it brought. Our discussion of the language, Avahaṭṭha, of *Kīrttilatā* earlier in the chapter, noted how one of its distinctive traits was the use of a large number of not just *tatsam*, Sanskrit loanwords, but also a range of Persian words. It is possible to argue that this 'language practice' signalled a deeper, if less visible, move towards a politico-ideological mutation.[127] The last chapter discussed how the Sanskritic ideal of puruṣārtha could

[126] David Shulman noted, in the context of Sheldon Pollock's formulation of a Sanskrit cosmopolis, 'that the cosmopolitan poets such as Bharavi and Magha were professionals, members of a non-official guild, practitioners of a well-defined craft—the production of polished (*ullikhita*) poetry in Sanskrit for consumption by a refined elite'. See Orsini, Shulman, and Venkatachelapathy, 'A Review Symposium: Literary Cultures in History', p. 381.

[127] It is fair to point out that on the rare occasions when Pollock does try to factor in the presence of the Delhi Sultanate and the Persian ecumene, he does vaguely hint at the possibilities discussed here. The closest he comes is when he mentions that '[t]here are dramatic instances of vernacularization largely contemporaneous with the expansion of Sultanate power and that actually remark on its presence, such as in Maharashtra. Reverberations of the rise of the new political powers, quite like those in the *chansons de geste*, may be heard in a wide variety of early north Indian vernacular works'. See Pollock, *The Language of the Gods*, p. 493.

be used to subsume a discrete discourse on political ethics. The detailed theoretical and empirical explication of puruṣārtha, not yet formulated by Vidyapati when he composed *Kīrttilatā*,[128] was an important operative ideal in *Kīrttilatā* too. Though the latter text's construction was shorter and vaguer, the very reason why the black bee narrates the story of Kīrttisiṃha is because he was the 'ideal man'. Like an ideal man he lived the life of a hero (vīra) with honour (māna). Later in the third pallava, when he finally got an audience with the Sharqi sovereign Ibrahim Shah, this is how Vidyapati describes the prince's state of mind:

> *Ajja ucchava ajja kallāna*
> *Ajja sudina sumuhūtta ajja mā-e majhu putta jā-ia*
> *Ajja punna purisattha pātisāha pāposa pā-ia*[129]
>
> (Today is merriment, today is bliss
> It is an auspicious day and occasion, truly am I my mother's son today
> My puruṣārtha is complete now that I got to kiss the King's feet.)

It is difficult to miss the alliterative positing (*punna purisattha pātisāha pāposa*) of the ideal of puruṣārtha with *pāposa* (Persian: *pabush*), the pre-Islamic Persian practice of kissing the feet of the Sovereign as a mark of submission. The particular reformulation whereby the realization of the Sanskritic ideal of puruṣārtha is represented as contingent on the protagonist's symbolic or real performance of the Persian practice of kissing the feet cannot be easily dismissed as a mere incidental observation of a poet. Let us bear in mind that the poet was not beholden for patronage to the Sharqi king, for whom he was probably a non-entity and his composition of no immediate value. In fact, as several such moves (digvijaya by the *Pātisāha*, for example) in the text would suggest, the deployment of Persian concepts and not just words was a critical component in Vidyapati's political imagination of the imperium. This was the reconfigured, and not 'forsaken', ideal of *rājyam*. This is surely interesting, if a little

128 Though the precise dates for neither text is certain, it is evident that *Kīrttilatā* was composed at least about a decade before *Puruṣaparīkṣā*.

129 *Kīrttilatā*, p. 98.

intriguing in the face of the present state of historiography of the 'early modern' period. That it was only with the Mughals, a century later, that the state proactively thrived on, even consciously cultivated, Sanskritic, Hindavi, and Persian literary sensibilities together, is something that cannot easily be explained.[130]

Yet, that does reopen the more general question of the fit between the actual territorial expanse of the states during the period, and the alleged shrinking of the poetic imagination. The relationship between language, literature, and power is undeniable, though not as yet fully fleshed out in the medieval Indian context. It would, however, be naïve to assume that poetic time and political time moved at the same speed. Poetic imagination is notoriously elusive. Even beyond nostalgia, a literary text might sometimes continue to hold on to an ideal and prefer to rework it rather than give up on it under adverse circumstances. On the other hand, it might sometimes even help do the spadework for an ideal that it conjured up at best as a 'realistic' fantasy. The distinction between 'code' and 'message' that Peter Burke made long ago, and that we discussed in Chapter 2 in this volume, assumes critical significance in this context.[131] The codes, not as precisely delineable as the algorithm of a computer programme, take root over time, while the message may 'instantly' be delivered. If we perceive *Kīrttilatā* as an expressive text with explicit political content, it is difficult to hold on to the idea that the 'new type of political space' was always 'historically co-present' with the new literary sensibilities. Where the political potency of a language and literary composition is concerned, it is equally important to cast one's glance diachronically, a practice that James Scott playfully called an 'occupational hazard' for historians.[132]

In the same vein, it might be pertinent to point out that the prehistories of imperial formations, such as that of the Mughals, are

[130] For a very interesting discussion of the role of Hindavi in Mughal court culture, see Phukan, 'Through Throats where Many Rivers Meet', pp. 33–58. For a very recent and detailed study of how Sanskrit was deployed in the service of Mughal imperial enterprise, see Truschke, 'Cosmopolitan Encounters'.

[131] Burke, *The Italian Renaissance: Culture and Society in Italy*, p. 3.

[132] Scott, 'Preface', *The Art of Not Being Governed*.

almost always written in terms of preceding theories of kingship, institutional legacies of previously existing states, or early politico-ideological affiliations of ruling dynasties. Rarely does such a study 'stoop down' to considering how a pre-state or proto-state populace is prepared for the final conversion into becoming a full-fledged imperial subject. My study suggests that the literary representations (such as *Kīrttilatā*) of an imperial formation, real or fantastic, that were made available to the would-be subjects of an empire might have played an important role in such a preparation. No instrumentalized teleology is implied here. Such a process is never simple, linear, terminable, or spectacular. Rarely would it be intended. Still, if the process of the 'emergence' of imperium has to be understood as anything more than the realization of the individual ambitions and ideological aspirations of a conqueror/dynasty, such a study is unavoidable.

Conclusion

Not that I assert poets to be prophets in the gross sense of the word, or that they can foretell the form as surely as they foreknow the spirit of events: such is the pretence of superstition, which would make poetry an attribute of prophecy, rather than prophecy an attribute of poetry.... Poets are the unacknowledged legislators of the world.[1]

—Percy Bysshe Shelley

Let me begin with a quick and brief summary of the ground covered so far in this volume. We began by noting that Vidyapati was a prolific author with an extraordinary range of compositions—covering a variety of themes in several languages—to his credit. His patrons were all local chieftains with very humble political ambitions, or so historians of larger imperial establishments assess. They belonged to a region, Mithila, which was not

[1] Shelley, 'A Defence of Poetry'.

located on the main arteries of commercial and military communication. Nor was it an integral and stable slice of the territorial possessions of any of the bigger kingdoms that laid claim over it, whether the Sharqis, the Bengal Sultanate, or, earlier in the fourteenth century, the Delhi Sultanate. Yet, its rich legacy of Sanskrit learning and emergent tradition of 'vernacular' creativity threw up a great crop of poets and scholars, from Jyotirīśvara and Caṇḍeśvara to Gaṅgeśa and Vācaspati Miśra during the fourteenth and fifteenth centuries. Vidyapati was part of this community of scholars. Yet he was so outstanding in his versatility that he becomes as much a puzzle for the historian, as he remains a delight for the local cultural chauvinist.

It is only when Vidyapati is located in the trans-local networks of the multilingual literary cultures of North India in fifteenth century that the puzzle starts to unravel slowly. As noted in Chapter 2 in this volume, the multilinguality of the fifteenth century itself had a very specific character. First, it was polymorphous: this is seen in the borrowings of words, bending of verbs, tweaking of genres, adaptation of metres, use of several languages in the same text, even occasionally in configuring liminal languages of the kind referred to by Sudipta Kaviraj.[2] Second, it was polycentric: this is evident not only in the centrally located bigger centres of power like Gwalior, Gujarat, and Malwa, but also in the 'outlying' areas like Bengal, Mithila, and Kashmir. Third, it affected all the named languages, as well as the as yet unnamed speech forms that either developed into vernacular dialects with time or disappeared altogether. Fourth, it was multi-directional: the traffic of 'influence' between languages might have been uneven but it was never unidirectional. Sanskrit and Persian too were affected by the 'vernaculars' and by each other as the latter were affected by the two cosmopolitan languages.

The addition of Persian to the conundrum and the steady 'mainstreaming' of a whole variety of disparate populations only made it more complex and multifarious. These disparate peoples included those who spoke Turkish, Persian, Arabic, and vernacular subsets of these. Sanskrit texts often described them with blanket terms like

2 See Kaviraj, 'The Two Histories of Literary Culture in Bengal'.

mleccha and *yavana*.[3] No less significant, however, was the coming into historical visibility of the other, indeed the 'original' mlecchas: those that the modern anthropologists, like the Sanskrit scholars of the Middle Ages, describe with a blanket term of their own, the 'tribals'.[4]

The aforementioned process gained in no small measure from the policies of Delhi Sultans moving into regions that the Persian chroniclers described as *mawas*.[5] It also gained from the activities of those who fell from the Sultanate's favour, and along with their retainers, turned the mawas into their habitat.[6] In the fifteenth century too, Vidyapati mentioned the continued initiative by the state to bring the deserted, or as yet uncultivated, lands (*ujjaṭabhūmi*) under cultivation.[7]

The emergence of multilingualism, it would appear then, was socially and politically powered by a long-term historical tendency towards closer interactions among people from diverse, part-shared and part-distinct, geocultural backgrounds. The point that emerged repeatedly, and from very different contexts, through the various chapters, is the continued vitality, indeed greater intensification, of

[3] 'Mleccha' literally meant impure/dirty. Sanskrit scholars often used the word to refer to lower castes or those without a caste. Frequently, the word was used to refer to Muslims, Christians, and people of any religion that did not have a varṇa/caste system. As such, one of the first people they called mleccha were the Greeks, who came to India during the ancient period. The proper Sanskrit word for the Greeks however, was 'yavana'. This later word too soon became a generic expression to loosely refer to those who came via the northwestern frontiers of the Indian subcontinent.

[4] The speech practices of these other 'mlecchas' remain below the radar of historians, but it would not be far-fetched to assume that traces of them must be buried somewhere in the continuously expanding vocabularies of the different forms of Apabhraṃśa as well as the local dialects.

[5] Hodivala, *Studies in Indo-Muslim History*, Supplement: Vol. II, 'He Proceeded into Mawās', pp. 226–9. Mawas literally means 'a sanctuary' or 'a place of refuge', usually because of its not-so-easily fordable terrain. From the perspective of the courts of Delhi Sultanate, mawas carried the added sense of being 'disturbed locales yet to be tamed'.

[6] Kumar, *Emergence of the Delhi Sultanate*, especially Chapter 5.

[7] Vidyapati, *Likhanāvalī*, letter no. 10, p. 8.

these processes in the fifteenth century. The strong culture of multilingual forms was visible in extensive and disconnected regions during this period. Mahmud Begada (r. 1458–1511) of Gujarat, primarily invested in Persian, also sponsored his own Sanskrit biography;[8] Sultan Zain al-Abidin (r. 1420–1470) of Kashmir got *Rājataraṅginī* translated into Persian and revived Sanskrit literary production in Kashmir;[9] Maithili songs were increasingly being introduced into Sanskrit plays in Nepal and Mithila;[10] sufis in Bengal used the *maṅgal-kāvya* genre of premodern Bengali literature to glorify their Sheikhs;[11] a version of Mahābhārata was produced in the local dialect in Orissa.[12] The examples might be multiplied.

The most noteworthy aspect of multilingualism was that it brewed over a long period of time. Perhaps it was slow in the making, and became starkly visible only from the thirteenth century. But, it most certainly indexed a new cultural vitality riding on a long history that refused to be arrested with the disintegration of the Delhi Sultanate.[13] Experiments with multilinguality were only one of the many intermediate consequences of these processes, though. A parallel but related phenomenon also noticeable during the same period, that is, from the eleventh century onwards and coming into its own in the fifteenth century, was an unprecedented proliferation of literary compositions. This is true as much in the case of Sanskrit, as in that of the so-called vernaculars. Dozens of texts were composed in Sanskrit for the first time, for example, on the theme of proper conduct and prescribed rituals for Śudras alone.[14] Persian, the latest cosmopolitan entry into

[8] Kapadia, 'The Last *Cakravartin*?'.

[9] Zutshi, 'Past as Tradition, Past as History', p. 203.

[10] Mishra, '*Bhumikā*' in Vidyapati, *Gorakṣavijaya*, pp. 6–8.

[11] Eaton, *Rise of Islam and the Bengal Frontier*, especially Chapter 8, 'Islam and the Agrarian Order in the East'.

[12] Sahu, 'Sarala's Odra-*desa:* Literary Representations of a Regional Society'.

[13] Chattopadhyaya noted 'integrative tendencies' emanating out of greater interactions between differently developed localities from at least the seventh century onwards. See Chattopadhyaya, 'Political Processes and Structure of Polity'.

[14] We have references to at least forty-nine such texts between the fourteenth and seventeenth century. See Benke, 'The *Śūdrācāraśiromaṇi* of Kṛṣṇa Śeṣa'. I thank Mayank Kumar for bringing this work to my notice.

the subcontinent, added in no small measure to this geometrical progression. As noted in Chapter 3 in this volume, texts have a tendency to thrive on each other, sometimes without acknowledging the debts.

The swelling mass of literary output in the fifteenth century was remarkably diverse in its themes, visions, genres, and novelty/orthodoxy. Yet, it is possible to identify a few powerful impulses. The common thread, weaving through each of my three case studies, was twofold: on the one hand, each composition was rooted in the deep histories of its own genre, theme, and orientation; on the other, each used its legacy flexibly and reconfigured the ideals that it articulated. The classicizing impulse is evident, but the contemporary flavour is unmistakable in each case. The debt to the Persian ecumene too, is present, although unevenly. In *Kīrttilatā*, it is explicit and ever present. In *Likhanāvalī*, it is implicit but substantive. In *Puruṣaparīkṣā*, it is somewhat indirect, mediated by a long history, and sublimated into the framing of the text. The insistent recurrence of visions of empire is evident in each of the three. It is significant, from the perspective of methodology, however, that the articulation of these visions differed with genre.

If we compare the genre of these texts, a pattern seems to emerge. *Likhanāvalī* was most beholden to the Persian genre of insha, but it was also clearly 'imagined' and hence entirely fictitious, gesturing towards a political setting, and catering to the professional needs of an occupation that was probably still in the process of reconstituting itself, that is, scribing. At a time when most of the major state formations conducted their official business in Persian, the appearance of a manual for framing official documents and writing letters in Sanskrit might appear incongruous. As we saw through the chapter (Chapter 3 in this volume), however, the system of documentation and the controversial occupation of the scribes had a long history in Sanskrit that seemed to have intermingled with the insha tradition in Persian in very interesting and productive ways. The expanding world of knowledge formations in various languages were thus constantly feeding upon and enriching each other.

Puruṣaparīkṣā, on the other hand, was largely historical with occasional legends and mythological tales being thrown in between. Where the presentation of a text on nīti (or naya) was concerned, this came in handy; the author conveniently deployed stories from imagined/mythic pasts to illustrate virtues for which no ready historical examples were available. It is in this text that we see an attempt on the part of one of the traditional elite (a Brāhmaṇa scholar) to use his knowledge of Sanskrit *śāstras* to produce what might be called a 'useable past': a collection of stories that claimed to do no more than illustrate the 'classical–universal' lore on nīti with the authority of history, Vedas, logic, and pragmatism. The fact that these tales were woven around the question of how to be an ideal man, and that they were told with the easy flair of a narrator in an oral context only made them more multivalent and easily accessible. In fact, Vidyapati was not the only person producing books on conduct with a classicizing impulse. As we saw, if there was a long history of kathā-driven nīti books in Sanskrit, the pre-Mughal period was also witness to a number of mirror-for-princes books in Persian that wove together ideas of manliness with political ethics. *Akhlaq-i Nasiri* was only one of the many such books available to North Indians during this period.

In *Kīrtilatā*, however, the tale remained largely historical and stuck to a known course of political events, even as the author took poetic liberties with the use of a 'vikaṭa' or vigorous style of retelling. This was particularly useful for creating the wide-eyed account of a cosmopolitan milieu that the author evidently wanted to eulogize. Such a style helped in a creative misrepresentation of the Sharqi court and capital as the ultimate earthly power (next only to the divine court of the mythic Indra): the abode of authority that extended into a limitless frontier, that upheld the tenets of dharma, that brooked no challenge and made no compromises, and where rajas from all directions waited for the royal grace in fear and hope. This was an imperium to look forward to. It was a political order worth preserving, and if not there, worth aspiring for.

In terms of their contents too, the three texts make for interesting comparison: *Likhanāvalī* hypothetically described a virtual checklist of a whole range of imperatives of state building that we are more familiar with from the kind of claims put forth by the Mughal state. It also sought to 'prepare' at least one kind of experts necessary for empire building—those well-versed in ideals of governance as well as techniques of appropriate documentation. In *Puruṣaparīkṣā*, the discourse on nīti and puruṣārtha readjusted caste and gender as essential components of social order and state power.[15] The text claimed to be non-sectarian and drew on diverse sources of authority: Vedic lore, recent history, and pragmatism. *Kīrttilatā*, on the other hand, juxtaposed two different but mutually compatible worlds. If the minor domain of Tirhut was local, unpretentious, and virtuous, the superior realm of the Sharqi 'imperium' was represented hyperbolically as unbounded in its expanse, extraordinarily prosperous, most powerful yet equally virtuous in protecting dharma.

The common thread running through each of the three compositions of Vidyapati, was a reformulated ideal of the imperium. The literary formation that supported the edifice of this imperium was composed of divergent, even contrasting contexts. Certainly, the socio-political and literary visions that sustained (and gained from) the establishment of big imperial states, whether that of the Cālukyas, Pratihāras, or of the Delhi Sultanate, did not disappear with their respective disintegration. They lingered and found hospitable ground in umpteen 'regional' locations, often—and this is the important point—without having to abandon their expansive tendencies. Vidyapati inherited and reworked these visions into newer, more 'actionable' knowledge forms. And as I have underlined earlier, he was not alone in this. Yet, these aspirational articulations seem to have been of no immediate consequence as far as the actual character of the polities in North India in the fifteenth century was concerned.

It was only in the sixteenth century that some of these ideals might have been actualized by the imperial state of the Mughals. In the absence of systematic research in the field, however, it is difficult to delineate with any degree of certainty as to how the Mughal state mediated and engaged with a society that was bred on visions of a socio-political order such as the ones articulated by Vidyapati in the fifteenth century. The political value of literature after all, can only be measured in the long duration. Recent research, however, does suggest that the Mughal court and its 'nobles' were not confined to Persian in their cultural engagements. Shantanu Phukan showed

[15] Clearly, political ethics for Vidyapati was not just about the state and its policies but also about validating entitlements and exclusions at the social level.

almost fifteen years ago that the 'ecology of Hindi' flourished fairly well in a world allegedly overwhelmed by Persian.[16] More recently, Audrey Truschke's research has underlined the significant place of Sanskrit in the 'political aesthetics' of the Mughal court.[17] How seriously the massive project of translating Sanskrit works into Persian was taken by the early Mughals is no longer a secret.[18]

Did Vidyapati, and others like him, anticipate and consciously prepare the ground for a grand empire like that of the Mughals? If historians wandered into this line of enquiry, they would—as Shelley so perspicaciously warned—risk taking 'poets to be prophets in the gross sense of the word'.

Studies of Mughal political culture or its public articulations of sovereignty in the sixteenth century tend to focus chiefly on Abul Fazl's sophisticated political theories. Akbar's claims of being the *insan-i kamil,* the establishment and disbanding of the *ibadat khana,* and the promulgation of *sulh-i kul* are the important components of this culture. The historical roots of these ideas, when they are not credited to the genius of a few men, or blamed on Akbar's upbringing in a Rājapūta household, are sought exclusively in the Persianate tradition: Turko-Mongol theories of kingship, Chingizid *torah,* Ibn al-Arabi's *Wahadat al-wujud,* or the *akhlaqi* ethics best represented by Nasir al-Din Tusi. While these might be valid areas to explore, it is difficult to see how non-Persian literary cultures could have been so irrelevant in a society as thoroughly multilingual as North India in the fifteenth century.

The land that the Mughals ruled over was not merely a 'territory' with the ability to throw up sufficient agrarian surplus to sustain a powerful state. The people who inhabited these lands and produced this surplus also had a history that any emergent political formation would have to contend with. Sheikh Mubarak, his sons, and countless others who participated in the making of the Mughal state and helped

16 Phukan, 'Through Throats where Many Rivers Meet'.

17 Truschke, 'Cosmopolitan Encounters'.

18 Badayuni, it seems, almost lost his job with the Mughal court because he was reported to have taken a short-cut while rendering a passage from Mahābhārata (*Razmnama*) into Persian. See Haider, 'Translating Texts and Straddling Worlds', pp. 121–2. Also see Ernst, 'Muslim Studies of Hinduism?'.

mediate this history were themselves a product of this, as were Sher Shah and Akbar himself. Any attempt to write about the ideological engagements of the Mughal state must also contend with the imperative force of that History that the fifteenth century exerted over the sixteenth. The methodological significance should not be missed here: if political culture is one of the critical forces that determine cultural politics, the vice versa is equally, if not more, true. Yet, the important point that emerges through my exploration in this volume is that both are subject to a prior history that historians must not ignore.

It is true that big imperial states often tend to be happy habitats for arts, including literature. But it is also frequently, and erroneously, assumed that the arts are so dependent on their imperial patrons that they rarely survive without them. Even a cursory survey of the cultural and intellectual milieu of the fifteenth century should suffice to prove otherwise. One might as well turn the presumption on its head, and ask whether large trans-local empires find fertile ground only in pre-existing fields of well-tended 'knowledge formations'? On the other hand, could it also be that the extraordinary vitality of literary cultures in the fifteenth century rode, in part at least, on the fact that it was a period unfettered by any imperial attempt to impose a singular vision of social order?

To come back to our protagonist in the fifteenth century, a period that was of unprecedented vitality for creative and scholarly pursuits, Vidyapati was indisputably one of the many luminaries of the time. But equally, many scholars would argue that some of his contemporaries and near contemporaries (Gaṅgeśa, the founder of *Navya-Nyāya* system of philosophy, for example), produced works of much greater sophistication and erudition than did our protagonist. Yet, as I have charted in this book, Vidyapati's genius lay primarily in the variety of themes and genres that he experimented in. It is no paradox then that it was in his unique versatility that Vidyapati most substantively embodied the spirit of the literary cultures of the fifteenth century.

Bibliography

Primary Literature

Abdul Rahman. *Sandeśarāsaka,* edited by C.M. Mayrhofer. Delhi: Motilal Banarsidass Publishers Private Ltd, 1998.

Abdur Rashid, ed. *Insha-i-Mahru* [Letters of 'Ain ud-din 'Ain ul-Mulk 'Abudullah bin Mahru]. Lahore: Research Society of Pakistan, University of the Punjab, 1965.

Abul Fazl Allami. *Ain- i Akbari,* vol. II, translated by H.S. Jarret, corrected and further annotated by J.N. Sarkar. Delhi: Low Price Publications, 2006.

Amir Hasan Sijzi. *Fawai'd al Fua'ad,* translated by B.B. Lawrence. New York: Paulist Press, 1992.

Amir Khusrau. *The Tughlaq Namah,* translated by Mirza as 'Appendix', in Mohammad Wahid Mirza, *Life and Works of Amir Khusrau,* pp. 245–53. Lahore: Punjab University Press, 1962.

Bhagwant Sahai, ed. *The Inscriptions of Bihar: From Earliest Times to the Middle of 13th Century* A.D. New Delhi: Ramanand Vidya Bhawan, 1983.

Bhāmaha. *Kāvyālaṅkāra*, edited and annotated by D. Sharma. Patna: Bihar Rashtra Bhasha Parishad, 1985.

Bhoja. *Ṣṛiṅgāraprakāśa*, edited by V. Raghavan. Cambridge: Harvard University Press, 1998.

Bilahaṇa. *Vikramāṅkadevacaritam*, edited by S.M.L. Nagar. Jaipur: Rashtriya Sanskrit Sahitya Kendra, 2004.

Caṇḍeśvara. *Rājanītiratnākara*, edited by V. Gairolā and T. Jha. Varanasi: Chowkhamba Vidyabhavan, 1970.

———. *The Rājanīti-ratnākara*, edited by K.P. Jayaswal. Patna: K.P. Jayaswal Research Institute, 1929.

Dāmodar Paṇḍita. *Uktivyaktiprakaraṇa*, edited by J.V. Muni. Mumbai: Siṃghī Jainśāstra Śikṣāpīṭh (Bhāratīya Vidyā Bhavan), 1953.

George Abraham Grierson. *Vidyapati's Puruṣaparīkṣā* translated by Grierson as *The Test of a Man*. London: Royal Asiatic Society, 1935.

Hemacandra. *Kāvyanuśāsana*, edited by T.S. Nandi. Patan: North Gujarat University, 2007.

Hemacandra. *Shri Siddhahemacandraśabdānuśāsanam*, edited by Muni Himanshu Vijaya. Shri Anandaji Kalyanaji Pedhi, 1934, 1991.

Jayanta Bhaṭṭa. *Nyāyamañjarī* (Āhnika-I), translated by V.N. Jha. Delhi: Sri Satguru Publications, 1995.

———. *Nyāyamañjarī*, part I, edited by S.N. Shukla. Varanasi: Chowkhamba Sanskrit Series, 1971.

———. *Nyāyamañjarī*, vol. 1, translated by J.V. Bhattacharyya. Delhi: Motilal Banarsidass, 1978.

Jyotirīśvara Kaviśekhara. *Varṇaratnākara*, edited by A. Mishra and G. Jha. Patna: Maithili Akademi, 1990.

———. *Varṇaratnākara*, as a part of Bibliotheca Indica Series, edited by S.K. Chatterji. Kolkata: Royal Asiatic Society of Bengal, 1940.

Kauṭalya. *Arthaśāstra*, edited by T. Ganapatisastri. Delhi: Bharatiya Vidya Prakashan, 1984.

Kṛiṣṇadāsa Kavirāja. *Caitanya Caritamṛita*, as a part of Harvard Oriental Series, edited by T.K. Stewart and translated by E.C. Dimock. Cambridge, MA: Cambridge University Press, 1999.

Lekhapaddhati: Documents of State and Everyday Life from Ancient and Early Medieval Gujarat, as a part of Aligarh Historians Society Series, translated by P. Prasad. New Delhi: Oxford University Press, 2007.

Lekhapaddhati, as a part of Gaekwad's Oriental Series, edited by C.D. Dalal, Preface, Notes, and Glossary by G.K. Shrigondekar. Baroda: Baroda Central Library, 1925.

Locanapaṇḍita. *Rāgataraṅgiṇī*, edited by D.K. Joshi. Mumbai: Bhalchandra Sitaram Sukhtankar, 1918.

Mādhavācārya. *Sarva-darśana-saṅgraha*, compiled, edited, and transliterated by M.M. Agrawal. Delhi: Chaukhamba Sanskrit Pratishthan, 2002.

Merutuṅga. *Prabandhacintāmaṇiḥ*. Mumbai: Kalidasasakalcandra, 1888.

———. *Prabandhacintāmaṇi*, translated by C.H. Tawney as *Wishing-stone of Narratives*. Delhi: Indian Book Gallery, 1982.

Minhaj al-Din Siraj Juzjani. *Tabaqat-i Nasiri*, edited by A.H. Habibi. Kabul: Anjuman-i Tarikh-i Afghanistan, 1963–4.

Paṇḍita Visnu Sharma. *Pañcatantra*, edited by B.S. Shastri. Jaipur: Hansa Prakashan, 2012.

Pushpa Prasad, ed. *Sanskrit Inscriptions of Delhi Sultanate, 1191–1526*. New Delhi: Oxford University Press, 1990.

Qeyamuddin Ahmad, ed. and trans. *Corpus of Arabic and Persian Inscriptions of Bihar, A.H. 640–1200*. Patna: K.P. Jayaswal Research Institute, 1973.

Radhakrishna Choudhary, ed. *Select Inscriptions of Bihar*. Patna; Saharsa: Shanti Devi, 1958.

Shaikh Rizq Ullah Mushtaqui. *Waqi'at-e-Mushtaqui*, edited and translated by I.H. Siddiqui. New Delhi: Indian Council of Historical Research and Northern Book Centre, 1993.

Shams-i Siraj Afif. *Tarikh-i Firuz Shahi*, edited by M.V. Husain. Calcutta: Bibliotheca Indica, 1888–91.

———. *Tarikh-i Firuz Shahi*, translated by R.C. Jauhri as *Medieval India in Transition*. New Delhi: Sundeep Prakashan, 2001.

Sharaf al-Din Ahmad ibn-Yahya Maneri. *Maktubat-i Sadi*, translated by P. Jackson as *The Hundred Letters*, Foreword by B. Lawrence. London: SPCK, 1980.

Udayarāja. *Rājavinodamahākāvyam*, edited by G.N. Bahura. Jaipur: Rajasthan Purātan Granthmālā, 1956.

Vācaspati Miṣra. *Sāñkhyatattvakaumudī*, edited by G. Jha. Delhi: Bharatiya Book Corporation, 2008.

———. *Vivādacintāmaṇi*, as a part of Gaekwad Oriental Series, edited by U. Mishra and translated by G. Jha. Vadodara: Oriental Institute, 1942.

Valmiki. *Rāmāyaṇa*, edited and translated by C.D.P. Sharma. Allahabad: Ram Narayan Lal Publisher and Book Seller, 1927.

Vidyapati. *Bhūparikramaṇa*, edited by V. Jha. Patna: Bihar Rashtra Bhasha Parishad, 1987.

———. *Gorakṣavijaya*, edited by H. Mishra. Patna: Bihar Rashtra Bhasha Parishad, 1984.

———. *Kīrttilatā*, edited and translated by G. Jha. Patna: Maithili Akademi, 1992.

———. *Kīrttilatā*, edited by V. Shrivastav. Patna: Bihar Rashtra Bhasha Parishad, 1983.

———. *Likhānavalī*, edited by I. Jha. Patna: Indralay Prakashan, 1969.

———. *Padāvalī*, part 1, edited by G. Singh. Patna: Bihar Rashtra Bhasha Parishad, 2000.

———. *Padāvalī*, part 2, edited by G. Singh, S.J. Shastri, L. Singh, B. Mishra, and J. Jha. Patna: Bihar Rashtra Bhasha Parishad, 2000.

———. *Puruṣaparīkṣā*, edited and translated by S. Jha 'Suman'. Patna: Maithili Akademi, 1988.

———. *Śaivasarvasvasāra*, edited by I. Mishra. Patna: Maithili Akademi, 1979.

———. *Vibhāgasāra*, edited by G. Jha. Patna: Maithili Akademi, 1976.

Viśākhādatta. *Mudrārākṣasam*, edited by R. Tripathi. Varanasi: Vishwavidyalaya Prakashan, 1969.

Vishnudas. *Mahābhārat: Pāṇḍav-carit*, edited by H.N. Dvivedi. Gwalior: Vidya Mandir Prakashan, 1973.

Viśvanātha Kavirāja. *Sāhityadarapaṇaḥ*, edited by S. Shastri. Delhi: Motilal Banarsidas 2014.

Zain Badr Arabi. *Khwan-i Pur Nimat*, translated by P. Jackson as *A Table Laden with Good Things*. Delhi: Idarah-i Adabiyat-i, 1986.

Secondary Literature

Agrawal, Madan Mohan. 'Introduction', in Mādhavācārya, *Sarva-darśana-saṅgraha*, compiled, edited, and transliterated by M.M. Agrawal, pp. i–xli. Delhi: Chaukhamba Sanskrit Pratishthan, 2002.

Ahmad, Manan. 'The Long Thirteenth Century of the *Chachnama*'. *Indian Economic and Social History Review* vol. 49, no. 2 (2012): 459–91.

Alam, Muzaffar. *The Languages of Political Islam in India*. New Delhi: Permanent Black, 2004.

Alam, Muzaffar and Sanjay Subrahmanyam. *Indo-Persian Travels in the Age of Discoveries, 1400–1800*. Cambridge: Cambridge University Press, 2007.

———. 'The Making of a Munshi'. *Comparative Studies of South Asia, Africa and the Middle East* vol. 24, no. 2 (2004): 61–72.

Ali, Daud. *Courtly Culture and Political Life in Early Medieval India*. Cambridge: Cambridge University Press, 2004.

———. 'Temporality, Narration and the Problem of History: A View from Western India c. 1100–1400'. *Indian Economic and Social History Review* vol. 50, no. 2 (2013): 237–59.

———. 'The Image of the Scribe in Early Medieval Sources', in *Irreverent History: Essays for M.G.S. Narayanan*, edited by K. Veluthat and D.R. Davis, Jr., pp. 165–85. Delhi: Primus Books, 2014.

———. 'The *Subhāṣita* as an Artifact of Ethical Life in Medieval India', in *Ethical Life in South Asia*, edited by A. Pandian and D. Ali, pp. 21–42. Bloomington: Indiana University Press, 2010.

Anand, Dineshwarlal and Shashinath Jha. 'Bhumikā', in Vidyapati, *Padāvalī*, part 1, pp. 1–114. Patna: Bihar Rashtra Bhasha Parishad, 2000.

Anooshahr, Ali. 'The King Who Would Be Man: The Gender Roles of the Warrior King in Early Mughal History'. *Journal of the Royal Asiatic Society* vol. 18, no. 3 (2008): 327–40.

Ansari, Hasan Nishat. 'Bihar under Firuz Shah Tughlaq and the Later Tughlaqs', in *The Comprehensive History of Bihar*, vol. II, part I, edited by S.H. Askari and Q. Ahmad, pp. 184–232. Patna: K.P. Jayaswal Research Institute, 1983.

———. 'End of the Karnata Kingdom and Assertion of Tughlaq Control over Bihar', in *The Comprehensive History of Bihar*, vol. II, part I, edited by S.H. Askari and Q. Ahmad, pp. 157–83. Patna: K.P. Jayaswal Research Institute, 1983.

———. 'Historical Geography of Bihār on the Eve of the Early Turkish Invasions'. *The Journal of the Bihar Research Society* vol. 49 (1963): 253–60.

Apte, Vaman Shivaram. *The Practical Sanskrit–English Dictionary*. Delhi: Motilal Banarsidass Publishers, 1965, reprint 2010.

Aquique, Md. *Economic History of Mithila*. New Delhi: Abhinav Publications, 1974.

Askari, Syed Ahmad. 'A Fifteenth Century Shuttari Sufi Saint of North Bihār'. *The Journal of the Bihar Research Society* vol. 37 (1951): 66–82.

———. 'Bihār in the Time of Akbar'. *Bengal: Past and Present*, vol. 64, no. 127 (1944): 31–42; vol. 65, no. 128 (1945): 7–28.

———. *Collected Works*, vol. 1. Patna: Khuda Baksh Oriental Public Library, 1985.

———. 'Historical Value of *Basatin-ul-Uns*: A Rare Literary Work of the Early Fourteenth Century'. *The Journal of the Bihar Research Society* vol. 48 (1962): 1–29.

Balachandran, Jyoti Gulati. 'Texts, Tombs and Memory: The Migration, Settlement, and Formation of a Learned Muslim Community in Fifteenth-century Gujarat'. Unpublished PhD thesis, University of California, Los Angeles, 2012.

Bangha, Imre. 'Early Hindi Epic Poetry in Gwalior: Beginnings and Continuities in the *Rāmāyan* of Vishnudas', in *After Timur Left: Culture and Circulation in Fifteenth Century North India*, edited by F. Orsini and S. Sheikh, pp. 365–402. New Delhi: Oxford University Press, 2014.

Behl, Aditya. 'Presence and Absence in *Bhakti*: An Afterword'. *International Journal of Hindu Studies* vol. 11, no. 3 (2007): 319–24.

Benjamin, Walter. *Illuminations*, edited by H. Arendt, translated by H. Zohn. New York: Schocken Books, 2007.

Benke, Theodore. 'The Śūdrācāraśiromaṇi of Kṛṣṇa Śeṣa: A 16th Century Manual of Dharma for Śūdras'. Unpublished PhD dissertation, University of Pennsylvania, 2010.

Bhattacharya, Sabyasachi. 'Reflections on the Concept of Regional History'. *Kameshwar Singh Memorial Lecture* delivered on 28 November 1997. Darbhanga: Maharajadhirāja Kameśwar Singh Kalyāṇī Foundation, 1998.

Bloch, Marc. *The Historian's Craft*. Manchester: Manchester University Press, 2004.

Brass, Paul R. *Language, Religion and Politics in North India*. New York and London: Cambridge University Press, 1974.

Bronner, Yigal and David Shulman. '"A Cloud Turned Goose": Sanskrit in the Vernacular Millennium'. *Indian Economic and Social History Review* vol. 43, no. 1 (2006): 1–30.

Burke, Peter. *The Italian Renaissance: Culture and Society in Italy* (Revised Edition). Cambridge: Polity Press, [1972] 1986.

Busch, Allison. *Poetry of Kings: The Classical Hindi Literature of Mughal India*. New York: Oxford University Press, 2011.

Carr, E.H. *What Is History?* Cambridge: Cambridge University Press, 1961.

Certeau, Michel de. 'The Historiographic Operation', in Certeau, *The Writing of History*, translated by T. Conley, pp. 56–114. New York: Columbia University Press, 1988.

Chand, Tara. *Influence of Islam on Indian Culture*. Allahabad: The Indian Press, 1922.

Chatterjee, Indrani. 'Renewed and Connected Histories: Slavery and the Historiography of South Asia', in *Slavery and South Asian History*, edited by I. Chatterjee and R.M. Eaton, pp. 17–43. Bloomington: Indiana University Press, 2006.

Chattopadhyaya, Braj Dulal. 'Anachronism of Political Imagination', in *Representing the Other? Sanskrit Sources and the Muslims: Eighth to Fourteenth Century*, pp. 98–115. Delhi: Manohar, 1998.

———. 'Introduction', in *The Making of Early Medieval India*, pp. 1–37. New Delhi: Oxford University Press, 1994.

———. 'Political Processes and Structure of Polity in Early Medieval India'. Presidential Address, Ancient India Section, Indian History Congress, 44th session, Burdwan, 1983.

———. *Representing the Other? Sanskrit Sources and the Muslims: Eighth to Fourteenth Century*. New Delhi: Manohar, 1998.

Choudhary, Radhakrishna. *A Survey of Maithili Literature*. New Delhi: Shruti Publication, 2010.

———. *History of Muslim Rule in Tirhut, 1206–1765 A.D.* Delhi: Chowkhamba Sanskrit Series, 1970.

———. *Mithila in the Age of Vidyapati.* Delhi: Chowkhamba Orientalia, 1976.

———. *Select Inscriptions of Bihar*. Patna: S. Devi, 1958.

———. 'The Karṇāṭa Kingdom of Mithila', in *The Comprehensive History of Bihar*, vol. 2, part I, edited by S.H. Askari and Q. Ahmad, pp. 107–56. Patna: K.P. Jayaswal Research Institute, 1983.

Clercq, Eva De. 'Apabhramsha as a Literary Medium in Fifteenth Century North India', in *After Timur Left: Culture and Circulation in Fifteenth Century North India*, edited by F. Orsini and S. Sheikh pp. 339–64. New Delhi: Oxford University Press, 2014.

Datta, Amaresh, ed. *Encyclopaedia of Indian Literature*, vol. 2. New Delhi: Sahitya Akademi, 1988.

De, Sushil Kumar. 'The Akhyayika and the Katha in Classical Sanskrit'. *Bulletin of the School of Oriental Studies, University of London* vol. 3, no. 3 (1924): 507–17.

De Vreese, K. 'Review of the Formation of the Maithilī Language'. *Journal of the American Oriental Society* vol. 82, no. 3 (1962): 402–6.

Dey, Nundo Lal. *The Geographical Dictionary of Ancient and Mediaeval India.* Delhi: Low Price Publications, 2005.

Digby, Simon. 'Before Timur Came: Provincialization of the Delhi Sultanate through the Fourteenth Century'. *Journal of the Social and Economic History of the Orient* vol. 47, no. 3 (2004): 298–356.

Doniger, Wendy. *The Hindus: An Alternative History*. New York: The Penguin Press, 2009.

Dvivedi, Hazari Prasad. 'Foreword', in Shivprasad Singh, *Kīrttilatā aur Avahaṭṭha Bhāṣā*, pp. 7–10. New Delhi: Vani Prakashan, 1988.

Eagleton, Terry. *Literary Theory: An Introduction*. Minnesota: University of Minnesota Press, 2008.

Eaton, Richard. 'Approaches to the Study of Conversion to Islam in India', in *Approaches to Islam in Religious Studies*, edited by R.C. Martin, pp. 106–26. Tucson: The University of Arizona Press, 1985.

———. *The Rise of Islam and the Bengal Frontier, 1204–1760*. New Delhi: Oxford University Press, 1994.

Ernst, Carl. 'Muslim Studies of Hinduism? A Reconsideration of Arabic and Persian Translations from Indian Languages'. *Iranian Studies* vol. 36, no. 2 (2003): 173–95.

Flatt, Emma Jane. 'Courtly Culture in the Indo-Persian States of the Medieval Deccan, 1450–1600'. PhD Thesis, School of Oriental and African Studies, University of London, 2009.

Flood, Finbarr Barry. *Objects of Translation: Material Culture and Medieval 'Hindu–Muslim' Encounter*. Ranikhet: Permanent Black, 2009.

Foucault, Michel. *The Archaeology of Knowledge and the Discourse on Language*, translated by A.M. Sheridan Smith. New York: Pantheon Books, 1972.

Gommans, Jos J.L. and Dirk H.A. Kolff, ed. *Warfare and Weaponry in South Asia, 1000–1800*. New Delhi: Oxford University Press, 2001.

Grierson, George Abraham. *Maithili Chrestomathy and Vocabulary*, edited by H. Jha and V. Jha. Darbhanga: Mahārājādhirāja Kameśwar Singh Kalyāṇī Foundation, 2009.

———. 'Vidyapati and His Contemporaries'. *The Indian Antiquary* vol. XIV (1885): 183.

Guha, Sumit. 'Bad Language and Good Language: Lexical Awareness in the Cultural Politics of Peninsular India', in *Forms of Knowledge in Early Modern Asia: Explorations in the Intellectual History of India and Tibet, 1500–1800*, edited by S. Pollock, pp. 49–68. Delhi: Manohar, 2011.

Habib, Irfan. 'Kabīr: The Historical Setting', in *Religion in Indian History*, edited by I. Habib, pp. 142–57. New Delhi: Tulika and Aligarh Historians Society, 2007.

———. *An Atlas of the Mughal Empire: Political and Economic Maps with Detailed Notes, Bibliography, and Index*. Delhi: Oxford University Press, 1982.

Habib, Mohammad and Khaliq Ahmad Nizami, ed. *A Comprehensive History of India*, vol. V, part II: *The Delhi Sultanate* AD *1206–1526*. New Delhi: Indian History Congress and People's Publishing House, 1993.

Haider, Najaf. 'Translating Texts and Straddling Worlds: Intercultural Communication in Mughal India', in *The Varied Facets of History: Essays in Honour of Aniruddha Ray*, edited by I. Alam and S.E. Hussain, pp. 115–24. Delhi: Primus, 2011.

Hanaway, William L. 'Secretaries, Poets, and the Literary Language', in *Literacy in the Persianate World: Writing and the Social Order*, edited by B. Spooner and W.L. Hanaway, pp. 95–142. Philadelphia: University of Pennsylvania Press, 2012.

Hawley, John Stratton. *A Storm of Songs: India and the Idea of the Bhakti Movement*. Cambridge: Harvard University Press, 2015.

———. *Three Bhakti Voices: Mirabai, Surdas, and Kabir in Their Time and Ours*. New Delhi: Oxford University Press, 2005.

Hegde, R.D. 'The Nature and Number of *Pramāṇas* According to the Lokāyata System'. *Annals of the Bhandarkar Oriental Research Institute* vol. 63, no. 1/4 (1982): 99–120.

Hinüber, Oskar Von. 'Did Hellenistic Kings Send Letters to Aśoka?' *Journal of the American Oriental Society* vol. 130, no. 2 (2010): 261–66.

Hodivala, S.H. *Studies in Indo-Muslim History: A Critical Commentary on Elliot and Dowson's History of India*, vol. II. Puna: The Popular Book Depot, 1957.

Jackson, Peter. *The Delhi Sultanate: A Political and Military History*. Cambridge: Cambridge University Press, 1999.

Jarrett, Jene Andrew. *Representing the Race: A New Political History of African American Literature*. New York: New York University Press, 2011.

Jha, Harimohan. *Bīchal Kahānī*. New Delhi: Sahitya Akademi, 1999.

Jha, Hetukar. *Man in Indian Tradition: Vidyapati's Discourse on* Puruṣa. New Delhi: Aryan Books International, 2002.

Jha, Indrakant. *Vidyāpatikālīn Mithilā*. Patna: Maithili Akademi, 1986.

Jha, Pankaj Kumar. 'A Table Laden with Good Things: Reading a Fourteenth Century Sufi Text', in *Moveable Type: Book History in India*, edited by A. Gupta and S. Chakravorty, pp. 3–25. Ranikhet: Permanent Black, 2008.

———. 'Beyond the Local and the Universal: Exclusionary Strategies of Expansive Literary Cultures in Fifteenth Century Mithila'. *Indian Economic and Social History Review* vol. 51, no. 1 (2014): 1–40.

———. 'Literary Conduits for "Consent": Cultural Groundwork of the Mughal State in the Fifteenth Century'. *Medieval History Journal* vol. 19, no. 2 (2016): 322–50.

———. 'Vidyapati: *Itihasakāroṃ kī pratīkṣā meṃ*'. *Pratimān* vol. 6, no. 2 (2016): 220–39.

Jha, Ramanath. 'Introduction', in Shashinath Jha, ed., *Puruṣaparīkṣā*, as a part of Darbhanga Series 1, edited by R. Jha, pp. 1–73. Patna: Patna University, 1960.

Jha, Shailendra Mohan. *Vidyapati*. Patna: Maithili Akademi, 1977.

Jha, Subhadra. *The Formation of the Maithilī Language*. London: Luzac, 1958.

Kapadia, Aparna. 'The Last *Cakravartin*? The Gujarat Sultan as "Universal King" in Fifteenth Century Sanskrit Poetry'. *The Medieval History Journal* vol. 16, no. 1 (2013): 63–88.

Kapur, Nandini Sinha. *State Formation in Rajasthan: Mewār during the Seventh–Fifteenth Centuries*. Delhi: Manohar, 2002.

Kastura, Shoryu. 'Dharmakīrti's Theory of Truth'. *Journal of Indian Philosophy* vol. 12, no. 3 (1984): 215–35.

Kataoka, Kei. 'The *Mīmāṃsā* Definition of Pramāṇa as a Source of New Information'. *Journal of Indian Philosophy* vol. 31 (2003): 89–103.

———. 'What Really Protects the Vedas? Jayanta on Sastra-prayojana'. *Journal of the Ganganatha Jha Kendriya Sanskrit Vidyapeetha* vol. 56 (2003): 249–76.

Kaviraj, Sudipta. 'The Two Histories of Literary Culture in Bengal', in *Literary Cultures in History: Reconstructions from South Asia*, edited by S. Pollock, pp. 503–66. Berkeley: University of California Press, 2003.

Khalidi, Tarif. *Arabic Historical Thought in the Classical Period*. Cambridge: Cambridge University Press, 1994.

Khan, Iqtidar Alam. *Gunpowder and Firearms: Warfare in Medieval India*. New Delhi: Oxford University Press, 2004.

Kielhorn, F. 'The Epoch of the Lakshmansena Era'. *The Indian Antiquary*, vol. XIX (1890): 1–7.

Kinra, Rajeev Kumar. 'Secretary–Poets in Mughal India and the Ethos of Persian: The Case of Chandar Bhān Brahman'. Unpublished PhD thesis, University of Chicago, 2008.

Knutson, Jesse Ross. 'History beyond the Reality Principle: Literary and Political Territories in Sena Period Bengal'. *Comparative Studies of South Asia, Africa and the Middle East* vol. 32, no. 2 (2012): 633–43.

———. *Into the Twilight of Sanskrit Court Poetry: The Sena Salon of Bengal and Beyond*. Berkeley: University of California Press, 2014.

———. 'The Consolidation of Literary Registers in the World of the Senas and the Beginning of Its Afterlife: Sanskrit and Bengali Social Poetics, 12th–14th Century'. Unpublished PhD dissertation. University of Chicago, 2009.

Koch, Lars-Christian. *My Heart Sings: Die Lieder Rabindranath Tagores Zwischen Tradition und Moderne*. Berlin: Ethnologisches Museum, 2012.

Kolff, Dirk H.A. *Naukar, Rajput and Sepoy: The Ethnohistory of the Military Labour Market in Hindustan 1450–1850*. Cambridge: Cambridge University Press, 1990.

Kumar, Sunil. '*Bandagī* and *Naukarī*: Studying Transitions in Political Culture and Service under the Sultanates of North India, Thirteenth–Sixteenth Centuries', in *After Timur Left: Culture and Circulation in Fifteenth Century North India*, edited by F. Orsini and S. Sheikh, pp. 60–108. New Delhi: Oxford University Press, 2014.

———. *Emergence of the Delhi Sultanate, 1192–1286*. Ranikhet: Permanent Black, 2007.

Lal, Kishori Saran. *Twilight of the Sultanate: A Political, Social and Cultural History of the Sultanate of Delhi from the Invasion of Timur to the Conquest of Babur, 1398–1526*. Bombay: Asia Publication House, 1963.

Majumdar, Biman Bihari. 'Vidyapati and His Age', in *The Comprehensive History of Bihar*, vol. II, part I, edited by S.H. Askari and Q. Ahmad, pp. 366–95. Patna: K.P. Jayaswal Research Institute, 1983.

Majumdar, R.C, ed. *The Delhi Sultanate*, Vol. 6, in *The History and Culture of the Indian People*. Delhi: Bharatiya Vidya Bhavan, 1960.

Majumdar, R.C., H.C. Raychaudhuri, and Kalikinkar Datta. *An Advanced History of India*. Delhi: Macmillan India, 1946.

Masumi, Sahir Hasan. 'Sunargaon's Contribution to Islamic Learning'. *Islamic Culture* vol. 27 (1953): 8–17.

Mayrhofer, C.M. 'Introduction', in Abdul Rahman, *Sandeśarāsaka*, edited by C.M. Mayrhofer, pp. ix–xiii. Delhi: Motilal Banarsidass Publishers Private Ltd, 1998.

McGregor, Ronald Stuart. *Hindi Literature from its Beginnings to the Nineteenth Century*. Wiesbaden: Otto Harrassowitz, 1984.

Mirza, Mohammad Wahid. *The Life and Works of Amir Khusrau*. Lahore: Panjab University Press, 1962.

Mishra, Harimohan. '*Bhumikā*' in Vidyapati, *Gorakṣavijaya*, edited by H. Mishra, pp. 6–8. Patna: Bihar Rashtra Bhasha Parishad, 1984.

Mishra, Madaneshvar. 'Prakāśakīya', in *Puruṣaparīkṣā* by Vidyapati, edited by S. Jha 'Suman'. Patna: Maithili Akademi, 1988.

Nizami, Khaliq Ahmad. 'The Sharqi Kingdom of Jaunpur', in *A Comprehensive History of India*, vol. V, part II: *The Delhi Sultanate* A.D. *1206–1526*, edited by M. Habib and K.A. Nizami, pp. 711–33. New Delhi: Indian History Congress and People's Publishing House, 1993.

Novetzke, Christian Lee. *The Quotidian Revolution: Vernacularization, Religion, and the Premodern Public Sphere in India*. Ranikhet: Permanent Black, 2017.

O'Hanlon, Rosalind. 'Manliness and Imperial Service in Mughal North India'. *Journal of the Economic and Social History of the Orient* vol. 42, no. 1 (1991): 47–93.

O'Hanlon, Rosalind and David Washbrook, ed. *Religious Cultures in Early Modern India: New Perspectives*. London: Routledge, 2011.

Olivelle, Patrick M. 'Manu and the *Arthaśāstra*: A Study in Śāstric Intertextuality'. *Journal of Indian Philosophy* vol. 32 (2004): 281–91.

Ollett, Andrew. *Language of the Snakes: Prakrit, Sanskrit and the Language Order of Premodern India*. Oakland: University of California Press, 2017.

Orsini, Francesca. 'How to Do Multilingual Literary History? Lessons from Fifteenth- and Sixteenth-Century North India'. *Indian Economic and Social History Review* vol. 49, no. 2 (2012): 225–46.

Orsini, Francesca and Samira Sheikh. 'Introduction', in *After Timur Left: Culture and Circulation in Fifteenth Century North India*, edited by F. Orsini and S. Sheikh, pp. 1–44. New Delhi: Oxford University Press, 2014.

Orsini, Francesca, David Shulman, and A.R. Venkatachelapathy. 'A Review Symposium: Literary Cultures in History'. *Indian Economic and Social History Review* vol. 42, no. 3 (2005): 377–408.

Pandey, Rajkishor. *Hindī Sāhitya kā Prārambhik Yug*. Hyderabad: Navhind Prakashan, 1966.

Pandey, Shambhunath. *Apabhraṃśa aur Avahaṭṭha: Ek Antaryātrā*. Varanasi: Chaukhambha Orientalia, 1979.

Pant, Ambadatt. *Apabhraṃśa Kāvya Paraṃparā aur Vidyāpati*. Varanasi: Nagari Pracharinị Sabha, 1970 (V.S. 2026).

Phukan, Shantanu. '"Through Throats where Many Rivers Meet": The Ecology of Hindi in the World of Persian'. *Indian Economic and Social History Review* vol. 38, no. 1 (2001): 33–58.

Pollock, Sheldon. 'Future Philology? The Fate of a Soft Science in a Hard World'. *Critical Enquiry* vol. 35, no. 4 (2009): 931–61.

———. 'India in the Vernacular Millennium: Literary Culture and Polity, 1000–1500', in *Early Modernities*, edited by S. Eisenstadt, W. Schluchter, and B. Wittrock, *Daedalus*, vol. 127, (special issue) no. 3 (1998): 41–74.

———. 'Introduction', in *Literary Cultures in History: Reconstructions from South Asia*, edited by S. Pollock, pp. 1–36. Berkeley: University of California Press, 2003.

———. ed. *Literary Cultures in History: Reconstructions from South Asia*. Berkeley: University of California Press, 2003.

———. 'Mīmāṃsā and the Problem of History in Traditional India'. *Journal of the American Oriental Society* vol. 109, no. 4 (1989): 603–10.

———. 'New Intellectuals in Seventeenth Century India'. *Indian Economic and Social History Review* vol. 38, no. 3 (2001): 2–31.

———. 'Pre-textures of Time', in *History and Theory* vol. 46, no. 3 (October 2007), in 'Forum: *Textures of Time*': 366–83.

———. '*Rāmāyaṇa* and Political Imagination in India'. *The Journal of Asian Studies* vol. 52, no. 2 (1993): 261–97.

———. 'Sanskrit Literary Culture from the Inside Out', in *Literary Cultures in History: Reconstructions from South Asia*, edited by S. Pollock, pp. 39–130. Berkeley: University of California Press, 2003.

———. 'The Cosmopolitan Vernacular'. *The Journal of Asian Studies* vol. 57, no. 1 (1998): 6–37.

———. 'The Death of Sanskrit'. *Comparative Studies in Society and History* vol. 3, no. 2 (2001): 392–426.

———. *The Language of the Gods in the World of Men: Sanskrit, Culture, and Power in Premodern India*. Berkeley: University of California Press, 2006.

———. 'The Languages of Science in Early Modern India', in *Forms of Knowledge in Early Modern Asia: Explorations in the Intellectual History of India and Tibet, 1500–1800*, edited by S. Pollock, pp. 19–48. New Delhi: Manohar, 2011.

———. 'The Theory of Practice and the Practice of Theory in Indian Intellectual History'. *Journal of the American Oriental Society* vol. 105, no. 3 (1985): 499–519.

Rao, Velcheru Narayana and David Shulman. *Śrīnātha: The Poet Who Made Gods and Kings*. Oxford: Oxford University Press, 2012.

Rao, Velcheru Narayana and Sanjay Subrahmanyam. 'Notes on Political Thought in Medieval and Early Modern South India'. *Modern Asian Studies* vol. 43, no. 1 (2009): 175–210.

Rao, Velcheru Narayana, David Shulman, and Sanjay Subrahmanyam. 'A New Imperial Idiom in the Sixteenth Century: Krishnadevaraya and His Political Theory of Vijayanagara', in *Forms of Knowledge in Early Modern Asia: Explorations in the Intellectual History of India and Tibet, 1500–1800,* edited by S. Pollock, pp. 69–111. New Delhi: Manohar, 2011.

———. *Textures of Time: Writing History in South India, 1600–1800.* Delhi: Permanent Black, 2001.

Ray, Rajat Kanta. 'What Ought to Be History'. *The Book Review* vol. XXVIII, no. 1 (January 2004).

Richards, John F. 'Warriors and the State in Early Modern India'. *Journal of the Economic and Social History of the Orient* vol. 47, no. 3 (2004): 390–400.

Sadhale, Nalini. *Kathā in Sanskrit Poetics.* Hyderabad: Sanskrit Academy of Osmania University, 1986.

Sahai, Bhagwant, ed. *The Inscriptions of Bihar: From Earliest Times to the Middle of 13th Century* A.D. New Delhi: Ramanand Vidya Bhawan, 1983.

Sahu, Bhairavi Prasad. Forthcoming. 'Sarala's Odra-*desa*: Literary Representations of a Regional Society', in *Early South Asian History Seen from Multiple Lenses: Essays in Honour of B.D. Chattopadhyaya,* edited by O. Boparachchi and S. Ghosh. Delhi: Primus Books.

Salomon, Richard. *Indian Epigraphy: A Guide to the Study of Inscriptions in Sankrit, Prakrit and the Other Indo-Aryan Languages.* New York: Oxford University Press, 1998.

Sarkar, Jagdish Narayan. *Glimpses of Medieval Bihār Economy: Thirteenth to Mid-Eighteenth Century.* Calcutta: Ratna Prakāśana, 1978.

Sarkar, Sumit. 'Post-modernism and the Writing of History'. *Studies in History* vol. 15, no. 2 (1999): 293–322.

Sartre, Jean Paul. *"What is Literature?" and Other Essays.* Cambridge: Harvard University Press, 1988.

Sastri, Haraprasad. 'Report on the Search of Sanskrit Manuscripts (1895–1900)'. Kolkata: Asiatic Society of Bengal, 1901.

Schöffer, Ivo. 'Did Holland's Golden Age Coincide with a Period of Crisis?', in *The General Crisis of the Seventeenth Century,* edited by G. Parker and L.M. Smith, pp. 88–108. London: Routledge, 1997.

Scott, James. *The Art of Not Being Governed: An Anarchist History of Upland Southeast Asia.* New Haven: Yale University Press, 2009.

Sharmma, Ramprakash. *Mithila ka Itihās.* Darbhanga: Kameshvar Singh Darbhanga Sanskrit Viśvavidyālay, 1979.

Sheikh, Samira. *Forging a Region: Sultans, Traders, and Pilgrims in Gujarat, 1200–1500.* New Delhi: Oxford University Press, 2010.

Shelley, Percy Bysshe. 'A Defence of Poetry', edited with introduction and notes by A.S. Cook. Boston: Ginn and Company, 1891.

Shrivastav, Virendra. 'Prastāvanā', in Vidyapati, *Kīrttilatā*, edited by V. Shrivastav. Patna: Bihar Rashtra Bhasha Parishad, 1983.

———. ed. *Vidyapati: Anuśilan evaṃ Mūlyāṃkan*, 2 vols. Patna: Hindi Granth Akademi, 1973.

Shukla, Ram Chandra. *Hindi Sāhitya ka Itihās*. Allahabad: Lokabharati Prakashan, 1929.

Siddiqui, Iqtidar Hussain. 'Social Mobility in the Delhi Sultanate', in *Medieval India 1: Researches in the History of India, 1200–1750*, edited by I. Habib, pp. 22–48. New Delhi: Oxford University Press, 1992.

Simpson, Edward and Aparna Kapadia, ed. *The Idea of Gujarat: History, Ethnography and Text*. New Delhi: Orient BlackSwan, 2010.

Singh, Namvar. *Pṛithvīrāja Rāso kī Bhāṣā*. Banaras: Sarasvati Press, 1956.

Singh, Shivprasad. *Kīrttilatā aur Avahaṭṭha Bhāṣā*. New Delhi: Vani Prakashan, 1988.

———. *Vidyapati*. Allahabad: Lokabhāratī Prakāśan, 1970.

Singh, Upinder. 'The Power of a Poet: Kingship, Empire and War in Kalidasa's *Raghuvaṃsa*'. *Indian Historical Review* vol. 38, no. 2 (2011): 177–98.

Sinha, Chandreshwar Prasad Narayan. *Mithila under the Karnāṭas, c. 1097–1325*. Patna: Janaki Prakāśana, 1979.

Spiegel, Gabrielle M. 'Genealogy: Form and Function in Medieval History Narrative'. *History and Theory* vol. 22, no. 1 (1983): 43–53.

Sreenivasan, Ramya. 'Alauddin Khalji Remembered: Conquest, Gender and Community in Medieval Rajput Narratives'. *Studies in History* vol. 18, no. 2 (2002): 275–96.

———. 'The "Marriage" of "Hindu" and "Turak": Medieval Rajput Histories of Jalor'. *The Medieval History Journal* vol. 7, no. 1 (2004): 87–109.

Steingass, F. *Comprehensive Persian–English Dictionary*. New Delhi: Munshiram Manoharlal Publishers, 1996.

Stewart, Tony. 'In Search of Equivalence: Conceiving Muslim–Hindu Encounter through Translation Theory'. *History of Religions* vol. 40, no. 3 (2001): 260–87.

Stoler, Ann Laura. 'Colonial Archives and the Arts of Governancc'. *Archival Science* vol. 2, no. 1–2 (2002): 87–109.

Storey, C.A. *Persian Literature: A Bio-bibliographical Survey*, vol. 3, part II. Leiden: The Royal Asiatic Society of Great Britain and Ireland, 1984.

Subrahmanyam, Sanjay. 'The Mughal State—Structure or Process? Reflections on Recent Western Historiography'. *Indian Economic and Social History Review* vol. 29, no. 3 (1992): 291–321.

Svami, Narottamdas. *Rāso Sāhitya aur Pṛthvirāj Rāso: Saṃkṣipta Parichaya*. Bikaner: B.S., 1885.

Syamaldas, Kaviraj. 'The Antiquity, Authenticity and Genuineness of the Epic Called the Prithvi Raj Rasa, and Commonly Ascribed to Chand Bardai'. *Journal of the Asiatic Society of Bengal* vol. 55, pt. I (1886): 5–65.

Tagore, Rabindranath. 'Adhunik Sahitya', in *Rabindra Rachanabali*, vol 8, pp. 441–5. Kolkata: Viswabharati, 1941.

Talbot, Cynthia. 'Contesting Knowledges in Colonial India: The Question of Prithviraj Raso's Historicity', in *Knowing India: Colonial and Modern Constructions of the Past*, edited by C. Talbot, pp. 171–212. Delhi: Yoda Press, 2011.

———. 'Inscribing the Other, Inscribing the Self: Hindu–Muslim Identities in Pre-colonial India'. *Comparative Studies in Society and History* vol. 27, no. 4 (1995): 692–722.

———. 'Rudrama-devi, the Female King: Gender and Political Authority in Medieval India', in *Syllables of Sky: Studies in South Indian Civilization, in Honour of Velcheru Narayana Rao*, edited by D. Shulman, pp. 391–430. New Delhi: Oxford University Press, 1995.

Thakur, Amarendra Kumar and Binod Kumar Verma. *India and the Afghans: A Study of a Neglected Region, 1370–1576 A.D.* Patna: Janaki Prakashan, 1992.

Thakur, Ramchandra. *Mithilāpabhraṃśaka Udbhav aur Vikās*. Patna: Janaki Prakashan, 2003.

Thakur, Shiv Nandan. *Mahākavi Vidyapati*, translated by Vidyapati Thakur. Patna: Maithili Akademi, 1979.

Thakur, Shrikant. 'Prakāśakīya Nivedan', in Vidyapati, *Vibhāgasāra*, edited by G. Jha. Patna: Maithili Akademi, 1976.

Thakur, Upendra. 'Institutions of Slavery in Mithila'. *Indian Historical Quarterly* vol. XXXV (1959): 217–19.

Thapar, Romila. 'Imagined Religious Communities? Ancient History and the Modern Search for a Hindu Identity'. *Modern Asian Studies*, vol. 23, no. 2 (1989): 209–31.

———. *Somanatha: The Many Voices of a History*. New Delhi: Viking Penguin India, 2004.

Tieken, Herman. 'On the Use of *Rasa* in Studies of Sanskrit Drama'. *Indo-Iranian Journal* vol. 43, no. 2 (2000): 115–38.

———. 'The Process of Vernacularization in South Asia'. *Journal of the Economic and Social History of the Orient* vol. 51, no. 2 (2008): 338–83.

Tor, Deborah Gerber. *Violent Order: Religious Warfare, Chivalry, and the 'Ayyār Phenomenon in the Medieval Islamic World.* Wurzburg: Orient-Institut Istanbul, 2007.

Trautmann, R. *Kautilya and the Arthaśāstra: A Statistical Investigation of the Authorship and Evolution of the Text.* Leiden: Brill, 1971.

Tripp, Susan. 'The Genres of Classical Sanskrit Literature'. *Poetics* vol. 10, nos. 2–3 (1981): 213–30.

Truschke, Audrey. 'Cosmopolitan Encounters: Sanskrit and Persian at the Mughal Court'. Unpublished PhD Dissertation, Columbia University, New York, 2012.

Varma, Bajrang.'Prākkathana', in Vidyapati, *Kīrttilatā*, edited by V. Shrivastav. pp. *ka–gha*. Patna: Bihar Rashtra Bhasha Parishad, 1983.

Vaudeville, Charlotte. *A Weaver Named Kabir: Selected Verses with a Detailed Biographical and Historical Introduction*. New Delhi: Oxford University Press, 1993.

Warder, A.K. *Indian Kavya Literature, vol. I: Literary Criticism*. Delhi: Motilal Banarsidass Publishers Private Limited, 1972.

———. *Indian Kavya Literature, vol. VI: The Art of Storytelling*. Delhi: Motilal Banarsidass Publishers Private Limited, 1992.

Woolford, Ian Alister. 'Renu Village: An Ethnography of North Indian Fiction'. Unpublished PhD Dissertation, University of Texas, Austin, 2012.

Yadav, Ramawatar. 'Maithili Phonetics and Phonology'. Unpublished PhD Dissertation, University of Kansas, Austin, 1979.

Zilli, Ishtiyaq Ahmad. 'Development of *Inshā* Literature till the End of Akbar's Reign', in *The Making of Indo-Persian Culture*, edited by M. Alam, F. 'Nalini' Delvoye, and M. Gaborieau, pp. 309–49. Delhi: Manohar, Centre de Sciences Humaines, 2000.

Zutshi, Chitralekha. 'Past as Tradition, Past as History: The *Rajatarangini* Narratives in Kashmir's Persian Historical Tradition'. *Indian Economic and Social History Review* vol. 50, no. 2 (2013): 201–19.

Index-Glossary

About the Author

Pankaj Jha is presently teaching at Lady Shri Ram College, New Delhi, India. He is giving final touches to his English translation of a fifteenth-century Sanskrit treatise on writing, entitled *Likhanāvalī*. He is also on the editorial board of the international journal *Indian Economic and Social History Review*. Earlier, Jha has taught at Ramjas College and St. Stephen's College, New Delhi.

Jha obtained his bachelor's and master's degrees in history from Ramjas College, and his MPhil and PhD degrees from the University of Delhi. Part of his doctoral work was done at University of Texas at Austin, U.S.A, on a Fulbright–Nehru fellowship. The primary area of his research interest is the literary cultures of the middle ages. Languages he has worked with include Persian, Sanskrit, Maithili, and Apabhraṃśa. He has published research articles extensively in peer-reviewed journals, in Hindi as well as in English.